Agricultural Crisis in Africa

The Nigerian Experience

David A. Iyegha

UNIVERSITY
PRESS OF
AMERICA

Lanham • New York • London

Copyright © 1988 by

University Press of America,® Inc.

4720 Boston Way
Lanham, MD 20706

3 Henrietta Street
London WC2E 8LU England

British Cataloging in Publication Information Available

Library of Congress Cataloging-in-Publication Data

Iyegha, David A., 1949–
Agricultural crisis in Africa : the Nigerian experience / David A. Iyegha.
p. cm.
Bibliography: p.
Includes index.
1. Agriculture and state—Nigeria. 2. Agriculture—Economic
aspects—Nigeria. 3. Agriculture—Nigeria. 4. Food supply—
Nigeria. I. Title.
HD2145.5.Z8I94   1988
338.1'09669—dc 19   88–17219 CIP
ISBN 0–8191–7080–1 (alk. paper)
ISBN 0–8191–7081–X (pbk. : alk. paper)

To those whose support made this work possible.
My mother
Dorcas Saraboh Iyegha
My brothers
Alfred, Zeblon, Anthony, and Allen
My wife
Diane Lynne

PREFACE

The work contained in this manuscript was triggered by a discussion of the failing performances of the agricultural economy of Nigeria (in the presence of a booming petroleum industry), which took place when I was enroute to Nigeria from the United States on one of my occasional visits to my home country. When a country like Nigeria started to import agricultural products such as gari (a product of probably the most staple crop in the country — cassava) from Brazil, rice from the United States and the Southeast Asian countries, and other products in large quantities, and when the population of Nigeria began to face hunger and malnutrition at a time when there were no immediate apparent natural hazards or historic events to incite such hardships, one wonders what has actually gone wrong in the country. The only explanation for this is that the country turned its back on agriculture and focused its attention on the immediate benefit that could be derived from the petroleum industry, which started to expand in the early 1970s, and used the oil money to replace its agriculture with imported foodstuffs. Apparently this would never have happened without some forces triggering it. The study, therefore, calls on the management style of the country's leaders of the economy to explain this dilemma and examines in critical terms the policy priorities made by the country that brought about the present situation.

Also, this work is the culmination of many years of personal interest and deep concern for the country, which was further enhanced by the visits made to the former Speaker of the House of Assembly, Ondo State, Mr. Richard Jolowo; the ousted President, Shehu Shagari; and key officials in some local and state goverments. Information gathered from these key policy makers was quite helpful in the decision to investigate the issues raised in this work.

Students of social sciences, especially geographers, are faced with an incredible problem in explaining the agricultural crisis on the continent of Africa, a continent which two to three decades ago used to supply its own food needs. It appears that some drastic, localized ecological changes have taken place on the continent. However, it seems that such localized natural events are highly unlikely, if not improbable. There are a few countries on the continent performing significantly well, and these countries are often surrounded by others that are not doing so well. Continent-wide natural events, especially drought, are often invoked to explain the problem. But, unless there are human elements intricately connected to this explanation, the natural element falls short in explaining the problem. In the case of Nigeria, an objective assessment of the climatic factor shows that it is not the overriding cause for the agricultural dilemma in the country.

Since natural conditions do not contribute an uncontrollable dimension in the present crisis, we have to look into the human factors. But even when we consider some of the human elements often cited as explanation — such as the past colonial legacy and the poor practices of African farmers —we still run into some difficulties. In this work, we are therefore forced to look into the often avoided repercussions of the management style of many post-independent African leaders, the Nigerian experience being a classic example of how limited resources have been mismanaged to the detriment of the population at large. This includes not only the mismanagement and imbalance distribution of the national wealth, but the gross neglect, exploitation, and abuse of the real producer (smallholder) by the government of Nigeria.

It took a great deal of help to produce the work contained in this book. However, the author is solely and fully responsible for the contents of the material therein. I gratefully acknowledge the untiring support, insight, and encouragement of Dr. Lutz Holzner, Chairman, Department of Geography, The University of Wisconsin-Milwaukee, my Ph.D dissertation supervisor. Appreciation is also extended to Dr. Karel Bayer, whose knowledge of climatology helped bring about a very clear analysis of the climatic factor in agricultural development. I am also grateful to Drs. Harold Mayer and Harold Rose of the Department of Geography, and Bruce Fetter of the Department of History,University of Wisconsin-Milwaukee, and Paul Erhunmwunsee for their helpful comments and suggestions.

This research would not have been possible without the financial support of the University of Wisconsin-Milwaukee. I gratefully acknowledge the fellowships the University awarded to me throughout the research period. Appreciation is extended as well to Linda Hawkins and Brenda Cullins of the Social Science Research Facility; Donna Genzmer Schenstrom and Timothy Moore, University of Wisconsin-Milwaukee Cartographic Laboratory; Miebi Akah, Ohio State University-Columbus; and Drs. Frank Stetzer and Kazimierz Zaniewski, for their computer, graphic, and cartographic assistance.

Special thanks are given to the Federal, Ondo and Sokoto States Permanent Secretaries and Directors of the Ministries of Agriculture, Statistics and Planning for providing me with the needed information for this research. I am quite indebted to

Mr. A. Babalola, Federal Ministry of Agriculture, and Mr. Joel Magi, Special Assistant to the Governor of Ondo State, for their effort in securing appropriate information from different ministries. I also wish to say thank you to the university students (Adeyemi College of Education and Sokoto State University) and high school teachers in Ondo and Sokoto State, who helped in conducting the interviews, and to many employees, especially those in the Inter-Library Loan Department of the Golda Meir Library, University of Wisconsin-Milwaukee and the AGS Collection, for their continuous help in locating materials. For suggestions in the final stage of editing and proofing, my thanks go to Pamela Pierce.

And finally, I want to thank God for the blessing of an understanding family, especially my dear wife Diane, for her support, sacrifice, and enduring love.

David Iyegha

TABLE OF CONTENTS

Chapter 4   CLIMATE AND AGRICULTURE IN NIGERIA

PART II

Chapter 5   THE PLIGHT OF THE SMALLHOLDER

Chapter 6   POLITICAL MISMANAGEMENT AND
                 AGRICULTURAL DEVELOPMENT IN NIGERIA

Chapter 7   RURAL-URBAN DICHOTOMY AND RURAL-URBAN
                 MIGRATION IN NIGERIA

PART III

Chapter 8 FIELD STUDY ANALYSIS – THE VOICE OF THE PEOPLE

Chapter 9 Summary and Conclusion

List of Tables

xv

List of Figures

Chapter 1

INTRODUCTION

Agricultural Crisis in Africa

The agricultural crisis on the continent of Africa has been on the international agenda for several decades. Agriculture has been on the decline in absolute terms in most Sub-Saharan Africa countries during the last two decades, reflected by the rapid disappearance of most of the export commodities from the international market, increasing importation of foodstuffs that can be produced domestically, and, more importantly, a deepening economic crisis that centers on the problem of food supplies. The crisis of food deficits has now become so consistent and so widespread that it can no longer be construed as the outcome of a particular historical or climatic occurrence such as war, ethnic strife, or drought. Governments and consumers both face serious problems in procuring the types and quantities of food they want at prices they can afford.

It is currently estimated that approximately 150 million of about 450 million Africans suffer from some form of hunger and malnutrition, originating in an inadequate supply of foodstuffs. This abysmal picture is further made darker by the fact that no fewer than 28 African countries are faced with food shortages so critical that famine is believed to be imminent (*Lofchie and Commins 1982*).

These data reflect a critical situation which is all the more alarming because the farming sector is the most important sector of the economy throughout the African continent. Indeed, farming is the single largest contributor to the Gross Domestic Product (GDP) in many African economies. More than 80 percent of the labor force in almost half of the African countries is employed in agriculture, and for most of these countries it provides over 50 percent of their export earnings (*Hinderink and Sterkenburg, 1983*). Yet, by all accounts, Sub-Saharan Africa is the only region in the world where food production per capita has declined during the past two decades, and it seems to be the center of mass starvation. As a result, the average per capita calorie intake is below minimum nutritional levels in most

1

countries, including those countries which were formerly self-sufficient.

This bleak situation has aroused considerable interest among individual researchers and research organizations. Researchers studying this problem have sought explanations and solutions that have varied considerably. The United Nations, which is very much aware of Africa's problems has assisted select countries in finding solutions. Many affluent nations such as the United States, West Germany, France, Canada, and Britain, have also acted in a humanitarian way in rendering assistance to the more seriously affected countries. But the situation clearly calls for more self help, as outside assistance can only be viewed as temporary. Numerous solutions also have been suggested as a means of helping the afflicted countries overcome problems associated with growing food deficits. The majority of these countries, however, especially those in Sub-Saharan Africa, seem to be unresponsive to the suggestions, and, as a result, they have suffered the most.

The Africans invariably have blamed harsh and uncompromising physical circumstances, especially drought, for their problem. But it seems that physical limitations (not unique to Africa) are just part of the problem. There are other explanations which also need to be addressed, the roots of which lie in the economic, political, and cultural institutions of each African country. The investigation of these will be the central focus of this work.

The Issue of Generalization in Explaining the Crisis

Students of political science, anthropology, rural sociology, economics, and geography, among other disciplines, are engaged in an effort to explain the bleak situation confronting Sub-Saharan Africa. Yet there seems to be little agreement among those who attempt to provide an appropriate explanation for the food crisis so prevalent on the African continent. The abundance of theories and explanations that have been put forth by various researchers indicate the complexity of the problem. However, if there is one thing held in common, it is that fact that there is a problem with regard to the agricultural economy of Africa, and that it is not simple. Rather, it is a complex problem, one which has passed from a chronic stage to an acute epidemic stage.

A number of generalizations, however, have been applied to Africa as a whole. On the top of the list of generalizations is the problem of drought, which many researchers feel is beyond the control of man because of the drought tendencies of Saharan regions (*Gusau 1981 and Derrick 1984*). However, not all countries in Africa lie near the Sahara Desert. Most of the coastal West African countries (Nigeria, Ghana, Liberia, Cameroon,

Ivory Coast, etc.) do not immediately border the desert, yet the majority of them are included on the list of countries with critical food shortages. The vegetation map of Africa does show a sharp contrast between desert and lush tropical conditions. But even if we consider the countries which are obviously on the drought-laden desert, such as Mali, Niger, Sudan, and Chad, we cannot conclusively attribute their crises to weather alone. Sudan, for example, was once one of the most successful agricultural countries on the continent before the advent of its border disputes. Furthermore, only a small portion of Ethiopia (one of the oldest independent countries in the world) is drought-prone, yet it has continuously used drought as an excuse to explain its agricultural underdevelopment, while it continuously wars with its eastern neighbors.

Significantly, history demonstrates that most of these drought-prone countries were once successful in confronting the problem of drought. Ironically, Egypt, which is almost entirely in the desert (and not necessarily wealthy, even by Third World standards), seems to have made a successful adaptation to the limitations of its environment. The same is true of Libya, Algeria, and Morocco. There was even a time in the history of Nigeria and other West African countries, as noted by Eicher, when they were generally not troubled by deficits of staple foods and were immune to chronic inflation and unequal distribution of land, problems that were only heard of in other underdeveloped countries in Asia and Latin America (*Eicher 1970, p. 10*). However, these problems exist now in most of the Sub-Saharan African countries, without exception, and all have been allowed to penetrate, with little or no resistance, the heart of each. A great portion of Africa is experiencing chronic food shortage, run-away inflation, and in some notorious cases, landlessness, which the governments of these countries have not been able to deal with effectively. A well articulated, long-term planning effort on the part of the people of these countries would probably have brought about a better understanding of the nature of climate and how to derive benefits from it, as some of these countries once did.

There are a few researchers who have directed their attention to the dynamics of land consolidation and the transition from land tenure to a private land market in West Africa. David Smock (1967), Victor Uchendu (1967), and more recently A. M. O'Connor (1978) among others, have made such a move. Eicher, who studied its traditional agricultural practices, contended that such a move would likely bring little economic growth, especially in the densely populated areas of West Africa. This kind of move has already been shown to create landlessness, unemployment, and poverty. William Hance (1967), a well known writer of Africa, stated that most African countries which have experimented with collective, communal, and state-controlled enterprises have found them to be ineffective methods of development, and that a far more powerful combination of government aid and private investment must be forthcoming for the problem to be dealt with properly.

Among other generalizations given by researchers are those based on the unproductive practices of African farmers including the land tenure system and intercropping, as opposed to the preferred plantation economy, and the "*laziness*" of the ignorant, uneducated African farmers who are not responsive to economic opportunities (*Dumont 1966: 59,166*). But too often, researchers are out of place in their condemnation of the people, without sufficient evidence. Dumont and others were ill-informed about Africans and their economic practices. Africans are probably one of the most capitalistic people the world has ever known. They may live poorly, but they are not stupid or ignorant. In fact, those who have thoroughly studied the African people have found them to be innovative and economic. William O. Jones, in "*Economic Man in Africa*," (1960) challenged this hypothesis of the noneconomic behavior of African farmers and pointed out that Africans are economic men who are highly responsive to economic opportunity, adding that the behavior of West African farmers could only be understood within the framework of traditional economic analysis. Similarly, others who have studied the Africans in their setting have found them to be efficient, productive, and innovative farmers, especially if they are given the same opportunities and incentives as government owned farm settlements and private plantations.

In regards to plantation economy, Eicher contended that under West African ecological, political, and social conditions, smallholders can produce almost any crop as efficiently as large-scale production units such as plantation or state farms, provided they have access to the new technology, credit, extension assistance, and central processing that is critical for crops. And considering all the implications of the plantation hypothesis, Eicher concluded that the over-simplification concept of plantation crops is not an operational guide to planners in West Africa. Given the present condition, in general, private plantations, government plantations, state farms, and farm settlements most probably cannot be operated efficiently under the likely political constraints in West African nations. Studies conducted by Oluwasanmi (1966) and Saylor (1968) in Nigeria pointed out that plantation schemes were insignificant, and that for all practical purposes, Nigerian small-farmers were still the mainspring of agricultural development before Independence. Since Independence, even though increasing attention has been devoted to government sponsored land settlements and government owned plantations, to the neglect of

4

small farms, the small farmers have been performing much better than the government sponsored schemes.

Similar findings have been made in Ghana by Bigelow (1973) and in Ivory Coast by Hecht (1983). Bigelow, in comparing the performances of the Agricultural Development Schemes and the small uninnovative, uneducated farmholders, found that formal education among farmers is not related to agricultural production and innovation, and that uneducated local farmers were still the backbone of the economy of Ghana, in spite of the near bankruptcy investment the government made on plantation type schemes to the neglect of the smallholders. In fact, during the time the schemes were in full force, Bigelow observed that there was an absolute decrease in the outputs. These failures, he commented, may be attributed in part to an inadequate understanding of the characteristics of the small local farmer. Ivory Coast, having learned its lesson, has ventured to encourage smallholders rather than large-scale agriculture, which brought about the economic miracle that Hecht found in the country. Zimbabwe, which gained her independence in 1980, is a net exporter of food to neighboring countries, which, though in the same climatic region with the former, have been stifled by distorted development strategies.

It should be noted that small-scale farmers often intercrop two or more crops on the same field. This practice has also been frowned on by some researchers who believe that it causes unproductivity. But recent studies have pointed out the contrary. In fact, there is enormous evidence which shows that a suitable combination of intercrops will always produce a greater total yield than only one crop (*Innis, 1980*). Furthermore, intercropping has been more effective in reducing the loss of nutrients from leaching and in maintaining the organic content of the soil. Intercropping, therefore, is highly desirable in the heavily leached soils of tropical areas.

The influence of the past policies of colonial powers and Westernization, which is still looked upon as an adverse factor in agricultural development in many African countries (*Federal Republic of Nigeria, Federal Ministry of Agriculture 1984*), should not be a primary consideration after over 25 years of political independence. While disruption under the colonial legacy may have been very significant and probably unwavering, the problems of today's Africa may not be adequately explained by those past policies. Moreover, countries in Africa (Liberia and Ethiopia, for example) whose independence outdated even some developed nations (and did not necessarily experience the well-known colonialism), have suffered the same fate as the younger nations. On the other hand, Zimbabwe, one of the countries that recorded the least production performance, has, since independence, become a net exporter of food to neighboring countries. Cameroon, a country just east of Nigeria, and Swaziland are performing well in their agricultural sector. Moreover, there are several African nations (Nigeria, Ghana, Sudan, Uganda, and others), whose post-independence agricultural development was significant enough to sustain the economy of those countries, but they were stifled by later development strategies. Therefore, gross generalizations should be avoided since agricultural planning and development anywhere in the world must be closely geared to the local conditions. The elements of climate (including microclimate), and social, cultural, and political conditions are different from society to society, and these factors are primary in the agricultural development in any society.

In order to avoid overgeneralization, a single country, Nigeria (Figure 1.1), has been selected for investigation. Since Nigeria is experiencing a severe agricultural crisis at this time, it is an excellent microcosm of greater Africa and an excellent basis of study. In the first place, the country has a great potential for growth, especially in the agricultural sector. In the second place, Nigeria is the most populous country in Africa (it holds about 95 million people, 20 percent of the continent's population) and one of the most affluent countries on the continent. However, it shares with its neighbors a serious agricultural crisis in spite of its very high potential for agricultural success and the revenue derived from the oil industry. Thirdly, the country's land is among the best on the continent south of the Sahara, in terms of climate. Fourth, like almost all other countries of the continent, Nigeria claims to place a great emphasis on unrestricted general assistance to farmers and to agricultural productivity in general. The country has adopted several verifiable measures of combatting the food shortage and, in effect, the overall agricultural problem. And finally, a study of Nigeria, a country with a high sphere of influence, can make important contributions to the debate on the merits and demerits of the generalizations regarding the agricultural crisis in developing countries, especially those in Africa. These countries have readily accepted these generalizations, and their acceptance has obscured the real problems.

The thesis raised in this work is that the agricultural crisis in Nigeria is much better explained by federal, state, and local mismanagement, and political corruption and neglect, as well as by displaced priorities in development strategy.

The Scope of the Study

The work examines, in critical terms, the underlying causes of the agricultural crisis in Nigeria. To do so, the study starts with the assumption that the crisis has its roots in the political, economic, and social environments of the country, which began approximately a decade after independence. While one might

6

FIGURE 1.1

hesitate to assign a point at which these factors operated to bring about the present crisis in the country, certain economic, political, and social developments strongly suggest that such a distinction is possible. The work, therefore, presents a thorough cause-effect analysis of broad economic, political, and social factors that are assumed to have led to the present dire state of affairs in the agricultural sector. And while the work is not aimed at solving all the problems facing the agricultural economy of the country, it seeks to explore the implications of the federal management decision-making processes that have been involved and the political environment in which they operated, and then make some practical suggestions for improving agricultural development policies.

Conditions Necessary for Agricultural Output

It is generally acknowledged that with all of the necessary natural conditions (land, rainfall, temperature, soil and relief) available, crops can generally thrive, and productivity can be increased if nutrients are added to the soil. In mathematical language, we can say that agricultural output is a function of the combined effects of moisture, temperature, quality of land, soil, and relief, and this can be represented in the equation below:

$Y = f(X_1, X_2, X_3, X_4, X_5, X_6)$ where

Y is the dependent variable representing the agricultural output, while

$(X_1, X_2, X_3, X_4, X_5, X_6)$ are the independent variables, controlling the agricultural output.

X_1 = the effect of moisture on the general performance of any given crop.

X_2 = the effect of temperature.

X_3 = the quality of land which of course depends upon climate

X_4 = the effect of soil and its nutrients.

X_5 = the effect of relief which holds the soil.

X_6 = other added nutrients.

The lack of any one of these independent variables may hinder agricultural activities. It would be unreasonable to think about high productivity without these conditions being properly met. While these basic factors are of prime importance in agricultural output, they are, by themselves, not enough to bring about high productivity. We have, in addition, the individual and/or collective decision-making processes and the social, economic, cultural, and demographic structures displayed in Figure 1.2 that interact to affect overall output.

In Nigeria, none of the five basic elements (including the climatic factor, which has been singled out in this study for more thorough scrutiny) poses an unusual problem for agricultural development. Yet the country is faced with an agricultural crisis that seems to be unresponsive to suggested solutions. Moreover, neither the governing body nor the population at large understands the factors that bring about the crisis or the problems farmers face, the solution of which is beyond the effort of the poor farmers in the countryside. This study, therefore, examines the impact of Nigeria's single resource (oil) economy, whose mismanagement is believed to be one of the major causes of the neglect of the rural economy.

Primary Assumptions for Investigation

A record of gains to the government will be provided to show that although heavy investment in the petroleum industry has resulted in a significant transfer of profit to Nigeria, the managerial impact of this on the basic constraints to social and economic development has been minimal, as exemplified by the case in the rural areas. Not only has the impact of the wealth from the oil industry been minimal in the rural areas, it has brought with it social and economic problems and ills that were never previously experienced in Nigeria.

The primary assumptions which serve as the basis for understanding this investigation are as follows:

1) *The elements of climate generally work in favor of agricultural expansion in Nigeria.*

2) *Scarcity of land is not a limiting factor in the development of the agricultural economy.*

3) *Agricultural output declined with the expansion of the oil industry in Nigeria, thus causing a deficit in the agricultural economy.*

4) *The present pattern of investment and development priorities in Nigeria seriously discriminates against the rural economy.*

5) *Dependence on foreign aid seems to discourage agricultural expansion.*

6) *The expansion of Nigeria's oil industry, its management, and its politics may have caused more harm than good.*

9

figure 1.2

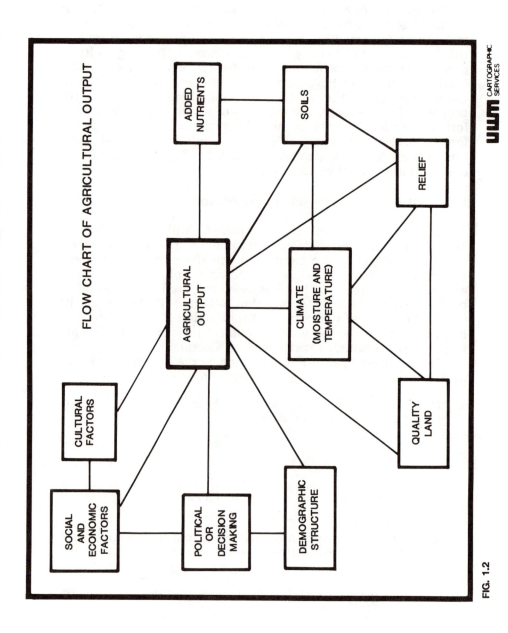

FLOW CHART OF AGRICULTURAL OUTPUT

ADDED NUTRENTS

SOILS

RELIEF

AGRICULTURAL OUTPUT

CLIMATE (MOISTURE AND TEMPERATURE)

QUALITY LAND

CULTURAL FACTORS

SOCIAL AND ECONOMIC FACTORS

POLITICAL OR DECISION MAKING

DEMOGRAPHIC STRUCTURE

FIG. 1.2

10

Justification for the Investigation

There are many reasons for undertaking this study. Firstly, Nigeria was formerly a world leader in exporting several agricultural cash crops, including cocoa, palm produce, and groundnut, and was also a secondary exporter of rubber, cotton, and beniseed. These former export products have virtually disappeared, and seldom find their way into the world market. Also, Nigeria was self-sufficient in food production prior to the expansion of the petroleum industry. The country must now increasingly import foodstuffs that it can produce domestically to satisfy the food needs of a growing population. In addition, it must even import some of the same cash crops it once exported. Interestingly, this low export volume and high import volume (the quantity of which is not known) of basic agricultural goods coincides with the period during which the country became a leading petroleum exporter. With the price revolution that grew out of the Arab Oil Embargo of 1973 and the price hike that followed, Nigeria experienced a more-than-record increase in oil revenue. Nevertheless, questions have been raised as to why Nigeria was unable to sustain continuing development of its agricultural sector in the face of the dramatic increase in revenue at its disposal.

It is perhaps necessary at this point to state that the above dilemma has been blamed, by several authors and government agencies, on the exploitative practices of past colonial powers. However, the wealth that Nigeria acquired in the decade 1970-1980 from its natural resources (especially petroleum) was greater than the total wealth the British colonial power exploited from the country, even after taking inflation into account. Therefore, the attribution of failure to past oppressive colonial practices appears inadequate. One is now inclined to look at the management, or the mismanagement, by various post-independence governments of Nigeria's natural resources, to satisfactorily explain the current dilemma. For instance, with the discovery of oil, the government's concern seemed to shift from providing a lasting agricultural economy to simply generating as much revenue as possible. There was inadequate planning for the development of the country, and Nigeria embarked on many wasteful development projects as a result of the availability of the oil revenue. However, the mismanagement of the country would perhaps have occurred without any "oil factor" involved, as seems to have been the case in other countries. But the oil factor seems to have played a major role in the decline of agriculture in Nigeria because it allowed decision-makers to overlook more significant, long-term development of the country and simply concentrate on immediate needs.

In short then, by examining the specific case of Nigeria, insights and conclusions can be more accurately drawn about the

11

geography of Sub-Saharan African countries and the problem of underdevelopment. One can see that other countries less fortunate in natural resources than African nations have made progress, and they are the envy of many more developed countries. It seems, then, that African nations who have relied too heavily on exploitation of their natural resources have encountered a problem of mismanagement, of the gains acquired from these resources.

Research Approach

To investigate the problem raised in this study, both structured and unstructured field interviews were conducted in Nigeria. The latter involved interviewing the somewhat rapidly changing high ranking government officials who were directly involved with matters of agriculture at both Federal and State levels. These government officials, as expected, could give little or no concrete information about the trend of activities in the agricultural sector, as they were almost new in their respective positions. They could only provide some data about past policies relating to the study, in addition to their condemnation of previous governments. In addition, a rich body of data addressing the problem has been extracted from reports and statistics published by different government units. These data are helpful in providing the most necessary information. These government documents are also useful in deciding which data to use where discrepancies are encountered. Some of the statistical information collected, even from government units, varies in its reliability. Thus a decision has to be made as to which of the varying information better represents the true story. Previous works by researchers and others appearing in scholarly publications also provide useful insights regarding the concerns, opinions, and attitudes of Nigerians as they relate to the crisis of agriculture. It is from these insights that the social, political, and economic factors can be more readily assessed.

The structured interviews involved in situ interviewing of local farmers by means of a written questionnaire. The interviews were conducted in two states that varied in physical character, cultural character, and size, but were representative of the country's two major regions. Within these states, several farming communities of varying sizes were randomly selected. The sample sizes of population chosen from the two local government areas were 302 and 326, respectively. The individual respondents were age 15 and older. Information was collected on the demographic characteristics of farmers, farming activities, problems encountered, and government involvement in their farming businesses. The sample was drawn from farmers who lived on their farms or worked in nearby towns and villages within a one-day walking distance from their farms. And, since more than 90 percent of the respondents had no formal education, the items appearing on the questionnaires had to be presented orally. This procedure generated a very high response rate.

Organization of the Work

This work is organized in three parts. Part I (Chapters 1-4) provides the background information considered necessary for understanding the problem of agriculture in Nigeria. The government factor and its implications are presented in Part II (Chapters 5-7). And finally, part III (Chapters 8 and 9) contains empirical research conducted in the field with its results, and an evaluation of the major findings, policy implications, and conclusions.

Some relevant physical and human conditions of the study area are summarized in Chapter 2. Chapter 3 provides information about the nature of the problem in the setting of Nigeria. In Chapter 4, an in-depth analysis of the climatic factor that is often viewed as a major explanatory variable of the crisis is discussed with some different conclusions about its role.

Chapters 5 and 6, which contain the center of the study, present the role of the government in the present agricultural crisis. Chapter 5 details the plight of the smallholder, who contributes so much to the country's economic development. The oil economy, its policies, and its management strategies are presented in Chapter 6, while Chapter 7 details the implication of such management strategies, believed to have led to mass migration of the able-bodied population to the cities neglecting the rural alternatives.

To find out whether or not differences exist between the two regions an analysis and evaluation of the questionnaire data are presented in Chapter 8, which provides information of the general demographic characteristics of farmers in the two study areas (Ondo and Sokoto States) and the problems they faced. This chapter also presents the general opinion of farmers regarding the government factor of agricultural development.

In Chapter 9, a summary evaluation of the major findings of the study is presented, which includes an exploration of the policy implications of the major findings for Nigeria's rural development strategy, a summary statement, recommendations for policy adjustment, and a conclusion.

Chapter 2

NIGERIA AS A STUDY AREA

The Country — Physical Characteristics

An analysis of the agricultural geography of Nigeria begins by examining the national and local settings within which the agricultural sector of the economy functions. Furthermore, to fully appreciate the changes that have occurred in the sector, an overview of the general condition of the country and the states involved is needed.

The Federal Republic of Nigeria is the largest country on the West African coast. With its estimated population of 95 million, the country contains about one-fifth of the continent's population, in an area of 356,669 sq. miles (923,768 sq. km.) (Figure 2.1.). Nigeria lies entirely within the tropics, between latitude 4° and 14° north of the equator, and longitudes 3° and 14° east of the Greenwich Meridian. A description of the physical characteristics will be limited here to a few salient features, since Chapter 4 is devoted to the most crucial aspects of the physical condition with respect to agriculture in the country.

Stretching for about 650 miles from north to south and 700 miles from east to west, Nigeria has two broad climatic and vegetational zones. The climate varies from tropical at the coast to subtropical further inland. There are two well-defined seasons. The dry season lasts from November to March in the south and September to May in the far north, and the rainy season lasts from March to November in the south and from mid-May to September in the north. Rainfall is heavier and more consistent in the south, particularly in the southeast, which receives more than 120 inches of rain a year compared with 70 inches to the southwest. The amount of rainfall decreases progressively away from the coast, and in the far north it is not more than 20 inches per year. This pattern, of course, naturally leads to north-south vegetational and occupational differences, which will be discussed later.

Figure 2.1

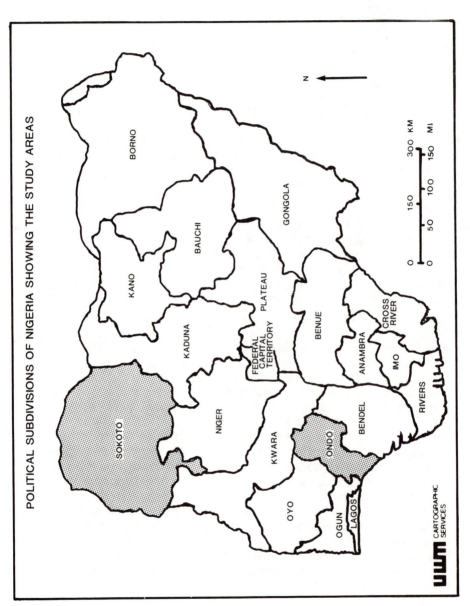

FIGURE 2.1

16

The country is located on the lower part of the great African Continental Plateau, which slopes gradually downward from south and east to north and west. Apart from a few isolated highlands in the major three regions (north, east, and west), the countryside ranges from slightly undulating to flat. The most prominent physical landmark is the Niger-Benue river system which, with its numerous tributaries, drains more than 75 percent of the country. In addition to the Niger-Benue Basin, the Lake Chad Basin in the northeast and the Gulf of Guinea Basin on the coast are drained by relatively short rivers.

Four main soil groups correspond closely with the country's main climatic and vegetational zones. Soils in the coastal areas are either sandy or swampy and, like the soils of the forest belt, are heavily leached. Soils derived from old, complex rocks in the forest belt are not as leached. Lateritic soils correspond with the dry climate north of the forest belt.

In short, Nigeria has a wealth of agricultural resources which, if well utilized, would bring about a better living standard for the population. There is a vast land area — 72 percent of the total land area — on which nearly all tropical crops could be grown due to the varied climatic conditions. In spite of all of this agricultural potential, the country is faced with an incredible food shortage and recently has been forced to import large quantities of food, food that it could produce locally to feed its population.

Agricultural Production and Development in Nigeria

Nigeria has a wealth of agricultural resources. The country has a vast area of arable land (over 70 million hectares). But only about 10 percent of the potentially arable land in the country is utilized, even when peak years are considered. In spite of this low utilization of available land, the economic growth which took place in Nigeria in the 1950s and 60s was generated by agricultural production for export; not only did the exportation of agricultural products generate income within the domestic economy, it also provided foreign exchange, which made possible the importation of machinery and other capital goods required for industrialization and general development.

Agricultural production consists of those crops grown for domestic consumption, those grown for export, and those products produced for both domestic and export purposes. Major domestic crops consist of yam, cassava, maize, millet, sorghum (guinea corn), rice, and beans, while major export crops include cotton, groundnut, and beniseed from the northern states and cocoa, rubber, palm oil, and palm kernels from the southern states. Among these products cited, palm oil, groundnut, and cotton are some of those produced for both domestic and export purposes.

17

Most of the major agricultural developments concentrated on export production during and after the colonial era. In spite of the low priority given to them, locally consumed foodstuff production continued to expand, and greatly exceeded in value the production of crops for export. Between 1950 and 1957 (the period for which reliable statistics are available), it is estimated that the value of foodstuffs produced in Nigeria for local consumption was over four times the export crops' value, and food production increased by about 50 percent during this period (*Ekundare 1973, pp. 279-80*).

The rapidly increasing population of the country necessitated increased production of foodstuffs, and even though food production kept pace with population growth up until the early 1970s, presently this need is not being met in Nigeria. Equally important was for the country's export crop earnings to increase in order to have revenue to bring about a more diversified export economy and to finance other sectors. The main problem of Nigerian agriculture has been that of expansion, which depends largely on the degree to which the country's leaders and population could succeed in overcoming and minimizing the problems farmers face.

Although farmers themselves are at times blamed for these problems, they are not as ignorant as they are sometimes portrayed to be. They have learned from experience that unless their land is cared for, an economically viable production level cannot be achieved. They invest as much as they can possibly afford to maintain their land to bring about good production. Intercropping is practiced generally in the country by most farmers, a practice, in fact, that the farmers themselves introduced to bring about better productivity and to reduce depletion of the heavily leached tropical soil. This practice has been deduced to be the best method of combatting the problem of tropical soils.

The Peoples of Nigeria

Nigeria is a melting pot of diversity with respect to peoples and cultures, a result of the great continental migration of people from north to south, west to east, and southeast to northwest. There are at least 250 distinct ethnic groups in the country, each of which has its own customs, traditions, and language. The four larger groups — Hausa, Yoruba, Ibo (Igbo) and Fulani — constitute over 60 percent of the population. Other prominent but less numerous groups include the Edo, Ijaw (Ijo), Nupe, Kanuri, Tiv, and the Ibibio. The greatest concentration of smaller ethnic groups, in which there are more than 180 linguistic groups, occurs in the middle belt. With ethnic diversity come intense cultural, social, language, and religious differences. Even though different ethnic groups have come a long

18

way in unifying themselves through marriage and trade contacts, such diversity creates problems of misunderstanding and intolerance, and such problems often affect decisions concerning the production and distribution of national wealth. Stereotypes exist in virtually all parts of the country which tend to color social, economic, and political relationships. The larger ethnic groups have always dominated the political and economic scene of the country, and their decisions have been "*law*" for the entire population.

It has been recently revealed that the largest ethnic group in the country (Hausa-Fulani) seems to dominate the highest posts in government because of their religious and linguistic affiliation with one another. Since the other two ranking ethnic groups (Ibos and the Yorubas) do not possess a similar mutual affinity, it is likely that the Hausa-Fulani groups will continue to occupy strategic positions in government. It is officially estimated that 47 percent of the Nigerian population is Muslim as compared to 35 percent Christian, while animists constitute only 18 percent of the population. On a regional basis the greatest concentration of Moslems is in the northern states, where at least 75 percent of the people are thought to profess the faith. A great number of the people in the western states are also Moslems.

The significance of this is that Moslem dominance has led to a majority rule in the country, which has manifested itself in the establishment of an Islamic utopian government in the last two elections. It is apparent that a non-Moslem president will not be elected to office in the near future. The Moslems are said to believe that the Christians are not fit to run the country, and they are looked upon as second class citizens. Moreover, Moslems believe that only a "*holy man*" can provide good government, and that there is no "*holy man*" outside of the Muslim community. This has been a problem in leadership selection in many countries where Moslems are a majority, as their own "*holy man*" will unanimously be selected as the political leader.

The Nigerian constitution does not permit leadership selection based on religious affiliation. Nevertheless, the Muslim population looks to its holy man as the ideal person to run the country. This occurs even in the face of a corrupt government like that experienced between 1979 and 1983 under Alhaji Shehu Shagari. Shagari was elected in 1979 and re-elected in 1983. He is a descendant of the ruling family of Othman dan Fodio, whose jihad made the greatest impact on Nigeria's Muslim population. To re-elect him was, therefore, a natural thing to do even though the corruptness of his government did severe damage to the entire nation's economy and put the country in debt for the first time since independence. He was also re-elected as the "*holy choice*" in spite of evidence of corruption, bribery, and violent assault (*West Africa August 15, 1983*).

The role of religion as to who is elected to public office, at least at the higher echelons, is pervasive. In the only two elections the country has ever experienced, religious affiliation seemed to transcend all other factors in affecting the election outcome. Because of widespread corruption, a military overthrow of the elected government occurred in December 1983. A subsequent overthrow of the government occurred again in 1985. In both instances, Muslim dominance prevailed and subsequently little change took place in policies relative to agricultural development.

Political Development

Nigeria became independent of British rule in 1960 and adopted a federal constitution and a parliamentary system of government. But this was obstructed by a military takeover in January 1966 and an ensuing succession of military governments until 1979, when a new constitution was adopted. Under this 1979 constitution the country adopted a presidential system of government in which the president, who was directly elected, exercised power as the Chief Executive and the Head of State. There was also a Federal Legislature which consisted of the Senate and the House of Representatives, from which the president sought support for his measures. Widespread mismanagement of public funds and corruption led to the downfall of the regime under President Shehu Shagari. Now, the country is once again back to a military government.

Political evolution in Nigeria has been rather painful at times. A destructive civil war was fought between 1967 and 1970 to preserve national unity and integrity. Following this crisis, a process of state restruction emerged in 1967, which made twelve smaller states out of the original four powerful regions of the first Nigerian Republic. In 1976, approximately 10 years later, the Murtala Muhammed regime expanded the number of states to nineteen with a federal territory. The idea obviously was to make the states as small and economically dependent on federal subvention as possible and to see that no one state was powerful enough to threaten secession, as did the former Eastern Region in 1967.

Social Condition

Most notable in the social condition of Nigeria is the wide gap that exists between the rural and the urban populations and the rich and poor. This difference is far greater in Nigeria than in industrialized countries. Even though the official minimum yearly wage by 1981 was about $2,300 (U.S.) most of the country's unskilled workers earned much less than this. Average earnings for lawyers, university teachers, engineers, and doctors in the public service was about $12,000/year, while professionals in the private sector and major contractors and merchants earned much more. And because of continuing price increases, many families found it difficult to eat adequately even though wages increased threefold during the 1970s (*Encyclopedia Britannica 1984, vol. 13 p. 95*). This situation was compounded by an acute shortage of staple food at the local level, and as a result, basic food items such as rice and corn, among others, had to be imported in large quantities every year. The Nigerian National Supply Company, established by the Federal Government to undertake the bulk purchase of essential items from foreign countries for distribution at controlled prices, proved ineffective. Prices of food continued to go up when food was very scarce or when local supply was inadequate due to the ineffective administration of the sector.

To continue, health conditions in Nigeria have met with little improvement over the years. Though modern medical facilities have made some progress in health conditions, the supplies have proven to be inadequate to meet the demand of the ever-growing population. Many people still die from malaria, water-borne diseases, and other preventable diseases because of inadequate medical facilities, and this problem is compounded by poor sanitary conditions (an outgrowth of the large concentration of people in the cities), water shortages, and even poor drainage.

It is axiomatic that the general quality of life in any human settlement depends to a large extent on the service level achieved. Such services as the provision of water for drinking and other uses, as well as in the disposal of refuse and sewage, are paramount in satisfying basic service expectations. Very little effort has been made by the government to bring these services to a satisfactory level. For example, Table 2.1, which shows the percentage of dwellings with pipe-borne water and sewage disposal systems in the state capitals, reveals in very clear terms the poor facilities of many towns and cities. Furthermore, in most of the towns served, the water supply falls far below the accepted per capital consumption of 21 liters per head per day, and in many parts of these towns, the supply often ceases completely. On the outskirts of such towns, and in towns where such services are not generally available (Table 2.2), people must resort to wells and streams to provide for their domestic needs. With such a seriously low service level, it is hardly surprising that water-borne or water-related diseases are usually among the major causes of sickness and death in Nigeria (*Fourth National Development Plan 1981-85 p.323*). Furthermore, while the water-related problems are very serious in the cities, they are virtually unattended to in the rural areas, where

21

about 75 percent of the country's population resides. This is depicted in Table 2.3; in 1978 most of the 15 states represented had no rural areas with piped water. The very small percentage of the country's population having access to safe drinking water underscores the governmental neglect of the mass majority.

Table 2.1

Water Supply in Selected Urban Areas

State	City	Percentage of Dwellings with Infrastructure Services			
		In house or In compound Water Supply	Sewage Pit Latrine	Disposal Flush Toilet	Power
Lagos	Lagos	66.0	30.0	30.0	94.0
Oyo	Ibadan	33.4	66.9	25.2	56.1
Ondo	Akure	23.8	57.1	1.6	37.7
Ogun	Abeokuta	25.3	25.4	9.3	47.4
Bendel	Benin City	24.9	95.0	4.0	59.3
Rivers	Port Harcourt	73.0	0.4	18.6	79.0
Imo	Owerri	63.3	3.1	3.6	70.8
Anambra	Enugu	49.9	5.6	26.4	68.7
Cross River	Calabar	11.3	51.6	3.5	26.2
Benue	Makurdi	21.9	18.2	-	23.1
Kwara	Ilorin	30.7	33.4	10.3	28.4
Niger	Minna	44.8	89.0	1.2	30.5
Sokoto	Sokoto	25.4	95.1	0.6	14.2
Kaduna	Kaduna	73.0	77.7	14.1	53.3
Kano	Kano	26.1	76.9	1.3	69.3
Bauchi	Bauchi	5.0	-	5.0"	25.0"
Plateau	Jos	73.0	48.8	4.8	61.8
Borno	Maiduguri	14.0	-	-	-
Gongola	Yola (Jimeta)	38.9	-	-	-

Source: Federal Republic of Nigeria, <u>Fourth National Development Plan 1981-85,</u> volume 1 p. 322.

In addition, the condition of the rural communities is made much worse than in the cities because of the hard and tedious way water has to be obtained. Many villagers must travel as far as six miles by foot to the nearest water point, usually a stream, to collect needed water, even though ground water is abundantly present. A lack of technological know-how places the ground water supply out of reach. Because people wash clothes, bathe, fish, and even dump their wastes in the same stream, the water drawn by anyone living in villages further downstream is often polluted. Wayside pits containing rain water are often used by both man and cattle, thus contributing to the high incidence of intestinal diseases and guinea worm in many rural areas. Efforts to ameliorate these problems in the rural areas have failed in the face of the widespread mismanagement and corrupt practices that have impeded rural development. Even though the rural areas constitute about 80 percent of the country's population, the people there have been the victims of brutal oppression and exploitation in spite of the heavy burden laid upon them in the development of the country.

Table 2.2

Urban Water Supplies by State 1977

	No. of towns served	Population served percent	No. of bore holes	No. of dams
Anambra	16	22	20	-
Bauchi	4	9	12	-
Bendel	20	24	61	1
Benue	8	4	12	-
Borno	7	10	8.10	-
Cross River	14	19	24	1
Gongola	5	6	21	-
Imo	16	13	26	-
Kaduna	11	16	13	6
Kano	19	8	29	5
Kwara	11	26	5	6
Lagos	4	98	6	-
Niger	7	14	2	-
Ogun	23	41	17	-
Ondo	21	38	9	2
Oyo	32	55	4	-
Plateau	8	12	6	2
Rivers	19	35	45	-
Sokoto	16	11	19	2
Nigeria	261	22	405	31

Source: Federal Republic of Nigeria, Fourth National
Development Plan 1981-85, volume 1 p. 325.

Table 2.3

Coverage of Water Supply in Fifteen States, 1978

	Total Pop. (m)	Urban centers	Percentages Served			
			Urban	Rural	Rural Piped Water	Pop. Served Piped Water (m)
Anambra	5.69	32	37	64	9	1.0
Borno	4.53	18	70	0	-	0.5
Benue	3.53	8	80	88	-	0.2
Cross River	5.08	19	85	8	5	1.1
Gongola	3.50	17	31	2	-	0.2
Imo	5.00	9	100	20	1	0.7
Kaduna	6.40	22	31	13	4	0.7
Kano	8.36	20	na	na	na	na
Kwara	2.70	21	85	13	2	0.8
Lagos	4.53	4	94	4	-	2.2
Oyo	7.60	24	79	na	na	6.0
Ogun	2.60	10	100	14	10	0.8
Plateau	3.19	19	83	0	-	0.6
Rivers	2.02	13	66	35	1	0.3
Sokoto	6.55	16	100	39	-	0.9
TOTAL	68.13	239	68	18	2	16.0

Source: Federal Republic of Nigeria, Fourth National
   Development Plan 1981-85, volume 1 p. 324.

Physical and Social Conditions in Ondo and Sokoto States

Since it was impossible, as well as unwarranted, to conduct extensive field work throughout the entire country, two states, Ondo State in the southwest and Sokoto State in the northwest, were selected for study. The selection and comparison of these two states makes the study meaningful and representative because they depict in a rather broad sense the ecological, social, and political climates of the entire country. The following sections describe the physical and social conditions of each of the states.

Physical and Social Condition in Ondo State

Ondo State was carved from the former Western Region (*later Western State*) of Nigeria during the Murtala Muhammed-Obasanjo Military Regime. The area was formerly known as the Ondo Province, a periphery of the former Western State. Within an area of about 14,400 sq. km. there is an estimated population of about 4.8 million. The Yorubas, who speak various ethnic dialects, constitute over 90 percent of the population. The Ijaws constitute a minority. The majority of the population is Christian. However, Moslems are numerous among the Yorubas in the upland, while the Ijaws are mostly Christians.

Geographically, the state lies in the tropical zone with temperatures in the 80s and a humidity of over 90 percent. Two well-defined seasons, dry and rainy, are present, with an annual rainfall ranging from 50 inches in the north to over 80 inches in the extreme southern part of the state. Adequate rainfall for farming activities is never a problem for farmers in this part of the country. Weather-related problems with regard to agricultural activities occur only when there is inadequate sunshine to dry the cocoa beans, as in the 1983 growing season.

The state is vegetated with mixed secondary forest and is, for the most part, well suited for agriculture. However, the land is undercultivated. With the exception of the small percentage of swampy high forest zone in the southern part of the state, the remaining land is ideal for agricultural activities. Cocoa and rubber are the principal cash crops, while yam, cassava, and rice are the major food crops. Production of these crops could be doubled if state and federal aids were made available to the more than 70 percent of the total working population engaged in the sector. However, such aid has never materialized due to the widespread corrupt practices and government policies which tend to suppress the farmers' ability to produce.

In the midst of these conditions are the compounding problems which the state government does not always have the technical know-how to deal with. Because of this, Ondo State has recently experienced more unemployment among the educated citizens per capita than any other state in the country. Many Grade II and III teachers and university graduates have been forced to give up their careers because the state is unable to provide them the minimum salaries consistent with their level of training. According to different independent sources, Ondo State has imposed a compulsory retirement on all Grade III teachers and those Grade II teachers who graduated as of 1983; it has also forced many public servants to give up their posts, a decision made to cut public expenditure as a result of the economic crisis. Decision-making of this sort indicates helplessness on the part of a government which sees no solution and often resorts to ill-conceived, overnight decisions.

As in any other part of the country, there is a very high poverty level in Ondo State, with well over 80 percent of the population living substandardly. Basic foodstuffs are gari, yam, rice, beans, fish, and meat, most of which are very scarce, and water is obtained mostly from ponds, rivers, and shallow wells, which are almost invariably polluted. The larger cities (Ondo, Akure, Ado-Ekiti, Owo, Okitipupa) receive unreliable pipe-borne water. Efforts made to improve the water problem with huge budgetary allocations have not been effective. Only 23.8 percent of the dwellings in Akure, the state capital, have pipe-borne water, and only 1.6 percent of its dwellings have flush toilets (Table 2.1). This obviously does not reflect an encouraging situation, in spite of the actual expenditure of more than ₦36.0 million out of the ₦76.5 million allocated to this sector in the state from 1975-80. Moreover, the 1981-85 plan allocated over ₦139 million for water supply, yet no evidence of improvement has been observed even in the cities. As always, the rural population is left to confront its own water problems.

In short, while Ondo State can pride itself on having the most educated population per capita in the country, the state is also one of the most corrupt and probably one of the least developed in Nigeria.

Physical and Social Condition in Sokoto State

Sokoto State, with an area of 102,500 square kilometers and a population of about 7 million, is one of the largest states in the country. The state was carved from the original Northwestern State, which in turn was created from the former Northern Region. The state lies in the subtropical zone, with temperatures mostly in the 90s during the day and in the 60s and 70s at night. The highest temperatures are experienced during the month of April, just before the rainy seasons starts. Humidity is relatively low, and precipitation is 20-50 inches annually, depending upon the location of places relative to the Atlantic ocean. Compared to Ondo State, this zone is marked by increased seasonality of rainfall. The bulk of the rain falls between May and September. In the southern part of the state, the rainy season usually extends from April to October. The heaviest rainfall is experienced in the month of August, with an average of 240 mm (about 10 inches) of rain in the south and 190 mm (about 8 inches) in the north. Here the dry season is longer and more severe, with low relative humidity. The harmattan season, which corresponds with the northern winter, extends from December to February and is characterized by winds from the Sahara Desert and chilly nights.

The mixed Cambretaceous woodland is the typical vegetation of the Sudan Savanna, with the Guinea Savanna culture dominant to the south. The grass is short, and acacia trees are the predominant Savanna tree in the state. Since most of the people are farmers (over 70 percent of the workforce), the open land there is better cultivated than the forested Ondo State. The light rainfall, short wet season, and low humidity restrict the principal food crops to grains, primarily millet and guinea corn. The land is undercultivated, and, as in all other states, aid from the government is minimal. The state is privileged in that almost 90 percent of its territory is covered by the Sokoto-River Basin, and two of the major dam systems are within reach of the people, but they are still plagued by erosion and other crop-related hazards.

Most people in the state speak Hausa, but Fulani is also widely spoken in Sokoto. It is a truly rural state compared to the states in the south. Estimates show that over 80 percent of the people live in settlements that have fewer than 5,000 inhabitants. Although it is extremely difficult to characterize the phenomenon of migration in Nigeria, it can be safely stated that the growing towns such as Sokoto, Gusau, and Birnin Kebbi, among others, have attracted a large number of migrants from rural areas in search of non-agricultural employment opportunities. The attractiveness of these cities has been enhanced by the disproportionate number of both public services and private industrial ventures located in these towns. The State also ranks high in illiteracy, but through the establishment of more secondary schools and a university, this condition is changing.

As in the rest of the country, the provision of water is inadequate in Sokoto. In Table 2.1 above, it is noted that only 25.4 percent of the urban population in the city of Sokoto is served with in-house or in-compound water supply, with just 0.6 percent having flush toilets. The rural population, which is invariably neglected, does not have these services at all, and, as a result, intestinal diseases are commonplace, a fact the population has been forced to live with. And because most of the people are poor, substandard living conditions are typical. Data show that about 48 percent of those between the ages of 15 and 65 have not been a part of the labor force because of sickness or disability. Underemployment is also a serious problem, and the female population contributes very little to the economy of the state, since less than 15 percent of it is in the labor force due to the Muslim tenet that discourages Muslim women working outside of the home.

Sokoto's development may best be described as being in a seminal stage. The several Niger Dam projects, along with the recently built dam on the Sokoto River, were constructed to help the industrial and agricultural sectors of the economy, but better utilization of these facilities depends upon the attention of the governments in that region.

Chapter 3

THE AGRICULTURAL DILEMMA IN NIGERIA

Introduction

The present situation of the agricultural sector of the Nigerian economy warrants investigation. Nigeria is facing a very serious agricultural crisis at a time when the prices of agricultural goods in the world are escalating. Most of its export commodities have disappeared from the export market. Even more disturbing is the absolute decline of the production of basic foodstuffs since about 1975, while the population has been increasing at an annual rate of about 2.5 percent. This dismal problem is further compounded by the average annual private consumption demand which, according to Onimode, increased almost 100 percent from 0.9 percent during 1960-70, to 1.6 percent for 1970-76 (*Onimode, 1982, p. 168*). The staggering inflation of prices for basic foodstuffs in Nigeria makes it impossible for a very high proportion of the population to feed itself adequately. As a result, malnutrition and related diseases are commonplace in a country so naturally blessed.

This reflects a grave situation in a country where the enormous importance of agricultural activities has been evidenced by the contribution of the agricultural sector to the development of the country before the expansion of the oil industry, in spite of the very high priority the government consistently claims to have given to its development. The irony of the matter is that Nigeria, with its high agricultural potential, extensive untilled arable land, and huge numbers of unemployed labor, increasingly imports food products that it could very well produce at home. While the import bill of food products has risen considerably, the agricultural export volume has declined since the late 1970s to less than half of what it was in the 1960s. Never in the history of Nigeria has the country experienced such a perverse agricultural crisis.

Historically, the only two instances of mild food shortage problems were associated with political disturbances. One such occasion was during the Second World War (1939-45) when, due to disruptions from the war, there was heavy food demand on the part of the British government to feed its population and army. The then Colonial Departments of Agriculture were mobilized to play important roles in the production of food for the empire. The second occasion was during the Nigerian Civil War fought between 1967 and 1970, but it was less severe, and was basically confined to the then Eastern Region, where much of the war was fought. Most of the remaining country's agricultural activities were unaffected by the war. Nigeria has fought no wars since 1970, yet the problem of food shortage has worsened at a time when the country has attained some political stability.

Decades before and after independence, Nigeria was self-sufficient in food production; in fact, its self-sufficiency was even taken for granted. Therefore, most of the major agricultural developments and efforts in the sector on the part of the government were directed to the export of cash crops like cocoa, rubber, groundnut, palm produce, beniseed, and cotton. Food crops were neglected since there was no real food shortage at that time. This was understandable because the government's revenue then depended heavily on farm exports, so the development of exports was of great importance.

Government effort towards agriculture should not, however, have been restricted to the development of cash crops alone; it should have emphasized the production of crops for the domestic agribusiness and consumption as well. It should be understood also that the government was consistently exploitative in its concern about the revenue it derived from export agriculture. It was not particularly concerned about how the farmers were faring, nor was it able to understand the problems farmers faced. The government's primary concern was made evident through its introduction of powerful Marketing Boards, which were set up to handle the major export crops processed for trading. That is the reason why, when an alternative income generating machine was introduced in oil production, the country abandoned its export oriented agriculture and plunged into the new, more lucrative money machine.

The Role of Agriculture in the Gross Domestic Product (G.D.P)

Even by world standards Nigeria has a very strong agricultural potential. This is evident from the performances of the agricultural sector of the economy before the country attained independence and during the decade after independence. The early stages of economic development witnessed an agriculture that provided almost all of the country's food needs, earned most of its foreign exchange, and generated the lion's share of the government revenue. In fact, all economic indicators attested to the importance of agriculture in the country.

The share of agriculture in the Gross Domestic Product (GDP) of any country is one of the most important indicators of the performance of the agricultural sector. According to Table 3.1, the sector contributed well over 60 percent of the GDP before and after independence in 1960. It then declined to about 48 percent in 1970 and to 18 percent in 1980. Since about 1975, the contribution of the agricultural sector has not increased. Even the very high inflation which took place during this period did not improve its share of the GDP. This is a very serious situation in a country that employs about 70 percent of its work-force in the agricultural sector. The percentage decline until the first part of the 1970 decade was quite gradual, but after 1973 a steep drop was experienced. The GDP share may be misleading, however, in a well diversified economy, which of course is not the case in Nigeria. Other economic indicators depict a frighteningly real agricultural crisis.

Agricultural Export-Import, A Paradox

In the 1950s and 1960s Nigeria commanded a comfortable position in the world's trade in at least three of the agricultural export crops. The country was the largest exporter of groundnut, with 36 percent of the world trade. It supplied about 20 percent of international trade for cocoa; in addition it had 18 percent and 11 percent shares respectively in the world export trade of cotton and vegetable oil (_Ekundare, 1973 p.16_). However, since the early 1970s, agricultural exports have become increasingly insignificant, and this can only be explained by governmental neglect of the agricultural sector in favor of a booming petroleum industry. Although the total value of agricultural export increased from ₦282.4 million (about $460.0 million U.S.) in 1960 to ₦498.5 million (about $800.0 million U.S.) (Table 3.2) in 1979 (not counting inflation), its share of the total value of all exports declined from 85.58 percent in 1960 to only 4.6 percent in 1979. This performance gives an indication of the drastic decline in the volume of agricultural exports over the years, only partially compensated for by higher export prices, especially for cocoa, which now accounts for over 80 percent of all agricultural exports. The decline in petroleum production and prices in the 1980s has not seemed to improve the percentage share of the agricultural exports.

31

Table 3.1

Share of Agriculture in Gross Domestic Product

	Total All Sectors (N million)	Agriculture Sector (N million)	% of Total
1950	1,377.4	930.0	67.52
1951	1,482.8	1,005.4	67.80
1952	1,587.0	1,022.4	64.42
1953	1,623.2	1,059.2	65.25
1954	1,744.2	1,115.6	63.96
1955	1,790.4	1,144.6	63.93
1956	1,747.4	1,103.6	63.16
1957	1,820.0	1,130.4	62.11
1958	1,800.0	1,239.8	68.88
1959	1,877.0	1,226.0	65.32
1960	1,962.6	1,280.0	65.22
1961	2,247.4	1,414.6	62.94
1962	2,359.6	1,453.2	61.59
1963	2,597.6	1,605.8	61.82
1964	2,745.8	1,673.8	60.96
1965	2,894.4	1,676.4	57.92
1966	3,110.0	1,691.8	54.39
1967	3,374.8	1,855.0	54.97
1968	2,752.6	1,527.8	55.50
1969	2,656.2	1,415.2	53.28
1970	3,549.3	1,711.2	48.23
1971	5,281.1	2,576.4	48.49
1972	6,650.9	3,033.7	45.61
1973	7,187.5	3,092.7	43.03
1974	12,118.0	3,352.1	27.66
1975	16,462.8	3,943.0	23.95
1976	19,437.7	4,579.5	23.56
1977	23,826.0	4,898.3	20.56
1978	26,758.5	5,143.4	19.22
1979	27,370.2	5,389.1	19.69
1980	31,424.7	5,656.8	18.00

Source: Federal Ministry of Agriculture, Information Bulletin on Agri-
culture, 1984, p. 12.
B. Onimode, Imperialism and Underdevelopment in Nigeria, The
Dialectics of Mass Poverty, 1982; p. 122.
D. Olatunbosun, Nigeria's Neglected Rural Majority, 1975, p. 92.

The figures in Table 3.2 also reveal the importance of the rural sector in the course of Nigerian development before the expansion of the oil industry. These figures show the crucial role this sector had been playing vis-a-vis other sectors. The trend was such that the economic growth in Nigeria had been due to export crops until the advent of the spectacular rise in crude oil. Yet the agricultural sector has been the least regarded in the economic development of the country since oil exports started. In fact, the virtual disappearance of most of Nigeria's traditional export crops from export trade is a clear testimony to the limited support of the agricultural sector by the government.

Table 3.3 quantitatively depicts the amount of export crops in tons. Considering these figures, it is quite apparent that the majority of the export crops, cotton, groundnut, and palm oil, are already out of the export market. Others are just barely holding their own. Only cocoa is holding up, though production of this crop is falling too. The corresponding value in Table 3.4 for each of the crops shows that only three crops are contributing to the agricultural export market of the country, with cocoa having accounted for over 80 percent since 1975. Nigeria, therefore, not only lost a relatively high world share for four of its basic agricultural exports (including beniseed), but its overall export volume declined by over 50 per cent, with, in some cases, four of the seven main export crops (along with timber) already out of the export market entirely.

The import bill for agricultural products (food in particular), as shown in Table 3.5, has increased from a mere ₦41 million, or about $65.0 million, in 1964 to over one billion naira in 1980 (a 2,700 percent increase over 1964). The figure was more staggering in the ensuing years when the import bill went close to 2 billion naira in 1981 and 1982, a more than fifty-fold increase from the 1964 value. And in fact, other sources put it at over ₦2 billion or 3.1 billion U.S dollars for 1980 (*Africa Report Jan.-Feb. 1982 p.41*) and ₦2.115 billion for 1981, the last year of unrestricted food imports (*West Africa May 19, 1986 p. 1041*). And while the export receipts from the agricultural sector paid for food imports and for all other imported goods in the 1960s, the value of agricultural exports could not pay for even half the imported food from 1976 on.

Once the leading exporter of groundnut, the second largest exporter of cocoa, and a leader in palm oil export (*Second National Development Plan 1970-74*), Nigeria was paying more than one billion naira a year for food imports including groundnut oil (*Fourth National Development Plan 1981-85*), and it imported over 300,000 tons of palm oil in one year (*West Africa. May 19, 1986 p. 1043*) and other vegetable oils, all of which the country previously produced locally. In addition, the country was importing cotton, once an export commodity, from

33

other countries to feed its textile industry. Regardless of the level of prices and earnings, which fluctuated widely, this low export volume and high import bill reflect falling gross output in different crops and, therefore, declining agricultural performance overall.

Table 3.2

Nigeria's Export Statistics, 1960-80

(₦ million)

Year	Total Agricult. as	Oil Export	Non oil Export	Agricult. Export	Export % of Total
1960	330.0	8.8	321.2	282.4	85.58
1961	346.9	23.1	323.8	283.0	81.58
1962	334.2	33.5	300.7	260.0	77.80
1963	371.5	40.4	331.1	286.0	76.99
1964	429.2	64.1	365.1	304.0	70.83
1965	536.8	136.2	400.6	327.4	60.99
1966	574.2	189.9	384.3	292.6	50.96
1967	483.6	144.8	338.8	264.6	54.71
1968	422.2	74.0	348.2	269.7	63.88
1969	636.3	261.9	374.4	278.2	43.72
1970	885.4	510.0	375.4	286.8	32.39
1971	1,293.3	953.0	340.3	265.5	20.53
1972	1,434.2	1,176.2	258.0	190.2	13.26
1973	2,277.4	1,893.5	383.9	288.7	12.68
1974	5,794.2	5,365.7	429.1	307.7	5.31
1975	4,925.5	4,563.1	362.4	256.5	5.21
1976	6,751.1	6,321.6	429.5	261.5	3.87
1977	8,673.5	7,969.2	704.3	437.7	5.05
1978	6,063.4	5,400.6	662.8	444.2	7.33
1979	10,836.8	10,166.8	670.0	498.5	4.60
1980	14,077.0	13,523.0	554.0	NA	NA

Sources: J.K. Onoh, The Nigerian Oil Economy, From prosperity to Glut, 1983, p.70.)

Federal Ministry of Agriculture; Information Bulletin on Nigerian Agriculture, 1984, p.14.)

D. Olatunbosun, Nigeria's Neglected Rural Majority, 1975, p. 61

Table 3.3

Major Agricultural Exports in Nigeria 1960-83
('000 tons)

Year	Cocoa	Palm oil	Palm Kernel	Ground nut	Rubber	Cotton
1960	154	na	418	379	57	na
1961	184	165	411	614	55	na
1962	195	118	367	681	60	na
1963	175	126	398	768	63	na
1964	197	134	394	763	66	25
1965	255	150	416	716	68	14
1966	190	143	394	810	70	15
1967	224	16	162	742	48	33
1968	206	3	159	918	52	14
1969	171	8	172	784	56	14
1970	193	8	182	536	59	28
1971	267	20	238	183	51	22
1972	228	2	209	105	41	1
1973	211	-	137	199	49	8
1974	180	-	185	30	59	-
1975	198	-	173	-	57	-
1976	231	-	472	-	39	-
1977	165	9	185	8	18	-
1978	205	8	58	-	29	-
1979	155	1	104	-	29	22
1980	135	1	77	0	41	0
1981	143	0	124	0	21	0
1982	150	2	50	0	17	0
1983	228	0	70	0	8	0

Sources: Federal Office of Statistics, <u>Economic Indicators</u>, Lagos, Nigeria
(various issues).
Federal Office of Statistics, <u>Annual Abstract of Statistics</u>, Lagos,
Nigeria (various issues).
Federal Office of Statistics, <u>Review of External Trade</u>, Lagos, Nigeria
1979-83.

Table 3.4

Values of Major Agricultural Exports, 1960-83

(₦ million)

Year	Cocoa	Palm oil	Palm kernel	Ground nut	Rubber	Cotton	Total
1960	73.6	na	52.1	56.2	28.4	na	210.3
1961	67.4	26.4	39.8	78.2	22.0	na	233.8
1962	66.6	17.8	33.6	82.2	22.6	na	222.8
1963	64.8	18.8	41.6	91.6	23.6	na	240.4
1964	80.2	21.5	41.9	94.0	na	na	237.6
1965	85.4	27.2	53.0	106.2	21.8	10.2	303.8
1966	56.6	22.0	44.8	111.0	23.0	14.2	271.6
1967	109.4	2.6	15.6	93.6	12.6	16.8	250.6
1968	103.0	0.2	20.4	104.8	12.6	8.4	249.4
1969	105.2	0.8	19.6	104.0	19.2	8.8	257.6
1970	148.4	1.2	32.2	77.6	17.6	13.4	290.4
1971	153.6	3.4	33.8	43.8	12.4	17.5	264.5
1972	123.4	0.2	22.2	36.0	7.4	3.2	192.4
1973	112.4	0	18.9	45.5	19.4	4.7	200.9
1974	159.0	0	43.7	13.0	33.2	0	248.9
1975	181.5	0	18.5	0.8	15.2	0	216.0
1976	218.9	0	27.0	3.6	14.4	0	263.9
1977	306.8	0	32.5	1.2	9.9	0	350.4
1978	405.3	0	13.0	0	13.5	0	431.8
1979	291.1	0.6	18.3	0.6	19.0	20.9	350.5
1980	202.4	0.2	15.6	0	19.6	0.2	238.0
1981	198.8	0	18.0	0	10.3	0	227.1
1982	170.1	0.6	7.1	0	7.7	0	184.3
1983	260.6	0	16.6	0	3.7	0	280.9

Sources: Quarterly Economic Review of Nigeria, 1968-82 (various issues)
Federal Office of Statistics, Annual Abstract of Statistics, Lagos,
Nigeria (various issues).
Federal Office of Statistics, Review of External Trade, Lagos, Nigeria
1979-83.
Federal Republic of Nigeria, Second National Development Plan ,1970-
74, p. 23.
Federal Republic of Nigeria, Second National Development Plan 1970-
74, Second Progress Report, p.15.
Federal Republic of Nigeria, Third National Development Plan 1975-
80, First Progress Report, p 19. for 1974/75.
Federal Republic of Nigeria, Fourth National Development Plan, 1981-
85, p. 21

Table 3.5

Actual Food Import (1961-84) in Nigeria

(₦ million)

Year	Food	Vegetable oil and fat
1961	45.44	0.13
1962	46.98	0.17
1963	43.80	0.17
1964	41.24	0.26
1965	46.08	0.35
1966	51.57	0.37
1967	42.56	0.60
1968	28.39	0.58
1969	41.73	0.38
1970	57.69	0.85
1971	87.91	0.72
1972	95.10	1.06
1973	126.26	1.39
1974	154.76	3.57
1975	297.86	8.92
1976	440.93	24.69
1977	736.46	47.01
1978	1,027.11	81.26
1979	952.40	97.99
1980	1,049.05	115.00
1981	1,820.22	128.74
1982	1,642.25	151.37
1983	1,296.71	105.56
1984	843.25	101.76

Source: Federal Office of Statistics, <u>Annual Abstract of Statistics</u>, Lagos, Nigeria
(various issues)
Federal Office of Statistics, <u>Nigeria Trade Summary</u>, Lagos, Nigeria
(various issues)

By the time the Second National Development Plan was introduced in 1970, the country was already sensing imminent food shortages, and four years later, at the end of the plan in 1974, the country's food import bill was more than double. Much of the import increase was experienced in the late 1970s, and a thorough assessment of the performance of the agricultural sector before this period accentuates the absurdity of Nigeria importing food that it could very well produce domestically.

Declining Production of Agricultural Products

This bleak situation is further demonstrated by the drastic drop in the production level of export crops as shown in Table 3.6 (which, of course, is incomplete because of a paucity of data). With the exception of the less pronounced decline of cocoa production, all crops experienced a sharp drop in production level. In fact, the production of cotton dropped from 347,000 metric tons in 1965 to 77,000 tons in 1981, about 78 percent, and, if we consider the peak year of 1975, the drop is well over 80 percent. Beniseed production fell from 32,000 tons in 1965 to 2,000 tons in 1981, while groundnut was surviving at less than one-third its 1974 peak year production level.

Table 3.6

Production of Principal Agricultural Export Commodities
(000 tons)

Year	Cocoa	Palm oil	Palm kernel	Ground nut	Rubber	Cotton	Beni- seed
1965/66	165	130	415	1385	na	347	32
1966/67	263	32	28	1185	na	112	23
1967/68	234	4	190	1091	na	209	16
1968/69	185	-	na	1269	na	446	-
1969/70	224	na	na	1292	na	372	16
1970/71	308	na	na	1581	na	357	22
1971/72	254	na	na	1380	na	425	21
1972/73	241	na	na	1350	na	105	4
1973/74	-	na	na	877	na	85	4
1974/75	214	na	na	1935	na	481	15
1975/76	-	na	na	458	68	311	15
1976/77	165	na	na	460	53	294	14
1977/78	-	na	na	603	59	269	9
1978/79	137	na	na	701	58	212	15
1979/80	-	na	na	453	58	125	7
1980/81	155	na	na	675	na	77	2

Sources: Federal Ministry of Agriculture, Department of Agricultural Planning, 1982.

Federal Republic of Nigeria, Second National Development Plan 1970-74, pg. 23.

Federal Republic of Nigeria, Second National Development Plan 1970-74, Second Progress Report, p. 15.

Federal Republic of Nigeria, Fourth National Development Plan 1981-85, p. 21.

Gill and Duffs: "Cocoa Market Reprint", Jan. 1982 Joint Planning Meeting on Tree Crops (1982) in Small Holder Rubber Development in Bendel State.

For convenience, the performance of some of the export cash crops is presented in diagrammatic form (Figure 3.1). From this diagram it is apparent that none of the cash crops survived the test of improvement. While their decline is apparent from the figures and the table, the government of Nigeria has never acknowledged such a stunning downfall. It recognizes only a situation which can be explained by population growth, an expanding agribusiness in the country, and higher domestic consumption. The government, in fact, depicts an overall production growth rate of about 1.5 percent, and another source pictured a 2.5 percent growth rate (*Onimode 1982, p. 168 and Ake 1985, p. 61*). Even this, for all practical purposes, is unacceptable for the economic sector which presumably receives the most attention from the government. Above all, it cannot bridge the supply-demand gap brought about by a relatively high (3.5 percent per annum) rate of growth in food demand (*Federal Ministry of Agriculture, Information Bulletin 1984, p.11*). However, data collected from the same Ministry show a negative production growth rate much closer to reality.

Unfortunately, food crop production also experienced a decline far more disturbing than that of the export crops. With the exception of millet and guinea corn (both of which are produced in the more drought-prone northern part of the country), the decline of which is not as pronounced, all food crops witnessed absolute decline in production from 1965 to 1984. And in fact, Sokoto State (supposedly drought-stricken) alone accounted for 60 percent and 40 percent respectively of the production of these two crops for the 1980/81 season. Kano (also a drought-stricken state) and Bauchi (a much more humid state) accounted for only 12.2 percent and 10.3 percent respectively for millet, and Kano and Gongola recorded 11.3 percent and 15.2 percent respectively for guinea corn for the 1980/81 season (Table 3.7). The majority of the crops, while having experienced some increases in the 60s and early 70s, started to decline from about the middle of the 1970s (Table 3.8). The production of yam and cassava, two of the most staple food crops in the southern and middle-belt states, fell from 14.74 million and 2.98 million tons in 1965 to 4.99 million and 1.17 million tons in 1984 (a 66 and 61 percent decrease respectively). Rice and beans, two of the main cereals, also dropped in production from their peak years by 85 and 57 percent respectively. Figures 3.2a and 3.2b demonstrate the performance of some of the crops. While these performances are somewhat compensated for by increased yield per hectare (Table 3.9 and Figures 3.3a , 3.3b and Appendix figure 2), they also unequivocally explain the increasing importation of foodstuffs that the country was producing locally.

Figure 3.1

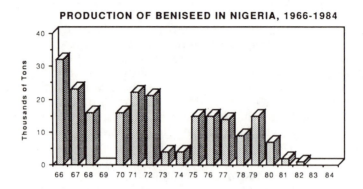

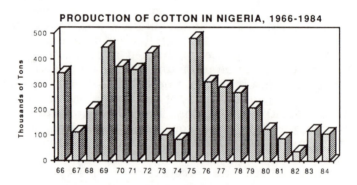

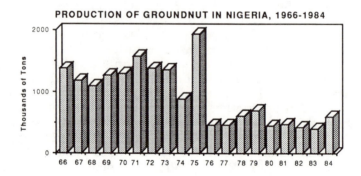

FIG. 3.1

Table 3.7

Production of Five Major Crops by State, 1978-81 ('000 tons)

	Millet			Guinea Corn			Yam			Rice			Cassava		
	78/79	79/80	80/81	78/79	79/80	80/81	78/79	79/80	80/81	78/79	79/80	80/81	78/79	79/80	80/81
ANAMBRA	-	-	-	-	-	-	265	219	414	5	1	0	85	48	18
BAUCHI	150	152	318	261	307	384	-	-	-	1	1	0	-	1	1
BENDEL	-	-	-	-	-	-	822	824	1,047	34	19	?	487	378	198
BENUE	89	99	48	114	194	34	1,739	1,029	939	28	4	11	173	171	71
BORNO	168	141	136	148	127	207	-	-	-	30	33	17	2	-	-
C. RIVER	-	-	-	-	-	-	239	314	264	4	1	2	73	59	82
GONGOLA	138	137	40	448	486	653	1,151	1,077	723	1	22	1	-	90	85
IMO	-	-	-	-	-	-	179	172	220	6	5	2	144	113	65
KADUNA	289	314	240	336	350	262	1	-	3	12	-	1	40	7	-
KANO	311	460	377	351	463	487	-	-	-	1	-	-	19	15	8
KWARA	5	11	22	35	25	84	259	262	340	-	1	0	15	9	15
LAGOS	-	-	-	-	-	-	1	0	-	-	-	-	3	1	4
NIGER	14	20	14	113	161	333	257	300	356	16	26	10	1	4	0
OGUN	-	-	-	-	-	-	17	9	5	3	1	2	62	16	29
ONDO	-	-	-	-	-	-	141	124	158	1	-	-	81	58	38
OYO	-	-	-	11	4	3	230	276	352	9	8	5	161	391	96
PLATEAU	38	66	50	228	201	130	385	399	390	17	11	5	27	8	3
RIVERS	-	-	-	-	-	-	95	45	70	1	-	0	205	129	159
SOKOTO	1,229	957	1,842	351	479	1,726	-	10	-	-	22	10	-	-	-
TOTAL	2,431	2,357	3,087	2,896	2,797	4,303	5,780	5,069	5,281	170	156	100	1,578	1,492	872

Source: Federal Ministry of Agriculture, 1982, Department of Agricultural Planning

Note: Figures may not add up because of rounding.

41

Table 3.8

Major Crop Production in Nigeria, 1965-84 ('000 tons)

Year	Millet	Guinea Corn	Ground nut	Beans	Yam	Cotton	Maize	Cassava	Rice	Melon	Beni-seed	Coco-yam	Soya beans
1965/66	2729	4235	1385	646	14736	347	1160	2976	231	115	32	2319	21
1966/67	1747	3160	1185	576	6987	112	975	1674	118	7	23	333	20
1967/68	2590	3389	1091	546	7806	209	950	3312	303	59	16	461	16
1968/69	2632	3236	1269	634	8233	446	1126	4104	275	47	-	183	-
1969/70	3081	4093	1292	884	9785	372	1255	4221	282	58	16	1074	19
1970/71	3106	4052	1581	884	12304	357	1443	5213	279	79	22	1383	15
1971/72	2834	3794	1380	798	9766	425	1270	4508	268	61	21	876	1
1972/73	2365	2298	1350	408	7601	105	638	2571	448	91	4	1400	1
1973/74	4017	3124	877	665	6935	85	1227	2901	486	191	4	1115	-
1974/75	4465	4732	1935	1099	7198	481	528	3582	535	48	15	478	-
1975/76	3552	2926	458	840	8621	311	1363	2321	643	262	15	477	4
1976/77	2893	2950	460	727	6556	294	1075	1876	218	165	14	532	0.05
1977/78	2579	3326	603	411	6661	269	777	1900	408	142	9	399	2
1978/79	2431	2396	701	339	5780	212	478	1576	170	106	15	196	111
1979/80	2357	2797	453	723	5069	125	491	1492	156	104	7	139	46
1980/81	2450	3690	471	529	5140	87	653	872	92	86	2	250	2
1981/82	2792	3698	419	615	5369	39	744	581	180	75	1	283	2
1982/83	2772	4081	396	741	5909	120	626	909	203	51	-	224	5
1983/84	3339	4231	591	475	4987	108	1027	1174	99	144	-	205	205

Source: Federal Office of Statistics, Annual Abstract of Statistics; Lagos, Nigeria. Federal Ministry of Agriculture, 1982, Department of Agricultural Planning.

Note: - Record not available.

Figure 3.2a

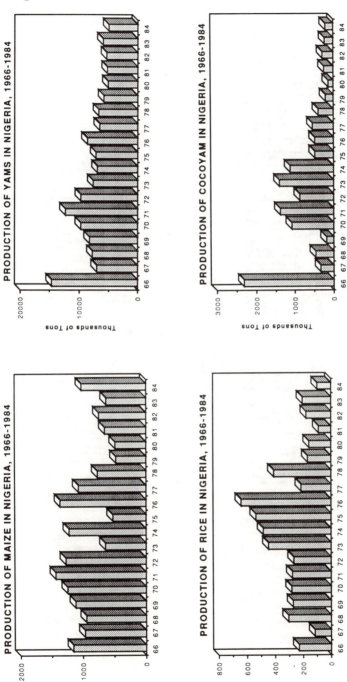

FIG. 3.2a

43

Figure 3.2b

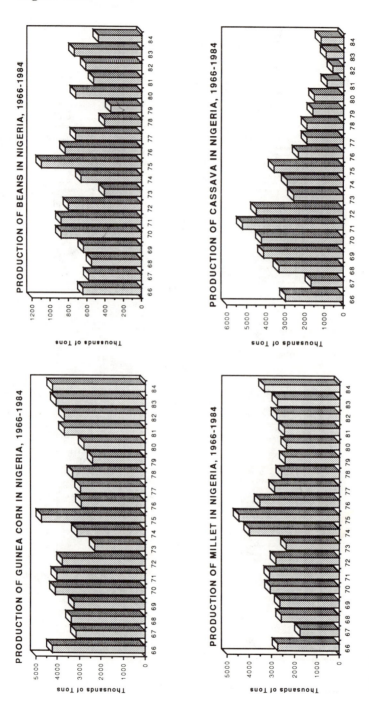

FIG. 3.2b

44

Table 3.9

Yield Per Hectare of Major Crops in Nigeria, 1965/66 1983/84 (in kg.)

Year	Millet	Guinea Corn	Ground nut	Beans	Yam	Cotton	Maize	Cassava	Rice	Melon	Beni-seed	Coco-yam	Soya beans
1965/66	590	713	621	230	8964	753	826	9854	1222	362	299	8194	309
1966/67	430	652	525	190	9416	365	852	9049	1168	114	426	5946	313
1967/68	591	716	483	139	10125	1066	817	8809	1347	551	262	4704	296
1968/69	588	630	653	188	7709	649	1028	9771	1335	180	0	3813	-
1969/70	628	524	706	215	9382	661	915	11286	1248	207	219	6671	306
1970/71	629	709	845	231	9947	545	996	13540	1120	219	282	6847	259
1971/72	602	704	769	210	7901	525	1043	10222	1347	151	955	3643	250
1972/73	841	606	665	166	8156	443	572	7142	1890	275	363	4878	500
1973/74	811	601	423	204	7315	697	1015	7289	1303	424	667	5310	-
1974/75	833	1013	1066	374	10727	1006	912	8631	1890	539	3659	4444	-
1975/76	787	1070	323	277	11110	771	1404	7415	2464	1110	349	4077	800
1976/77	736	609	671	267	9655	766	1205	5168	1130	903	412	5216	1000
1977/78	1035	955	790	265	11544	968	1274	9596	1659	843	500	4807	667
1978/79	1070	698	987	241	12272	1050	1921	9017	1478	797	1071	5351	550
1979/80	910	1041	853	514	10520	919	1155	10891	1950	920	1750	3564	2190
1980/81	868	1123	837	362	10526	664	1405	9241	1483	1142	1000	5093	400
1981/82	894	1165	645	525	11303	848	1456	8183	1957	1210	1453	4493	556
1982/83	806	1108	797	488	11024	1412	1126	11363	2137	944	-	4571	-
1983/84	838	989	909	402	9517	1161	971	10870	1868	1274	-	5694	-

Source: Federal Office of Statistics, Annual Abstract of Statistics; Lagos, Nigeria. Federal Ministry of Agriculture, 1982, Department of Agricultural Planning.

Note: - Record not available.

Figure 3.3a

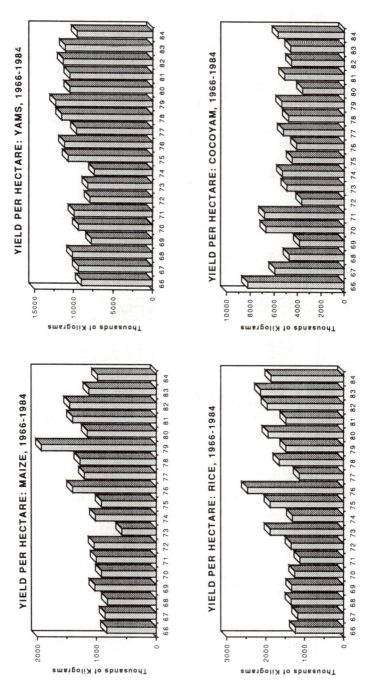

FIG. 3.3a

46

Figure 3.3b

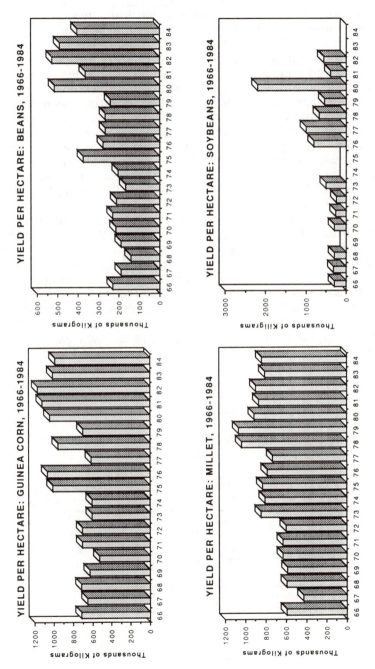

FIG. 3.3b

47

The argument of the government and other sources that there is not an absolute decline in production of food crops, even though there may be a general decline relative to population increase (*Ake 1985, p. 61 and West Africa May 12,1986 p. 990*) is impossible. While we may say that individual producers produce enough to feed their families and maybe produce even as much as they did in the past, or even more, we still cannot conclude from this information that the country as a whole has not experienced an absolute decline in food production. The decline of the amount of land under cultivation (discussed below) attests to the fact that production of basic foodstuff has actually gone down. The agricultural technology of Nigeria has never been advanced enough to offset such a decline in land use under production. Yield per hectare would have had to increase beyond the realm of possibility in Nigeria in order to compensate for this. For all practical purposes, the production of marketable food at least should have still stayed the same, but that was not the case. Production went down. On the other hand, food importation was doubling every year. The most disturbing aspect of the situation is the multi-fold increase in the volume of rice and maize import that started around 1974, as shown in Table 3.10. While these figures are frightening, the outlook in the following years was even worse, when Nigeria imported 1 million tons of wheat in 1980, and 600,000 tons of rice, 300,000 tons of maize, and 350,000 tons of vegetable oil in 1982 (*Africa Report Jan-Feb. 1982 p. 41*) to feed its population. The 2.5 per cent demographic growth rate could not in any way explain the rapidly increasing volumes and values of imported food every year.

Table 3.10

Volume of Import of Some Grains in Nigeria, 1974-77
(Quantity in 1,000 Kilogram)

	Wheat	Rice	Maize	Barley	Other cereals
1974	318,269	4,805	2,440	13	588
1975	407,309	6,652	2,211	37	945
1976	733,132	45,377	9,861	17	847
1977 (Jan Aug)	505,742	225,224	20,172	94	79

Source: Abalu, G.O.I. and D'Silva, B. 1980, "Nigeria's Food Situation — Problems and Prospects" Food Policy, Vol. 5, February 1980. p.50.

The case of palm produce, of which the country is a substantial consumer, undercut the governments even further. While two products (palm oil and palm kernel) are extracted from the fruit, only palm oil is consumed mainly in the country; the kernel has very little use. Therefore, no matter how inaccurate the data may have been, it would not have resulted in the exportable kernel being unduly represented in both value and quantity in the export market, the way it is reflected in the Tables. The fact of the matter is that production of palm produce went down in absolute terms (as did all other cash crops represented in Tables 3.6 and 3.8 above), since the output of the oil and kernel is a function of the fruit from the tree. Furthermore, the production of the kernel doesn't have to decline with the oil, which depends on the texture of the fruit, since the kernel must always be extracted whether or not the fruit produces oil. So, from all indications, the output of kernel should increase over the year if the production of palm produce goes up. But that was not the case; consequently, it was no wonder that the country imported more than twice as much palm oil as it had formally exported.

Under-Utilized Land Area, A Contradiction

Even according to the government, the scarcity of arable land is not a problem in Nigeria. The country's estimated cultivable land area is 71.2 million hectares or 72 percent of the total land area of 98.3 million hectares (_Fourth National Development Plan 1981-85, p. 98_). But much less than half of this arable land is actually cultivated. As a matter of fact, land area under cultivation for the thirteen major crops has declined since 1971. Table 3.11 and Figure 3.4 show the trend of the cumulative performance of the thirteen major annual crops produced in the country from 1965 to 1981, with respect to the total land area devoted to them. It is interesting that the total land area under cultivation for these major crops has declined from over 20 million hectares in 1965 to 9.6 million hectares in 1981, a drop of over 53 percent. It is interesting to note from this Table that the Civil War years (1967-70) witnessed better performances than years after the war, and, in fact, it was during the 1969/70 season that the country devoted the highest portion of land (22.94 million ha.) for these major crops. This fact, at least in principle, rules out the effect of war on the future performance of the agricultural sector and gives credence to the idea that the government neglected the farming sector in favor of an expanding oil economy, which the population believed would change their lives (and in a negative way it did).

Table 3.11

Total Land Area Under Cultivation in Nigeria for Thirteen Major Crops ('000 ha)

Year	Total Land Under Production
1965/66	20,377
1966/67	16,196
1967/68	18,345
1968/69	18,694
1969/70	22,944
1970/71	20,336
1971/72	15,489
1972/73	19,929
1973/74	16,816
1974/75	14,939
1975/76	15,009
1976/77	11,057
1977/78	9,507
1979/80	8,626
1980/81	9,648

Source: Federal Ministry of Agriculture, <u>Department of Agricultural Planning</u>, 1982.

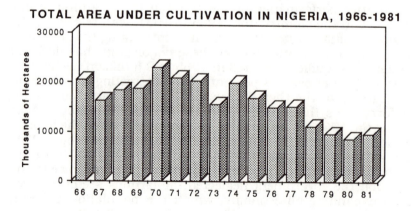

Figure 3.4

Table 3.12 depicts land area devoted to the cultivation of individual crops from 1965 to 1981. For easy reference, some of these numbers are also presented in Figures 3.5a , 3.5b and Appendix figure 3. From these tables, it is clear that land area devoted to millet and yam (two of the most important staple foods), for example, fell from 4.6 million ha. in 1965 to 2.96 million ha. in 1981 (a 36 percent decline), and from 1.6 million ha. to just 496 thousand hectare (a 70 percent decline) respectively during the same time period. With the exception of guinea corn and maize, which had a 45 percent and 48 percent decline respectively, each of the other major crops experienced at least a 60 percent decline in land area under cultivation between 1965 and 1981, and for three of the crops, cocoyam, beniseed, and soyabeans, the decline was very steep, over 80 percent. This decline in land area under cultivation explains the decreasing production level of each of the crops, as depicted in Table 3.8, and the increasing level of food importation. It is not difficult to explain why the absolute production level declined. For example, a total land area of 1.64 million ha. was planted for yam that produced 14.7 million tons in the 1965/66 seasons; however, in the 1980/81 season, 15 years later, only 498,000 ha. were planted and the production level dropped with the land area to 5.281 million tons, a difference of about 64 percent from the 1965/66 level, which of course was compensated for only by improved yield per hectare. (For convenience some examples are extracted from Tables 3.8, 3.9 and 3.12, and for easy reference are shown in Table 3.13.) If this was the pattern of all the major crops in the country, it is no wonder that the country imported more than 50 percent of its necessary food, and even imported some of the export agricultural products in the late 1970s that the country was still a world leader in exporting.

The only explanation for this is the response of the population to the oil economy, the management and politics of which created a false belief that led people to mass migrate to tap its benefits. It was considered positive if only about 50 percent of Nigeria's food was imported to meet the need of the growing population, which had almost doubled between 1960 and 1980. However, this brought about "*multifold*" inflation of basic foodstuffs. Prices for basic foodstuffs increased 10, 20 and at times 50 fold between 1965 and 1984. Not many people could afford this, and the increasing prices resulted in mass starvation and malnutrition.

Table 3.12

Area Planted of Major Crops in Nigeria, 1965-81 ('000 ha)

Year	Millet	Guinea Corn	Ground nut	Beans	Yam	Cotton	Maize	Cassava	Rice	Melon	Beni-seed	Coco-yam	Soya beans
1965/66	4628	5937	2231	2805	1644	461	1404	302	189	318	107	283	68
1966/67	4064	4043	2256	3030	742	307	1145	185	101	149	54	56	64
1967/68	4384	4735	2258	3917	771	196	1163	376	225	107	61	98	54
1968/69	4479	5138	1943	3369	1068	667	1095	420	206	261	-	48	-
1969/70	4906	7809	1831	4111	1043	714	1371	374	226	262	73	161	63
1970/71	4967	5414	1872	3820	1237	655	1449	385	249	360	78	202	58
1971/72	4789	5387	1795	3790	1236	809	1218	441	199	405	22	241	4
1972/73	3690	3791	2033	2464	932	236	1115	360	237	331	11	287	2
1973/74	5651	5193	2076	3256	948	122	1246	396	373	450	6	210	2
1974/75	4787	4651	1815	2937	671	478	579	414	283	89	4	108	-
1975/76	4629	2734	1418	3033	776	403	971	313	261	236	43	117	5
1976/77	3930	4845	684	2721	679	384	892	363	193	184	32	102	0.05
1977/78	3089	3480	763	1552	517	278	610	190	246	168	18	83	3
1978/79	2273	3433	710	1406	471	202	519	175	115	132	14	37	20
1979/80	2565	2686	531	1408	481	136	425	138	80	112	4	39	21
1980/81	2962	3276	563	1463	498	116	485	93	62	76	2	48	5

Source: Federal Ministry of Agriculture, 1982, Department of Agricultural Planning.

Figure 3.5a

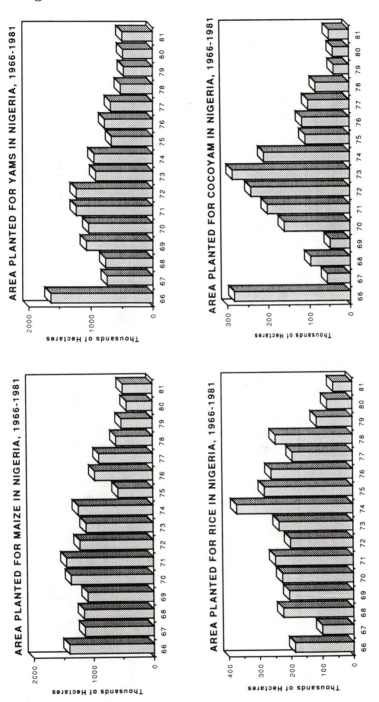

FIG. 3.5a

53

Figure 3.5b

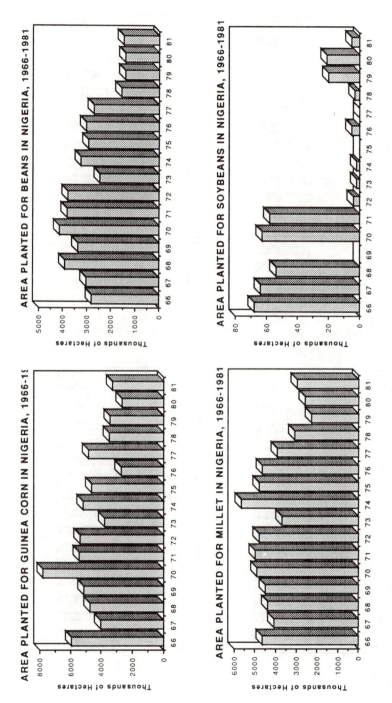

FIG. 3.5b

54

Table 3.13

Area Planted, Production and Yield Per Hectare of Three Major Crops in Nigeria 1965-81

Years	Yams			Rice			Cassava		
	Area	Prod	Yield	Area	Prod.	Yield	Area	Prod.	Yield
1965/66	1644	14736	8964	189	231	1222	302	2976	9854
1966/67	742	6987	9416	101	118	1168	185	1674	9049
1967/68	771	7806	10125	225	303	1347	376	3312	8809
1968/69	1068	8233	7709	206	275	1335	420	4104	9771
1969/70	1043	9785	9382	226	282	1248	374	4221	11286
1970/71	1237	12304	9947	249	279	1120	385	5213	13540
1971/72	1236	9766	7901	199	268	1347	441	4508	10222
1972/73	932	7601	8156	237	448	1890	360	2571	7142
1973/74	948	6935	7315	373	486	1303	396	2901	7289
1974/75	671	7198	10727	283	535	1890	414	3582	8631
1975/76	776	8621	11110	261	643	2464	313	2321	7415
1976/77	679	6556	9655	193	218	1130	363	1876	5168
1977/78	577	6661	11544	246	408	1659	190	1900	9596
1978/79	471	5780	12272	115	170	1478	175	1576	9017
1979/80	481	5069	10520	80	156	1950	138	1492	10891
1980/81	498	5281	10604	62	100	1613	93	872	9376

Source: Federal Ministry of Agriculture, 1982, Department of Agricultural Planning.

Area = Area Harvested (in '000 hectares)
Prod. = Production ('000 tons)
Yield = Yield per hectare (Kilograms

The sharpest expression of the agricultural situation in Nigeria (especially in the 1970s and 80s) was the juxtaposition of the oil boom with the agricultural stagnation and the ensuing breakdown of the entire agricultural sector. As the OPEC oil price hikes generated billions of fortuitous *"petro naira"* from booming export sales, agricultural export earnings fell systematically into relative insignificance, and the food crisis worsened (*Onimode, 1982*). This drastic decline in agricultural production could be explained only in terms of the country's misconception of the easily acquired oil wealth and the gross mismanagement, dire neglect, blatant corruption, and inconsistent policies of the government toward the agricultural sector, as alluded to in Chapter 1. The people of Nigeria are the ones who have suffered most from this dilemma.

Chapter 4

CLIMATE AND AGRICULTURE
IN NIGERIA

Introduction

The decline of food production and the entire agricultural failure in Nigeria and in many countries of Africa have been consistently linked to unfavorable weather and climatic conditions, especially drought. It is easy to credit or blame the weather for many of a society's successes and failures, such as a bumper harvest or a famine following drought. And certainly adverse natural conditions are often a factor. But while taking into account weather and climate as important and sometimes controlling factors, we cannot neglect other influences. A society's economic structure, level of technological sophistication, political responsiveness, and long-term planning vision, among other things, must be considered when we try to evaluate the impact of weather, climate, and climatic change on human affairs. It is true that when it comes to food production, water supplies, and even human health, adverse weather and climate can play a major role and even take a heavy toll (*Schneider and Londer 1984, p.369*). In this sense, abnormalities of weather, like unusually severe winters, exceptional drought, or a catastrophic hurricane, represent short-term hazards. In most cases we are unprepared to deal with such sudden weather events.

Of course, weather is not only a hazard. Climate — weather conditions observed over a long period of time — can be a resource, to be used to improve the quality of life. Many a country has benefited from the exploitation of climatic resources. The warm and humid summer conditions in North America, South America, and Australia, for example, have made portions of these regions principal granaries for much of the world. And the warm and humid to sub-humid conditions in the tropics have made it possible for societies in this region to practice subsistence agriculture to sustain their lives. While no one expects weather in individual years to be without fluctuation, society does expect the climate to be stable enough over any length of time to allow sensible long-term investments in agricultural activities in tropical regions.

Unfortunately, not all nations have made sensible long-term planning decisions to tap economically the benefit of climate. Sometimes nations are quick only to point out the ills of weather as the sole cause of their failure. However, it is imperative also to see social, political, economic, and other culturally related factors as contributions to such failure. How well people can utilize the benefit of weather and climate depends on how seriously the people take the issue of weather, and how well they can adjust to the new conditions weather can impose when climatic conditions change.

This chapter attempts to describe what is and what is not available climatically to the local farmer in Nigeria. An assessment of the general climatic conditions and a consideration of potential climatic change will be made, and their relation to the agricultural dilemma in the country will be explored.

Weather Zones and Seasons of Nigeria

Nigeria is situated in the southeastern sector of West Africa between latitudes 4° and 14° N, and covers an area in excess of 900,000 km^2. The geographical location, size, and shape of the country allows it to experience a variety of the West African climate and weather within its boundaries. In other words, the country is climatically a microcosm of West Africa from central Africa to the Atlantic. The study of the climate of Nigeria in this context will allow one to understand a cross-section of the West African climate and the agricultural economy of the region.

Nigeria enjoys a tropical climate with distinct wet and dry seasons whose duration and intensity steadily decrease from the coast in the south towards the hinterland in the north. This pattern dictates the types of agricultural activities practiced in different parts of the country. The wet and dry seasons are associated with the prevalence of the moist maritime southwesterly monsoon from the Atlantic Ocean and the dry continental northeasterly harmattan from the Sahara Desert. Seasonal variation in rainfall is therefore attributed to the fluctuations of the boundary between two different air masses that influence the entire West Africa climate. Between November and April much of the country is dominated by the dry harmattan-bearing air mass from the Sahara. On the other hand, between late April and October, the moisture-bearing monsoonal air mass from the Atlantic Ocean prevails. The boundary between these two air masses, the Intertropical Discontinuity (ITD), is significant because it separates two distinct patterns of weather on either side and helps determine the prevalence of one or the other of the two air masses over a given place and period of the year.

This means that the sequence of weather types experienced at given place in the country during the course of a year is determined primarily by the location of that particular place relative to the fluctuating surface of the ITD.

The surface position of the ITD in Nigeria varies not only seasonally but from day to day. The ITD assumes its average northernmost position close to 20° N latitude in July, when a flow of moist maritime air covers the area. However, in January ITD migrates southward to about 7° N latitude, when the whole region is experiencing the dry continental air from the Sahara Desert.

The five distinctive weather zones in the region are associated with the position of the ITD, as illustrated in Figure 4.1, which is a schematic and idealized cross-section of the ITD. Figure 4.2 illustrates the average position of the ITD in summer and winter and the extreme location of the weather zones as related to the seasonal shift of the ITD.

Weather Zone A, located farthest north, lies poleward of the ITD and hence is completely within the easterly flow of dry, anticyclonic, Saharan air. Cloudless skies with hot days and marked night cooling prevail (*Trewartha 1981, and Ayoade in Barbour et al. 1982*). Harmattan periods, characterized by extensive dust haze, are frequent, especially in the winter months. Relative humidity is low, about 40 percent in some places, and rainfall is practically nil.

Zone B, immediately to the south of the ITD, extends 250 to 400 km from it. Surface winds are southwesterly, but the maritime air mass is shallow. On a few days each month thunderstorms develop, though not all of these bring rain. Rainfall varies from 25 to less than 75 mm per month; relative humidity also varies from about 90 percent at night to 50 percent during the day.

Weather zone C extends from about 350 km to 1250 km south of the ITD. Here the maritime surface current is deeper and the total rainfall is greater than in zone B. This is the zone of frequent lines of thunderstorms or disturbance lines; cumulus and cumulonimbus clouds yield thunderstorms, frequently with heavy rain, usually in the afternoon. Relative humidity is generally high in the zone, and the diurnal temperature range is small.

Zone D lies approximately between 1,250 km and 1,600 km south of the surface positions of the ITD. This is a region of large cloud cover (mainly stratus), high humidity, and relatively low and constant temperature (*Griffiths 1975*). Here the deeper maritime flow creates an increasingly favorable environment for precipitation, and days with rain are the rule rather than the exception. The rainfall is more prolonged and less intense. Monsoonal climate is associated with the belt dominated by this weather zone.

Figure 4.1

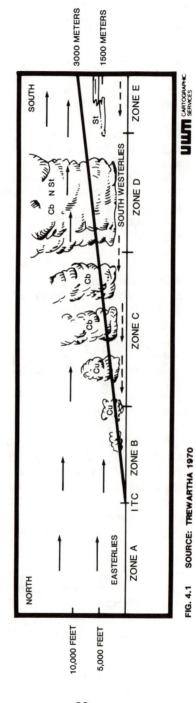

FIG. 4.1   SOURCE: TREWARTHA 1970

60

GENERAL LOCATIONS AND APPROXIMATE BOUNDARIES OF WEST AFRICA'S 5 WEATHER ZONES IN SUMMER (A) AND IN WINTER (B)

Figure 4.2

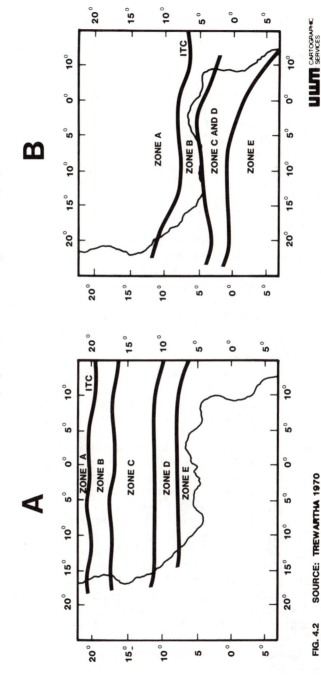

FIG. 4.2   SOURCE: TREWARTHA 1970

61

Weather Zone E, the most southerly of the weather zones, is located much of the year over the ocean and is able to penetrate over the coastal areas only in a narrow strip for a short period between July and September. This is a region of decreasing stratocumulus and stratus cloud cover with increasing alto-stratus, altocumulus, or cirrus clouds. Although the southwest-erly flow is steady and strong and clouds are abundant, rainfall in it is usually modest and temperatures are not excessively high.

Not all of the five weather zones discussed above are experi-enced in all parts of Nigeria. Weather Zone A, the only weather zone north of the ITD, which extends as far as the seasonal sur-face location of the ITD, is rarely experienced at the coast, whereas Zones D and E are confined to the south (*Ayoade, 1982*). As a matter of fact, weather zone A predominates over much of the northern part of the country during the dry season months of November to April, when the harmattan bearing northeast-erly flows over most of the country. During this period, most of the southern part of the country enjoys a weather type associ-ated with zone B, with weather zone C very much confined to the coastal areas, particularly the Niger Delta area (Figure 4.2b). From May to October, when the moisture-bearing southwesterly air mass prevails over the country, the weather zones shift ac-cordingly as the ITD is pushed northward. During this time, the northern part of the country experiences weather zones B and C as weather Zone A is pushed out of the country into the 20th parallels; this allows B and C weathers to dominate in the north, thereby generating the rainy season, while zones C, D and E flourish over the south with varying frequencies (Figure 4.2a).

A regional classification of the weather zones has been sug-gested by Garnier as shown in Figure 4.3 (*Garnier in Griffiths 1975*). In the figure region 1 experiences Zone A conditions for at least half the year, has little Zone B weather, and has about four months of Zone C weather corresponding to the rainy sea-son of this part of the country. Region 2 experiences a definite spell of Zone B weather, especially during the northward move-ment of the ITD. Region 3, while experiencing only limited pe-riods of zone A conditions, is nevertheless the only area of Nigeria wherein the effects of the four major zones are felt. In region 4, Zone C dominates while Zone A is seldom experienced.

To be noted in this context also is the influence of the weather zones on each other in their respective locations in a given year. There is a mutual modifying effect of the conditions of one weather zone on another adjacent weather zone. This is very important to agriculture practices because the kind of crop to be planted is influenced by the duration of rain in a particu-lar location. For example, the southern part of the position of Zone B is influenced by the weather in Zone C, and vice versa.

Figure 4.3

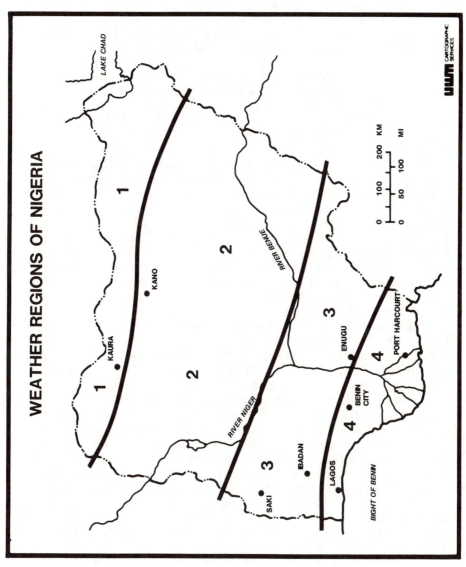

FIG. 4.3   SOURCE: GRIFFITHS, J.F. 1975 p. 173

The influence is mutual in that each weather type in each zone has a modifying effect on the other. Therefore, each zone is named according to the prevalence of one zone over the other in a particular location and time of the year. But it could be observed that, because of the influence of a more rainy zone, the southern edge of Zone B may have more rainfall than the rest of the zone, which is influenced by the drier Zone A weather to the north. On the other hand, the northern end of Zone C may receive less rain than the rest of the zone because of the influence of Zone B to the north. This mutual influence is observed in all zones that border other zones.

As noted, the climate in the country alternates between very well defined wet and dry seasons throughout the year. Distinctive weather or rainfall belts have been observed to migrate with the surface movement of the ITD (*Griffiths 1975*). These distinctive rainfall occurrences are connected with the prevalence of each of the different weather zones discussed above. During the northern winter, when the surface location of the ITD lies at about 7° to 9° N across Nigeria, there is only a shallow depth of moist maritime westerly air covering the coastal areas, giving rise to occasional showers in the delta between December and February. Most of the land south of the ITD enjoys Zone B weather, with weather Zone C confined to the Niger Delta area. The rest of the country north of the ITD during these months is under the desiccating influence of the dust-bearing northeasterly harmattan, associated with Zone A weather. These months mark the climax of the dry season the country experiences in any given year.

From March onwards, the southwesterly maritime air mass begins to advance inland in response to the increasing insolation and decreasing pressure in the continental interior, and the surface location of the ITD shifts northwards correspondingly. As the depth of the southwesterly increases, it brings clouds and rain, which begin at the coast and advance inland, until, between June and September, the whole country is experiencing abundant rainfall, which corresponds to the wet season (*Oguntoyinbo 1982*). While the rainfall in the northern part of the country during these months is associated with weather conditions associated with B and C zones, the southern third of the country receives its rainfall from conditions dominated by Zones C, D and E weather types (Figure 4.3). Conditions associated with A zone are pushed completely out of the country into the 20 parallels where the southwesterly maritime air mass is least effective.

The amount of rainfall a given place receives, as pointed out earlier, depends upon the distance of that particular place from the coast. Along the coast the annual total rainfall ranges from over 70 inches in the west to about 120 inches in the east. Northwards the mean annual rainfall decreases progressively inland to less than 30 inches in the far northeast in the Lake Chad Basin (Table 4.1 and Figure 4.4). This condition could also be explained in terms of the different conditions imposed by the weather zones in the country. While southern Nigeria lies under the alternating influence of wet weather conditions associated with Zones B, C, D, and E through most of the year, for six months out of the year the north is under the influence of a dry air mass associated with Zone A; only weather types B and C are prevalent in the north during the rainy season. When the rain-bearing southwesterly retreats southward at the end of the rainy season, the zones shift positions in the same order; this shift again provides favorable conditions for rain in the south sequentially, but leaves the north under the rainless condition of the A zone type weather. This therefore explains why the annual rainfall decreases northward in response to the prevailing conditions associated with the different weather zones in the country, not only in amount, but also in duration. Even though this pattern exists latitudinally, it is interrupted by the relief in the interior. While the Niger-Benue Trough receives less than average rainfall for its latitude, and with respect to the zones associated with rain, the Jos Plateau Region, which lies north of the Trough, receives much more than the latitudinal mean. In fact, the amount of rain the Jos Plateau Region receives is comparable to the amount received by most areas south of the Niger-Benue Trough. This unusual situation can be explained by the orographic type of rain associated with higher altitudes.

The duration of the rainy season is influenced by latitudinal differences as well as the conditions imposed by the weather zones. With the exception of the regions in which relief interrupts the pattern, the length of the rainy season decreases progressively from the lower latitudes at the coast (about 10 months) to the higher latitude in the extreme north, where the length of the rainy season is less than four months (Figure 4.5).

The onset of the rainy season in the extreme south has been calculated from rainfall frequency to occur in the middle of February. There is, however, an enclave near the coast (especially in the eastern half) in which there is no break in rainfall throughout the year. In the extreme north, the rainy season starts in mid-May, ending in the middle of September, and runs to about the end of December in the Niger Delta Area. The number of days rain falls varies from 360 days in the extreme southeast to about 80 days in the extreme northeast (*Oguntoyinbo 1982*). The kind of agriculture practiced, therefore, corresponds to the amount and duration of rainfall a particular region experiences.

Table 4.1

Average Rainfall for Selected Stations in Nigeria (in inches)

	JAN	FEB	MAR	APR	MAY	JUN	JUL	AUG	SEP	OCT	NOV	DEC	TOT. inch	YEARS of Avg.
P. Harcourt	1.3	2.1	6.3	8.1	9.6	11.1	14.6	11.1	17.0	10.9	4.3	1.3	97.7	22
Enugu	1.3	0.9	3.9	7.2	8.0	8.9	8.8	7.5	10.6	8.7	1.7	0.6	68.1	65
Lagos	1.2	1.7	3.9	5.9	10.9	18.3	11.2	3.0	5.9	8.0	2.7	0.7	73.6	78
Ibadan	0.3	1.0	3.6	5.3	6.0	7.4	6.2	3.7	7.0	6.4	1.7	0.4	49.0	66
Benin	0.7	1.3	4.1	6.7	8.2	11.8	13.5	8.9	12.7	9.5	3.0	0.7	81.1	65
Markurdi	0.3	0.2	1.2	4.3	7.0	8.0	6.6	8.4	10.4	5.4	0.5	0.1	52.4	27
Jos	0.1	0.1	1.0	3.7	7.5	9.0	12.8	11.1	8.2	1.7	0.1	0.1	55.4	50
Kaduna	0.0	0.1	0.4	2.9	5.7	7.0	8.5	11.5	10.8	3.2	0.2	0.1	50.1	33
Maiduguri	0.0	0.0	0.0	0.3	1.4	3.1	7.1	9.2	4.2	0.8	0.0	0.0	26.1	56
Kano	0.1	0.0	0.1	0.4	2.6	4.7	8.2	12.1	5.4	0.5	0.2	0.0	34.3	67
Sokoto	0.0	0.0	0.0	0.4	1.9	3.8	6.6	9.6	5.5	0.7	0.0	0.0	28.9	56

Source: Federal Office of Statistics, Annual Abstracts of Statistics, Lagos Nigeria

Figure 4.4

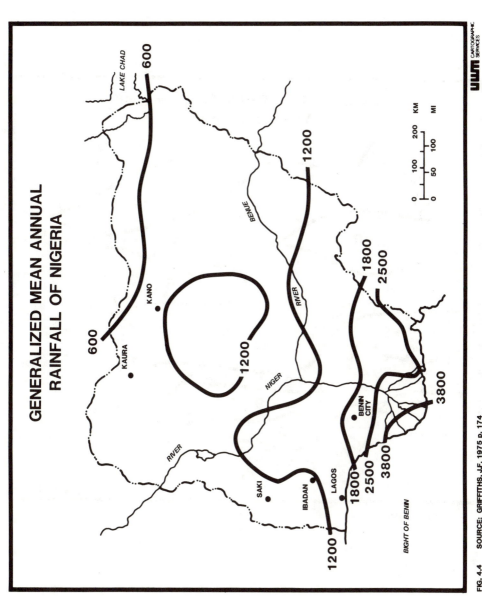

GENERALIZED MEAN ANNUAL
RAINFALL OF NIGERIA

FIG. 4.4   SOURCE: GRIFFITHS, J.F. 1975 p. 174

67

Figure 4.5

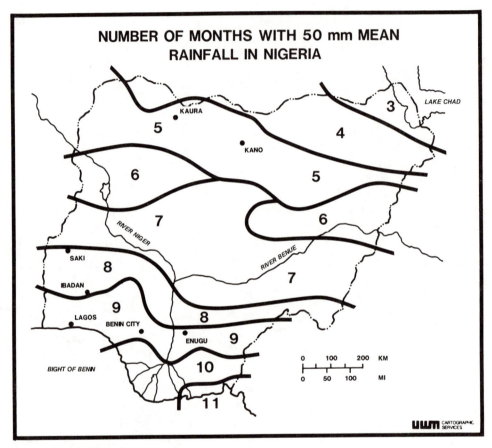

FIG. 4.5   SOURCE: GRIFFITHS, J.F. 1925 p. 177

Rainfall Variability and the Changing Climatic Conditions

The pattern of annual rainfall variability closely mirrors that of mean annual precipitation. In absolute figures, it is greatest in the humid south and least in the north. When expressed as a proportion of the mean annual values, the pattern is very different. While in the south the annual variability amounts to less than 20 percent of the mean total, it is over 30 percent in the extreme north. The latter situation could pose a serious problem in farming where the variability is over 30 percent in a region with an annual rainfall of less than 30 inches. A succession of years with about 30 percent variability could have a pronounced effect on the farming success of the inhabitants.

There has been some concern about changing climatic conditions worldwide. This change is obviously not confined to Africa's Sahel. While some parts of the world receive heavier than average rainfall as a result of this climatic trend, others receive less than their normal average. It has been noted that the monsoon rains, which sweep from the South Atlantic and across the southern coast of West Africa and then diminish toward the Sahara, have, since the 50s, stayed farther south than before. The sections most likely to experience drought in this kind of climatic trend are located at the northern edge of the monsoon's range, far from the sea. These areas used to lie in the 20th parallels in Africa, but have now shifted to the 19th parallel. These are the climatic borderlands (ecotones) which are very sensitive to climatic change and have the most variable weather (*Bryson and Murray 1977*).

The climatic sensitivity of these borderlands is not a new phenomenon. Over different time periods people had adjusted to what the climatic changes imposed. Today, however, people in some regions of the world with similar conditions have made better use of them. A well-articulated long-term planning strategy would most likely ameliorate the problem of drought in the Sahel. But most of these nations in the Sahel presumably have allowed the retreat of the monsoon, which of course is predictable, to completely alter their lifestyles. Nothing has happened to human intuition. However, man cannot successfully utilize his intuitiveness in an unstable political climate. People cannot till the ground or produce to feed others while they themselves starve and reap no benefit. In addition, widespread government corruption has always stifled farmers' intuition and their efforts to produce, as is now the case in Nigeria. Proper management of the Sahel would have resulted in a more bountiful life. Yet after more than 20 years of international aid and more than constructive advice, the Sahel is closer than ever to becoming a wasteland.

But only a negligible portion of Nigeria, lies in the Sahel. Nigeria is situated between latitude 4° and 14° N of the equator. Within these limits, Nigeria is in no way threatened by a world-wide climatic change that long-term constructive planning cannot help divert. Available data with regard to the present trend of weather and climatic condition does not point to a serious problem in the country. A. Babalola at the Nigerian Federal Ministry of Agriculture noted that weather is not a serious problem in agricultural development in Nigeria. In fact, the implementation of policies with regard to agriculture is the major problem. The data available obviously supports what Babalola stated privately. Tables 4.2 to 4.9 are strategically compiled from World Meterological Organization (WMO) reports and the Nigerian Federal Office of Statistics. With the exception of the years with missing data, there has been no year when rainfall was low enough in all stations to cause a prolonged drought in the country. Moreover, most of the missing data are from months of high rainfall, and there are no other years without rainfall in those months.

Tables 4.2 and 4.3 represent the Sokoto (one of the two study areas) and Kano stations, the two northernmost of all the stations and the ones which fall within the drought prone section of the country. Again, most of the years with low rainfall are missing data at the peak months. There were no periods in which the rainfall was below 500 mm (20 inches) in any given year that has little or no missing data, except of course for the Sokoto Station, the northernmost of all the stations, which received 19 inches of rain each for only 1971 and 1981. That, of course, rules out the theory that prolonged drought may affect agricultural development in the northern part of the country. Moreover, most of the missing data occurred primarily during the Civil War or lost due to the pure neglect of agents.

About 2° south of the Kano station are Jos and Minna stations (Tables 4.4 and 4.5), neither of which had less than 30 inches of rainfall in any given year, except in 1973 and 1974 for Minna and only 1974 for Jos, when missing data affected the result. There are no years without missing data that had less than 40 inches of rain in both stations, except in Minna where the rainfall was 32 inches in 1983.

South of the Jos and Minna stations is the Ilorin station (Table 4.6) which experiences not less than 35 inches of rain in any given year, except in the years with missing data. The Ilorin station, however, represents the Niger-Benue Trough, which receives less than average rainfall for its latitude.

Finally Tables 4.7, 4.8, and 4.9 represent the Lagos, Ondo (the second study area), and Port Harcourt stations which receive no less than 50 inches of rainfall in any given year with-

Table 4.2

Rainfall Statistics in Sokoto (Lat. 13° 01'N)

YEAR	JAN	FEB	MAR	APR	MAY	JUN	JUL	AUG	SEP	OCT	NOV	DEC	TOTAL mm.	TOTAL in.
1963	0	0	0	5	43	100	188	245	115	88	0	0	784	32
1964	0	0	3	0	48	165	223	145	135	0	0	0	719	29
1965	0	0	0	0	45	280	125	315	195	5	0	0	965	39
1966	0	0	0	13	25	—	138	173	153	68	0	0	570	23
1967	0	0	10	3	10	88	123	250	128	3	0	0	615	25
1968	0	0	0	45	35	85	115	—	20	50	0	0	350	14
1969	0	0	0	20	40	103	210	185	—	13	0	0	571	23
1970	0	0	0	0	13	33	303	170	98	3	0	0	620	25
1971	0	0	0	0	35	18	130	230	65	0	0	0	478	19
1975	0	0	0	4	89	85	123	147	109	0	0	0	557	22
1976	0	0	0	0	68	98	176	286	107	114	0	0	849	34
1977	0	0	0	0	40	116	188	335	134	0	0	0	813	33
1978	0	0	0	11	0	105	195	245	139	19	0	0	714	29
1979	0	0	0	0	11	114	129	265	69	0	9	0	597	24
1980	0	0	0	7	59	138	106	193	41	20	0	0	564	23
1981	0	0	0	0	8	54	208	133	76	0	0	0	479	19
1982	0	0	0	0	6	38	161	300	52	11	0	0	568	23
1983	0	0	1	0	45	154	229	128	63	0	0	0	620	25

Source: Federal Office of Statistics, Annual Abstract of Statistics, Lagos, Nigeria.

Note: — No record available.

Table 4.3

Rainfall Statistics in Kano (Lat. 12° 3'N)

YEAR	JAN	FEB	MAR	APR	MAY	JUN	JUL	AUG	SEP	OCT	NOV	DEC	TOTAL mm.	TOTAL in.
1951	0	0	0	0	51	113	209	158	267	12	0	0	810	32
1952	0	0	2	0	224	109	187	339	150	24	0	0	1035	41
1953	0	0	—	0	55	143	172	258	85	2	0	0	715	29
1954	0	1	—	28	164	112	355	287	118	34	4	0	1103	44
1955	—	0	0	2	58	171	215	456	138	33	0	0	1073	43
1956	0	0	2	—	1	76	292	315	63	10	0	—	759	30
1957	0	0	2	3	151	168	234	256	185	12	0	0	1009	40
1958	1	—	0	14	26	248	217	258	63	0	0	0	827	33
1959	0	0	—	6	75	93	181	409	255	2	0	0	1021	41
1960	0	0	0	31	30	73	293	252	77	1	0	—	757	30
1961	1	0	—	—	20	70	220	340	120	0	0	0	771	31
1962	0	0	—	3	80	280	290	330	200	40	0	0	1220	49
1963	0	0	5	0	43	78	130	355	80	0	0	0	694	28
1964	0	0	3	0	60	145	203	255	70	0	3	0	739	30
1965	0	0	0	0	5	243	265	268	100	13	0	0	894	36
1966	0	0	0	15	110	93	95	300	175	3	0	0	791	32
1967	—	—	—	103	—	—	248	228	95	0	0	0	571	23
1968	0	0	0	8	75	145	118	120	48	0	—	0	609	24
1969	0	0	0	0	20	188	233	283	95	70	0	0	897	36
1970	0	0	0	13	18	55	325	283	230	3	0	0	914	37
1971	0	0	0	3	68	25	173	220	200	0	0	0	699	28
1972	0	0	0	0	100	128	71	239	45	5	—	0	591	24
1973	—	0	0	—	—	—	164	172	—	—	0	0	336	13
1974	0	0	0	18	42	42	262	197	112	5	0	0	660	26
1975	0	2	0	0	40	128	125	224	178	0	0	0	713	29
1976	0	—	—	—	44	117	132	123	66	60	0	0	544	22
1977	0	0	0	35	7	198	33	439	106	4	0	0	787	31
1978	0	0	0	0	69	198	309	271	30	29	0	0	941	38
1979	0	0	0	0	32	111	192	—	111	20	0	0	466	19
1980	0	0	0	20	94	123	283	311	68	35	0	0	914	37
1981	0	0	0	19	36	62	143	203	112	0	0	0	576	23
1982	0	0	0	0	66	62	158	261	71	1	0	0	638	26
1983	0	0	0	0	27	47	91	266	67	0	0	0	498	20

Sources: Federal Office of Statistics; Annual Abstract of Statistics, Lagos, Nigeria .
World Meterological Organization (WMO) Reports

Note: — No record available.

Table 4.4

Rainfall Statistics in Jos (Lat. 09° 52'N)

YEAR	JAN	FEB	MAR	APR	MAY	JUN	JUL	AUG	SEP	OCT	NOV	DEC	TOTAL mm.	TOTAL in.
1951	0	0	4	41	249	155	255	392	181	85	1	0	1363	55
1952	5	0	28	61	255	220	408	122	260	28	0	0	1387	55
1953	0	15	36	36	328	191	185	263	184	21	0	0	1259	50
1954	0	2	42	109	351	159	367	208	230	47	33	0	1548	62
1955	2	0	—	76	146	258	337	249	234	87	0	14	1389	56
1956	0	13	113	66	82	240	227	184	286	25	1	0	1251	50
1957	0	0	2	90	221	209	427	276	319	139	14	0	1697	68
1958	10	2	1	178	143	294	189	232	297	35	0	0	1381	55
1959	0	0	36	97	267	209	349	282	316	10	0	0	1566	63
1960	—	0	2	196	159	261	276	299	267	5	—	—	1465	59
1961	10	0	—	—	90	140	300	200	160	20	0	0	920	37
1962	0	0	—	130	100	210	260	180	320	50	0	0	1250	50
1963	0	3	60	170	120	200	420	320	140	140	0	0	1573	63
1964	0	0	0	70	165	223	313	318	183	28	3	0	1303	52
1965	0	3	3	100	98	253	245	295	190	10	0	0	1197	48
1966	0	0	8	115	163	258	353	307	—	—	—	0	1204	48
1967	0	0	5	113	153	195	355	285	175	48	0	0	1329	53
1968	0	5	18	208	180	268	378	318	150	20	0	0	1545	62
1969	0	0	0	200	142	195	420	383	228	115	13	0	1696	68
1970	0	0	8	70	158	115	238	253	195	15	0	0	1052	42
1971	0	0	10	40	243	190	333	308	263	25	0	0	1412	56
1972	—	0	39	49	235	181	248	427	198	6	0	10	1393	56
1973	0	—	12	174	121	153	372	341	—	—	—	0	1173	47
1974	0	0	—	—	87	188	—	—	308	18	—	0	601	24
1975	0	0	0	53	116	155	332	366	341	12	0	4	1379	55
1976	3	9	19	78	101	192	344	306	237	58	0	0	1347	54
1977	0	0	13	6	233	162	307	262	159	34	0	0	1176	47
1978	0	0	18	116	104	236	297	366	223	111	0	0	1471	59
1979	0	0	9	81	179	205	254	309	156	15	7	0	1215	49
1980	0	18	14	11	238	166	240	237	114	70	0	—	1100	44
1981	0	0	0	100	191	206	249	295	191	41	0	0	1273	51
1982	0	0	8	205	144	169	382	253	136	34	0	0	1331	53
1983	0	0	21	0	—	250	317	356	81	0	—	0	1025	41

Sources: Federal Office of Statistics, Annual Abstract of Statistics, Lagos Nigeria.
World Meterological Organization (WMO) Reports,
Note: — No record available.

73

Table 4.5

Table 4.5

Rainfall Statistics in Minna (Lat. 09° 37'N)

YEAR	JAN	FEB	MAR	APR	MAY	JUN	JUL	AUG	SEP	OCT	NOV	DEC	TOTAL mm.	TOTAL in.
1951	0	0	31	55	77	119	273	249	310	251	1	0	1366	55
1952	1	0	2	32	225	161	263	123	285	141	0	0	1233	49
1953	0	65	4	17	235	64	234	201	182	152	0	0	1154	46
1954	0	—	77	101	58	174	270	274	253	220	3	0	1430	57
1955	—	0	3	75	81	156	293	215	404	122	0	0	1349	54
1956	0	—	25	46	45	221	110	133	252	129	7	25	1003	40
1957	0	0	—	51	172	226	384	307	217	160	45	0	1562	62
1958	10	0	—	45	192	126	86	241	225	77	16	0	1018	41
1959	—	14	21	37	83	232	169	345	347	50	23	0	1321	53
1960	0	0	24	68	107	171	323	154	296	100	—	38	1281	51
1961	10	0	0	—	100	—	340	150	280	90	0	—	970	39
1962	—	0	—	120	130	180	150	410	330	220	30	0	1570	63
1963	0	3	2	60	40	140	260	260	160	160	—	0	1085	43
1964	0	0	4	70	132A	—	229A	292A	533A	122A	2A	0	1372	55
1965	—	48A	—	3	129A	251A	195A	193A	206A	107A	0	—	1135	45
1966	0	0	0	71A	76A	231A	—	320	—	145A	—	—	896	36
1967	0	0	5A	126A	94	180A	170A	307A	409A	—	—	—	1273	51
1968	—	0	74	—	—	253	253	209	172	81	0	0	1136	45
1969	0	—	10	14	66	128	—	201	202	220	24	0	775	31
1970	0	0	7	26	140	98	173	345	341	69	0	0	1116	45
1971	0	5	47	31	227	213	233	245	242	29	0	0	1140	46
1972	0	—	4	22	—	83	316	408	187	51	0	0	1350	54
1973	0	0	5	—	120	85	85	393	—	—	0	0	589	24
1974	—	—	21	15	—	120	—	—	252	128	0	0	625	25
1975	0	19	0	5	23	—	113	142	380	78	0	0	768	31
1977	0	0	0	5	23	139	282	390	323	95	0	0	1257	50
1978	0	0	21	108	262	123	194	402	250	122	5	0	1487	59
1979	0	0	15	15	139	—	—	—	—	—	—	—	169	8
1980	0	0	0	8	239	131	204	250	150	142	0	0	1124	45
1981	0	0	0	23	58	188	239	276	183	92	0	0	1059	42
1982	0	0	13	100	45	138	289	353	160	105	0	0	1203	48
1983	0	0	0	12	37	85	167	245	207	41	0	0	794	32

Sources: Federal Office of Statistics; Annual Abstract of Statistics, Lagos, Nigeria . World Meterological Organization (WMO) Reports

Note: — No record available.

Table 4.6

Rainfall Statistics in Ilorin (Lat. 08° 29'N)

YEAR	JAN	FEB	MAR	APR	MAY	JUN	JUL	AUG	SEP	OCT	NOV	DEC	TOTAL mm.	TOTAL in.
1951	1	—	129	84	238	95	299	162	191	155	64	0	1418	57
1952	40	—	63	74	143	206	237	45	325	145	6	81	1365	55
1953	0	24	109	66	309	265	211	36	286	215	—	25	1546	62
1954	20	12	103	179	181	242	29	139	247	310	14	—	1476	59
1955	122	0	65	146	128	258	361	177	309	107	1	—	1674	67
1956	0	28	128	109	104	251	40	30	379	207	20	65	1361	54
1957	5	0	45	151	144	120	133	157	289	136	40	72	1294	52
1958	26	17	12	113	156	132	1	88	333	119	61	2	1060	42
1959	21	10	46	80	174	231	280	115	265	138	25	—	1385	55
1960	—	—	63	148	154	189	184	155	338	335	14	1	1586	63
1961	1	0	10	130	120	180	130	40	170	50	0	—	831	33
1962	—	0	—	130	230	310	170	130	270	260	160	1	1661	66
1963	0	20	80	110	140	290	360	220	250	200	—	—	1670	67
1964	1	0	50	90	200	—	107	—	206	59	56	79	848	34
1965	61	23	50	130	163	135	173	124	218	193	0	0	1270	51
1966	15	0	41	94	86	368	—	140	—	142	1	0	887	35
1967	0	—	—	86	84	—	63	—	176	178	19	—	606	24
1968	—	51	22	—	110	290	289	349	269	91	6	0	1477	59
1969	—	—	—	—	161	263	156	157	—	—	—	0	566	23
1970	0	6	50	86	156	131	126	42	262	61	0	0	919	37
1971	0	18	32	102	144	202	111	113	253	167	0	0	1142	46
1972	0	0	25	106	183	216	129	89	156	240	0	0	1162	46
1973	0	18	23	120	—	269	221	208	—	—	—	0	841	34
1974	0	0	27	—	173	157	122	97	273	107	0	0	856	34
1975	0	18	28	92	153	182	272	29	265	172	0	3	1214	49
1976	0	35	33	192	189	164	64	65	62	327	42	0	1173	47
1977	0	0	26	46	170	186	65	28	245	162	0	0	928	37
1978	8	3	57	180	252	136	154	134	196	66	31	0	1206	48
1979	8	0	91	61	110	145	166	196	238	160	18	0	1193	48
1980	0	19	4	44	135	215	124	280	215	197	3	2	1238	50
1981	0	0	118	86	266	226	163	77	253	98	0	0	1287	51
1982	8	29	22	142	151	127	77	183	248	229	0	0	1216	49
1983	0	9	15	92	175	146	92	216	228	34	2	149	1158	46

Sources: Federal Office of Statistics; Annual Abstract of Statistics, Lagos, Nigeria .
World Meterological Organization (WMO) Reports

Note: — No record available.

Table 4.7

Rainfall Statistics in Lagos (Lat. 06° 35′N)

YEAR	JAN	FEB	MAR	APR	MAY	JUN	JUL	AUG	SEP	OCT	NOV	DEC	TOTAL mm.	TOTAL in.
1951	30	—	31	34	267	183	335	108	209	371	30	0	1598	64
1952	46	36	47	140	328	247	139	5	300	228	137	55	1708	68
1953	8	76	94	64	227	450	109	13	197	195	80	14	1527	61
1954	155	180	226	116	132	560	51	63	188	268	85	16	2040	82
1955	104	6	122	115	167	378	120	43	238	282	74	5	1654	66
1956	—	86	189	115	129	180	49	6	126	178	57	39	1156	46
1957	4	16	108	157	250	400	291	144	424	245	56	54	2149	86
1958	38	46	100	112	152	355	2	12	119	75	34	101	1146	46
1959	1	63	44	86	265	266	302	83	107	216	145	29	1607	64
1960	17	56	43	216	234	343	99	110	231	160	70	98	1677	67
1961	30	3	150	290	130	490	320	3	100	260	100	10	1866	75
1962	3	20	—	140	370	520	450	140	120	120	110	30	2023	81
1963	20	30	90	280	180	320	410	170	190	150	40	30	1910	76
1964	3	30	98	155	215	188	675	50	70	123	35	5	1637	65
1965	5	55	100	213	258	428	638	138	295	133	25	3	2291	92
1966	13	20	67	195	193	268	415	50	133	218	78	13	1663	67
1967	50	20	56	108	113	127	400	435	5	130	218	65	1727	69
1968	13	52	47	180	170	587	583	520	525	187	30	17	2911	116
1969	30	3	215	160	363	498	278	133	68	218	53	5	2024	81
1970	125	8	35	100	298	578	470	35	323	300	68	0	2340	94
1971	8	95	25	58	210	350	350	28	217	58	48	18	1465	59
1972	35	32	46	126	278	568	48	7	178	70	—	0	1388	56
1973	0	11	77	389	145	190	74	155	—	—	—	31	1041	42
1974	36	69	95	—	246	276	276	54	126	128	8	0	1314	53
1975	0	97	34	320	101	119	255	44	16	146	117	22	1271	51
1976	4	165	83	188	94	214	76	24	134	84	76	2	1144	46
1977	104	0	28	108	223	418	211	23	87	147	7	9	1365	55
1978	18	61	101	298	294	189	269	24	84	275	101	27	1741	70
1979	3	19	60	136	378	364	468	269	239	161	120	4	2221	89
1980	133	47	52	74	267	342	142	400	201	122	170	0	1950	78
1981	7	3	52	169	256	449	96	84	241	115	22	1	1495	60
1982	0	17	25	215	288	66	280	5	64	109	32	0	1701	68
1983	0	0	30	67	433	604	69	14	175	35	48	0	1515	61

Sources: Federal Office of Statistics; Annual Abstract of Statistics, Lagos, Nigeria.
World Meterolgical Organization (WMO) Reports

Note: — No record available.

Table 4.8

Rainfall Statistics in Ondo (Lat. 07° 6'N)

YEAR	JAN	FEB	MAR	APR	MAY	JUN	JUL	AUG	SEP	OCT	NOV	DEC	TOTAL mm.	TOTAL in.
1960	8	22	80	149	156	217	155	140	228	123	35	70	1383	55
1961	21	—	71	101	94	190	388	39	218	148	48	31	1349	54
1962	0	15	162	82	184	184	283	102	144	312	167	49	1684	67
1963	15	80	85	87	132	377	234	481	246	479	4	14	2234	89
1964	—	8	85	214	123	235	237	59	137	183	76	8	1365	55
1965	69	24	92	104	154	215	379	260	138	153	20	0	1608	64
1966	7	29	114	183	189	160	229	272	189	91	97	1	1561	62
1968	11	55	103	238	124	185	308	521	385	172	65	39	2206	88
1969	1	40	133	201	84	219	260	191	223	204	96	0	1652	66
1970	22	0	129	106	176	217	50	79	289	230	21	—	1319	53
1971	3	60	92	125	145	131	277	79	318	108	60	25	1423	57
1972	31	63	105	80	147	200	131	104	178	118	58	38	1253	50
1973	—	31	55	119	187	175	268	285	274	178	3	16	1591	64
1977	19	33	56	138	165	275	210	106	105	188	3	40	1338	54
1978	0	63	126	288	204	233	426	72	296	168	8	2	1886	75
1979	9	13	96	115	140	169	297	291	364	174	101	5	1774	71
1980	0	51	127	189	125	304	186	361	349	304	52	22	2070	83
1981	0	5	99	140	166	253	210	150	183	133	50	0	1389	56
1982	10	101	61	209	165	177	156	45	186	182	0	0	1292	52
1983	0	18	35	127	157	283	129	45	312	80	46	22	1254	50

Sources: Ministry of Economic Development, Statistics Division, Digest of Agricultural Statistics, Ibadan, Western State of Nigeria.
Federal Office of Statistics, Annual Abstract of Statistics, Lagos, Nigeria.

Note: —   No record available.

Table 4.9

Rainfall Statistics in Port Harcourt (Lat.04° 5'N)

YEAR	JAN	FEB	MAR	APR	MAY	JUN	JUL	AUG	SEP	OCT	NOV	DEC	TOTAL mm.	TOTAL in.
1951	25	37	116	84	211	374	130	269	392	348	102	0	2088	84
1952	30	52	112	369	252	383	560	227	610	168	37	9	2809	112
1953	39	85	226	84	277	130	232	201	325	179	53	30	1861	74
1954	21	215	204	118	234	213	147	394	434	205	83	50	2318	93
1955	1	97	193	191	206	267	684	234	420	335	131	14	2773	111
1956	14	86	359	167	198	224	329	92	443	278	40	88	2318	93
1957	42	2	190	164	256	215	388	582	459	344	147	5	2794	112
1958	14	21	64	128	314	357	72	196	253	93	150	71	1733	69
1959	53	15	117	324	271	235	359	175	524	315	131	18	2537	101
1960	56	73	289	122	272	295	421	413	566	395	55	33	2990	120
1961	40	30	130	310	320	310	500	90	550	300	50	10	2640	106
1962	30	10	—	170	210	300	460	460	510	370	280	50	2850	114
1963	10	58	80	208	235	220	253	348	315	245	38	25	2035	81
1964	15	33	185	193	310	283	308	40	485	458	225	8	2543	102
1965	38	70	229	193	313	520	535	218	238	28	28	88	2498	100
1966	80	90	113	430	255	220	400	425	345	345	193	28	2924	117
1967	0	25	125	—	—	—	—	—	—	—	—	—	150	(6)
1969	28	30	285	213	163	228	473	375	383	418	140	13	2749	110
1970	60	38	60	198	180	213	533	408	263	315	80	0	2348	94
1971	15	33	68	43	165	280	308	438	308	135	42	105	1940	78
1972	10	128	80	116	169	263	412	454	282	169	76	62	2221	89
1973	32	89	93	124	243	—	198	273	—	—	82	69	1203	(48)
1974	69	60	48	—	240	217	—	361	381	242	116	23	1757	70
1975	0	36	357	229	193	287	534	179	293	193	216	13	2530	101
1976	1	180	182	171	98	293	204	357	238	402	201	0	2327	93
1977	62	56	41	108	205	260	272	359	527	509	12	27	2438	98
1978	29	85	179	310	224	375	92	187	456	247	92	15	2291	92
1979	0	187	222	255	101	407	296	317	215	281	121	11	2413	97
1980	8	28	64	159	361	265	375	282	359	432	212	1	2546	102
1981	76	28	140	102	311	273	349	306	337	171	66	0	2159	86
1982	70	49	169	86	187	379	339	234	349	228	57	26	2173	87
1983	0	0	30	221	227	229	184	130	454	262	73	8	2118	85

Sources: Federal Office of Statistics, Annual Abstract of Statistics, Lagos, Nigeria .
World Meterolgical Organization (WMO) Reports

Note: — No record available.

out missing data. Of course, these stations, except for Ondo Station, are coastally located, and they receive rainfall every month of the year.

From this information, it is clear that Nigeria is not threatened by a prolonged drought, even in the northern part where such conditions might occur at all. This, of course, is not to say that there is not a downward trend in the weather and climatic conditions in the country. But we have seen so far that weather has no bearing on the agricultural problems in Nigeria. All the stations, with the exception of the two northern stations, fall outside the boundary of the drought-prone section of the country. Moreover, Nigerians have been adjusting to the more unpredictable rainfall variability for decades; and it is this variability in the climate that hurts crops most. In this sense, a change in the mean can be accommodated by the farmers over time, because the knowledge of the change in the mean permits adjustment in agricultural strategy. But when high variation comes without warning, few farmers are prepared for it (*Schneider in Kopec 1975*). Furthermore, production and yield per acre have remained higher for crops (Chapter 3) in the near Sahel region than in the rest of the country, which possesses much more favorable climates. These facts rule out the present trend of agricultural activities dictated by variability and change of climate which are important parts of the climatic record.

Temperature Condition

Temperatures in the country are generally high, and they increase with increasing latitudes toward the interior. The hottest season usually precedes the rainy season. In the north, where there is little cloudiness, temperatures commonly soar into the 90s or even above 100°F before the rainy season. On the other hand, temperatures in the south are quite moderate (between 70° and 80° F) because of the greater incidence of cloud cover and rainfall.

The mean annual range of temperature increases progressively from the coast (5° to 10° F) to the interior, where it reaches 20° F or even more in the far north. This increased mean annual range of temperature is due to the poleward extent of the hot and dry tropics, which produces a definite hot season and a cooler season. The relative humidity that comes with temperature and moisture reflects this association. In fact, it decreases with the increasing latitude. While the relative humidity is about 90 percent in the south, where the rainfall is more reliable, it is less than 50 percent in the north, where the average annual rainfall is lower..

Both evaporation and evapotranspiration rates increase from the south to the north with increasing temperature and latitude. The importance of these two parameters is seen in their role in the supply of available water for crop cultivation.

Climate and Vegetation

The climatic regime in Nigeria naturally leads to a north south vegetational and occupational difference. The main vegetation patterns run, therefore, in broad east west belts parallel to the equator (Figure 4.6). Mangrove and fresh water swamps occur along the coast and in the Niger Delta, and fishing is the most important occupation along the coast. A few miles inland, the swamp gives way to dense tropical rain forest in which the most important economic trees include such hardwoods as mahogany, iroko, and obeche. The economically valuable oil palm grows wild in this forest belt, and cocoa and rubber trees are also widely grown here.

North of the forest belt is the more extensive tree-studded savanna (tropical grassland). This wooded grassland becomes more open toward the extreme north, where it phases imperceptibly into the drought-prone sahel of the Central African Sudan. While root crops for domestic food and plantation culture for export are the basis of the southern economy, cotton, groundnut, and a variety of grain crops (millet and guinea corn), along with fibers and animal husbandry, are the basis of the northern economy. This will be discussed in detail later under Climate and Agricultural Zones.

Climate and Soil Formation

The five main soil groups in Nigeria correspond closely with the country's main climatic and vegetation zones (Figure 4.7). The coastal soils are either sandy or swampy, and are heavily leached. In the rain forest belt further inland, soils derived from old complex rocks are not as leached. The ferruginous tropical soils comprise the most important group of soils in Nigeria because they cover the greatest portion of the country and support most of the important cash and food crops. These are developed mainly from basement complex and old sedimentary rocks. Other important soil groups include the weakly developed soils, the Ferralitic, Ferrisols, and Hydromorphic soils.

The importance of climate is fundamental in that its factors influence the rate and depth of weathering and soil formation, the influence of which decreases generally from the humid south to the subhumid north. The soil moisture regime, which is very important in agricultural productivity, correlates strongly with the incidence of rainfall in different parts of the country (*Areola in Barbour et al. 1982*).

Figure 4.6

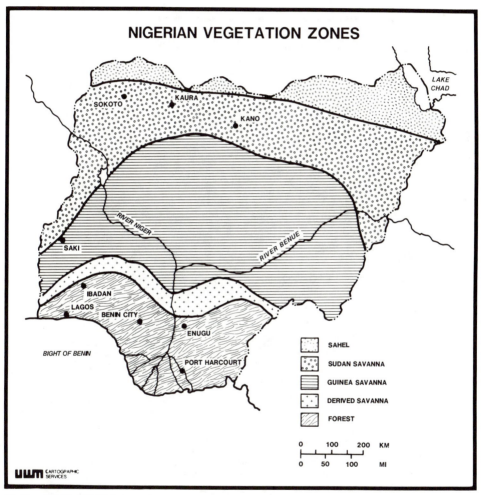

FIG. 4.6   SOURCE: BARBOUR, K.M. et al 1982

Figure 4.7

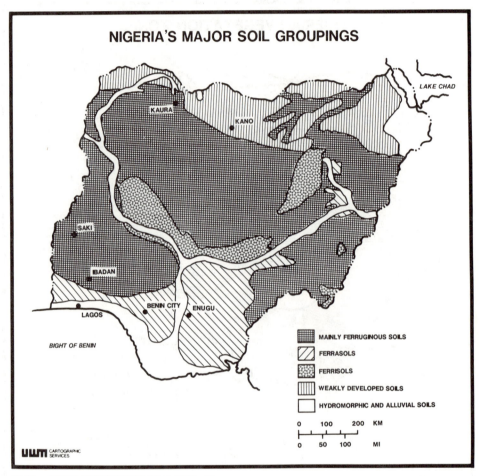

NIGERIA'S MAJOR SOIL GROUPINGS

LAKE CHAD

KAURA

KANO

SAKI

IBADAN

BENIN CITY   ENUGU

LAGOS

BIGHT OF BENIN

MAINLY FERRUGINOUS SOILS

FERRASOLS

FERRISOLS

WEAKLY DEVELOPED SOILS

HYDROMORPHIC AND ALLUVIAL SOILS

0   100   200   KM

0   50   100   MI

UWM CARTOGRAPHIC SERVICES

FIG. 4.7   SOURCE: AREOLA IN BARBOUR, K.M. et al 1982 p. 23

82

Characteristic regulation which depends on climate also conditions soil moisture. Soil becomes more prone to desiccation towards the north, not only because of less humid conditions, but also because of the scantier vegetation cover. This condition is less serious in the more humid and vegetated south.

Climate and Agriculture

Nigeria has great agricultural potential. Most of the land in Nigeria is located favorably with regard to climate. In fact, only the very northern extreme of the country falls within the Sahel, and neither temperature nor moisture are seriously limiting factors in agricultural development. Over 80 percent of the land receives at least 30 inches of rain annually, and only a negligible portion of the land in the northeastern extreme receives less than 30 inches of rain in a year, and most of this falls during the growing period. With the exception of the eastern coastal forest area, which receives over 120 inches of rain, the rest of the country falls within a climatically favorable agricultural belt. This being the case, Nigeria should be in a good position to deal with its agricultural problems in case of any water shortage.

Effect of Climate on Crops

The significance of climatic factors in setting the limit for crop production should not be underestimated. Both vegetation and crops, and even animals, respond to climatic differences. Even though the actual distribution of crop plants is determined by the combined influence of physiological, ecological, social, technological, and historic forces, no crop can become important in an agricultural system unless it has adapted to prevailing environmental conditions.

The principal climatic factors affecting crop production are the same as those influencing all vegetation. Of importance in this case are moisture condition, temperature, length of growing season, sunlight, and wind. A drastic change of any one of these major elements could be detrimental to the production of a particular crop. Practically, all crops have climate limits for economic production — limits which can be moderately extended by plant breeding and selection as well as by cultivation method (*Critchfield 1974*). If this is the case, the various crops cultivated in Nigeria must be adaptive to the climatic conditions that persist in the country. It is logical that a nonadaptive crop should not be introduced into an environment which may bring about uneconomic practices.

The climatic factors are closely related in their influence on crops. The effect of each is modified by the other. Daily, seasonal, or annual variations in any or all of the climatic elements are of importance in determining the efficiency of crop growth. The following paragraphs highlight the importance of some of the major climatic factors (moisture, temperature and wind) in agricultural production.

The temperature of the air and of the soil affects all the growth processes of plants. Every variety of every crop plant has minimum, optimum, and maximum temperature limits for each of its stages of growth. Some, such as the winter rye, can do well in relatively low temperatures and can withstand freezing temperatures during a winter period of dormancy. Others, like the tropical cocoa beans, will die in low freezing temperatures, but do very well in a year-round high temperature environment. While some plants can easily stand the direct rays of the sun, others need to be protected from it.

Within rather wide temperature limits, moisture is more important than any other environmental factor in crop production. There are optimum moisture conditions for crop development just as there are optimum temperature conditions. Because crop plants obtain their water supplies primarily through their root systems, maintenance of soil moisture is the most compelling problem in agriculture. There must be a balance in water supply for crops to grow well. Excessive amounts of water in the soil affect various chemical and biological processes, thus limiting the amount of oxygen and increasing the formation of compounds that are toxic to plant roots. Inadequate supply of water can actually bring about drought, which has in many areas of the world become one of the most serious problems facing farmers. Inadequate water supply can be brought about by low relative humidity, wind, high temperatures, and soils which lose their moisture rapidly through evaporation or drainage. A good maintenance of the crop plant environment could alleviate the problem of water shortages. Irrigation has become a widespread method for providing all or a part of the water need of crops, and rapid evaporation and drainage can be corrected through good drainage practices. Cover-crops and addition of humus to the soil help reduce rapid runoff and drainage. While the problem of high temperature is serious, it can be solved under field conditions by increasing the moisture supply through irrigation or moisture-conserving tillage practices (*Ibid 1974*).

The effect of wind in crop production is great. Its most important effects on crop production are indirect, through the transport of moisture and heat in the air. The movement of air increases evapotranspiration and the transport of pollen and seeds, which is done indiscriminately. The latter function can be detrimental when weed seeds are spread and when unwanted cross-fertilization of plants occurs. Excessive evapotranspiration can be averted through irrigation employed to combat drought. The effect of strong wind can be corrected through the practice of effective windbreak measures, to avert the damage that strong wind does to crops and fruits.

It is obvious from the discussion above that the effects of climate in the production of crops is indisputable, and that it plays both constructive and destructive roles which man has either to accept or correct. The following section will deal with how climate has caused the creation of agricultural zones in Nigeria.

Climate and Agricultural Zones in Nigeria

Nigeria can be divided into three major agricultural zones (*Nwafor in Barbour et al. 1982*) that coincide with the country's three broad ecological zones: the southern tree and root crops zone of the rain forest belt, the mixed crop zone of the Guinea Savanna (Middle Belt), and the northern grain crops zone of the Sudan Savanna (Figure 4.8).

The real pattern of these zones reveals the combined influence of rainfall, humidity, vegetation, and available soil moisture. The most important factor in the creation of the major crop zones is the relation between available water and the water needed by the crops. The amount and distribution of rainfall are, therefore, the most important single environmental influences on agriculture, effectively determining the types and period of cultivation. Temperature is not as important in this regard because it is adequate in virtually every part of the country. The soil catena, though, may occasionally have a sufficiently marked effect upon agricultural production for the boundary to be taken as a zonal one (as in the case of cocoa), however, they are less essential to agricultural zonation in Nigeria than rainfall, which varies from nine months of reliability in the south to about four months in the extreme north.

a) The Southern Tree and Root Crop Zone

The southern tree and root crop zone occupies the rain forest belt. This is a region of high and well distributed rainfall in which moisture supply to the plant-soil system is always adequate. The rainy season lasts from seven to over nine months, depending upon the distance of the region from the coast. This is where most of our root crops (yam, cassava, and cocoyam) and other water dependent crops (vegetables, plantains, beans, maize, etc.) are grown. This is also the region in which the economically important cash crops (cocoa, oil palm, rubber, and kola) and citrus trees can do well. The cultivation of swamp rice is gaining in importance in the southeastern part of the zone.

Figure 4.8

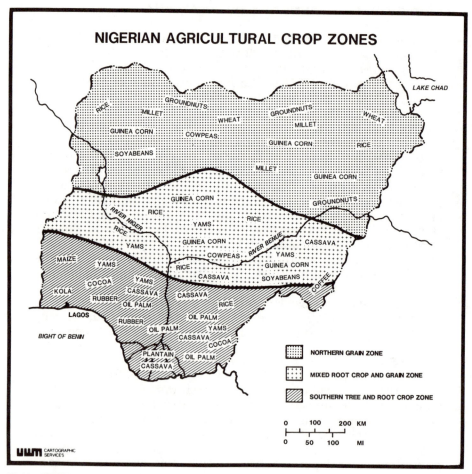

NIGERIAN AGRICULTURAL CROP ZONES

LAKE CHAD

RICE
MILLET
GROUNDNUTS
GROUNDNUTS
WHEAT
GUINEA CORN
COWPEAS
MILLET
WHEAT
SOYABEANS
GUINEA CORN
RICE
MILLET
GUINEA CORN

RIVER NIGER
GUINEA CORN
RICE
RICE
YAMS
RICE
GROUNDNUTS
RICE
YAMS
GUINEA CORN
RIVER BENUE
CASSAVA
MAIZE
YAMS
COWPEAS
YAMS
YAMS
RICE
GUINEA CORN
KOLA
COCOA
YAMS
CASSAVA
SOYABEANS
RUBBER
CASSAVA
CASSAVA
COFFEE
LAGOS
OIL PALM
RICE
RUBBER
OIL PALM
BIGHT OF BENIN
OIL PALM
YAMS
CASSAVA
COCOA
PLANTAIN
OIL PALM
CASSAVA

NORTHERN GRAIN ZONE

MIXED ROOT CROP AND GRAIN ZONE

SOUTHERN TREE AND ROOT CROP ZONE

0   100   200 KM
0   50   100   MI

UWM CARTOGRAPHIC SERVICES

FIG. 4.8   SOURCE: NWAFOR IN BARBOUR et al 1982 p. 73

86

b) The Mixed Crop Zone

The mixed crop zone falls within the Guinea Savanna (Middle Belt) where rainfall is adequate for the kind of agriculture practiced there. In the southern part of the zone is a region of moisture supply sufficient for satisfactory root crop cultivation. This area is characterized by the output of yams, cassava, and rice. Northward, cereals such as maize, guinea corn, and millet are the dominant crops. The Jos Plateau constitutes a sub-zone in which tropical crops are grown at varying levels, while temperate and sub-tropical crops are cultivated at the highest altitudes. The northern limit of the Mixed Crops Zone corresponds with the limit of high expectation of a rainy season long enough, and with sufficient rain, to make root cropping worthwhile.

c) The Northern Grain Zone

North of the Middle Belt mixed crop zone is the grain economy of the Northern zone, which lies within the Sudan Savanna. Here the light rainfall, short wet season, and low humidity restrict the principal crops to grains (millet, Guinea corn, acha, rice, beans, cowpeas, and groundnuts). Millet is the dominant crop and occupies the greatest area of any one crop in Sokoto, Borno, and the rest of Hausaland, with the exception of the Kano emirate, where there is permanent cultivation of market garden crops. Again, the rainfall toward the southern limit of the zone is more reliable than toward the northern end. Here a wide variety of cereal is planted and is supplemented by flood-land cultivation. This is also where most of the livestock is raised. Toward the northern border of the zone, cropping is restricted to quick-growing varieties of grain, chiefly millet, and there is, in effect, one short growing period.

It should be stressed, though, that each agricultural zone merges gradually into the next. It should also be noted that the boundaries or transition zones do not represent the same kind of relationship throughout. The reason for the sequence is complex and may not be explained solely by water-balance and plant-soil relationship. Pest problems and the effect and pattern of disease (plant, animal and man) are all factors, and they need to be assessed to fully appreciate the ecological conditions responsible for the agricultural zones in Nigeria.

Conclusion

Considering the climatic conditions within the country, it is obvious that Nigeria has a high potential for agricultural development. Neither of the major climatic factors poses a threat to the agrarian economy of the country. The country has to examine factors other than climate to fully understand the problems that have persisted in the agricultural sector for years.

Moreover, climate had never been a persistent problem in the development of the agricultural economy in the 50s and 60s or even in the early 1970s. This is not to say that the climate has always been favorable. There have been variability and change in climate. But the change has not posed an unsolvable problem for the country. This is certified by both field study and literature. The Sahelic condition that is shifting southward has not done so without warning. Moreover, yield per acre in all agricultural products in the drought-prone Sahel has been steadily increasing, and that does not show an uncompromising weather condition. It is obvious from this assessment that Nigeria is not threatened by a prolonged drought. Therefore, the government can no longer use climate as an excuse to explain the agricultural development problem in Nigeria.

Chapter 5

THE PLIGHT OF THE SMALLHOLDER

Introduction

As indicated earlier, the smallholder is the main producer of all the food and cash crops in Nigeria. He accounts for over 95 percent of all agricultural output even today, but he does this without any strong support from the government or from any other agencies or institutions. There are several ways by which the interest of the smallholder, who contributes so much to the national economy, could be protected. Incentives in the form of reasonable price increases, a little credit, and perhaps some break in the taxes farmers pay would be desirable means of motivating him to produce more. The government's failure to deal with some of the basic needs of a broadly destitute population, which produces almost all of the nutritional need of the country, shows a gross misplacement of priority.

This chapter details the plight of the smallholder in the context of some of the incentives mentioned above. A detailed description of the role of the government in the plight of the peasants brings to light the betrayal by the government of the peasants who actually feed the country.

Price Increases and the Role of the Marketing Boards

Farmers generally respond well to properly applied incentives. For example, price increases and agricultural credit could be used to motivate farmers to produce more. Nigeria's poor pricing policy may have contributed to the absolute decline in export crop production. Even today there exists a striking similarity between the colonial policy that exploited the resources of the colonial territories and the national policy that now exploits the resources of the countryside, to develop the domestic urban areas. The Nigerian policies, originally intended to minimize international price fluctuations, were increasingly used as methods of taxing farmers, and resulted in a 20-60 percent decline in real income of the rural population

(*Ogbona 1979, p. 131*). The generated funds were used very little for agricultural improvement, to the detriment of long-term production (*Hinderink and Sterkenburg 1983, p. 10*), and farmers received very little for their labor.

The situation led to a dramatic decline in the officially marketed output of crops for export in Nigeria, while the world market price for these products was rising. In the face of the crisis, the federal government was compelled to play a prominent role in the determination of producer prices (a role dominated by the Regional and State governments by means of the Marketing Boards). The government decided to raise the prices of export crops to stimulate production, which was slipping. As Table 5.1 shows, producer prices increased from ₦81 per ton in 1972-73 to ₦250 in 1974-75, and to ₦495 by 1980-81 for palm oil, a 511 percent increase for the 10 year period, and ₦79 to ₦165 and to ₦450 for groundnut during the same periods, a 470 percent increase. It should be noted, however, that the smallest increase in prices was for crops (cocoa, rubber and palm kernel) which still were in the export market, while those crops (especially oil palm and groundnut) which were almost out of the export market were given the highest percentage increase.

Table 5.1

Producer Price for Selected Export Commodities 1972-83

(₦ per ton)

Year	Cocoa	Palm kernel	Palm oil	Ground-nut	Cotton	Beni-seed	Rubber
72/73	279	59	81	79	102	58	-
73/74	450	65	200	103	181	122	-
74/75	550	135	250	165	202	176	-
75/76	660	150	265	250	308	264	-
76/77	660	150	265	350	308	264	-
77/78	1,030	150	295	275	330	290	-
78/79	1,030	150	355	290	330	300	575
79/80	1,200	180	450	350	330	300	692
80/81	1,300	200	495	420	400	315	795
81/82	1,300	N A	N A	450	465	315	1,000
82/83	1,300	N A	N A	450	510	N A	1,200

Sources: Federal Republic of Nigeria, Third National Development Plan, 1975-80, p. 17.
Federal Republic of Nigeria Fourth National Development Plan, 1981-85, p. 35.
Federal Department of Agriculture, 1982, Meloney Street, Lagos, Nigeria.

These producer price increases did not have the expected effect — they were not accompanied by any increase in production. Instead, the production of almost all export crops declined radically. Because Nigerian peasants had in the past responded positively to price increases, the situation of the 1970s and 80s calls for some explanation. It is likely that the beneficiaries of the increases in producer prices were not the peasant producers but the intermediaries between the producers and the states (The Marketing Boards), and probably the few capitalist farmers, whose production was never large enough to make much difference. It is doubtful that the peasants received any benefit from the price increases; otherwise there appears no logical reason for them not to have responded. What then might have triggered the change in attitude? Perhaps it was a lesson the farmers learned from the gross exploitation they suffered at the hands of the monopolistic commodity Marketing Boards, which had regulated the major agricultural exports of Nigeria since World War II.

The Marketing Boards grew out of attempts by the colonial power to tie the colonial economies more closely to the urban areas. The entire country was mobilized for production of the so-called "*scheduled crops*" (export crops handled exclusively by the Marketing Boards) at the expense of crops for domestic consumption. Such crops in Nigeria are cocoa, groundnut, cotton, rubber, palm produce, beniseed, and coffee. The boards were vested with sole authority to purchase commodities from the farmers at monopoly prices, and to sell these at bargain prices on the European markets. Because peasant producers had no representation on these bureaucratic boards, they had no say in the determination of its exploitative and arbitrary pricing and surplus disposal policies. While their stated objective was to stabilize producer prices against the fluctuation of world commodity markets, the boards (one for each of the major export commodities) ran very high surpluses by keeping producer prices deliberately low. This made large surpluses possible, surpluses which were important sources of government revenue to be channeled into the urban industrial and commercial activities or, in some notorious cases, into private banks associated with regional political leaders (*Ogbona 1979 p. 131-33, Onimode 1982 p. 166*).

In addition, the Marketing Board System, after its postcolonial transformation, was an instrument of indirect heavy taxation and unremitting exploitation of the peasantry. This heavy taxation, along with the monopolistic pricing policies, greatly determined the discouraging return farmers received on their products. Table 5.2 illustrates how the Nigerian Cocoa Marketing Board was an instrument of a tax burden to the poor farmers. While the figures do not include the income tax and other community taxes producers had to pay, it is apparent they were being used for the benefit of the Boards and the government. For instance, in 1958 the total revenue the government realized from the F.O.B. price per ton was 43.7 percent, which represents the exact proportion by which the farmer was underpaid under the colonial power. A decade later, in 1968, under an independent government, this proportion climbed to 49.1 percent and did not ease much until its reform in 1977, in spite of the heavy role petroleum played in the export market. Producers paid as much as a 62 percent implicit tax on the world prices of their products, in the difference between world prices and prices offered the peasants by the Board. In addition, they paid produce, income, community development, tenement, and other oppressive multiple taxes (*Onimode 1982, p. 166*), some of which are listed in Table 5.2. Yet the large surpluses and tax proceeds were not channeled back into the agricultural sector to diversify production; rather they were used primarily to finance, elitist projects for the benefit of the urbanized bourgeoisie. "*The Agbekoya riots*" of 1969 in the former Western State, which involved the killing of many chiefs and police officers, among others, were provoked by such oppression of the indigent peasantry. These riots indicated that the peasant farmers were aware of the abuse they had received politically. Such a politically neutralized but increasingly restive population could not be expected to fulfill the agricultural responsibility of any nation (*Ibid, p. 167*).

The price increases in the 1970's and 1980s were, therefore, seen as a means of resigning the farmers to the Boards' selfish marketing policies. Some looked for more lucrative internal and local non-monopolistic markets for their products. Others migrated to the cities to obtain more lucrative jobs created by the advent of the oil industry. This, therefore, implies that export crops could no longer be a priority for those farmers who could afford to do without them. For the northerners it was an easy shift, for they did not grow perennial crops such as cocoa, rubber, and oil palm, which depend mainly on external markets. The two major export crops — groundnut and cotton — as well as beniseed were simply not important to them. They focused instead on locally consumed food crops sold at the local markets, which were not controlled by the government. For the southern areas dominated by perennial crops (oil palm, cocoa, and rubber), the effect of competition from more lucrative food crops was less immediate, but production of all the export tree crops declined. Those farmers who could afford it simply abandoned their farms to migrate to the cities, and the majority of those who moved were young, able-bodied citizens. The older farmers obviously did not have the same option, because their homes were established in the rural area. And since they could

Table 5.2

Nigerian Cocoa Marketing Board Structure of F.O.B. Cocoa Bean Price for the Period 1957-71 in Nigeria
(₦)

	57/58	58/59	59/60	60/61	61/62	62/63	63/64	64/65	65/66	66/67	67/68	68/69	69/70	70/71
Product price per ton	292.0	292.0	312.0	264.0	192.0	202.0	212.0	232.0	122.0	172.0	182.0	192.0	292.0	302.0
Buying allow.	31.0	27.0	26.2	24.4	25.4	22.0	20.2	19.6	19.4	19.4	23.2	23.4	25.0	23.8
Export duty & product sales tax	121.6	111.8	83.0	54.2	41.8	42.6	60.2	37.0	33.2	68.0	71.6	96.6	106.0	112.0
Shipping and handling charges less refunds	4.2	3.4	3.8	4.4	3.6	3.4	3.6	4.4	4.2	4.4	4.0	3.6	9.6	9.8
Other costs	0.6	19.4	3.6	6.2	15.8	1.0	6.2	2.2	32.8	12.6	25.8	40.8	21.0	20.0
Profit/loss	+132.6	+108.4	+9.4	-3.4	+31.4	+43.0	+57.8	-35.2	+26.4	+108.6	+103.4	+153.6	+96.4	+106.4
F.O.B. price/ton	582.0	562.0	438.0	348.0	310.0	314.0	360.0	260.0	238.0	384.0	410.0	510.0	550.0	574.0
Contrib. to govt. revenue * per ton	254.2	220.2	92.4	49.0	73.2	85.6	118.0	1.8	59.6	176.6	175.0	250.2	202.4	218.5

Source: Olatunbosun, D., Nigeria's Neglected Rural Majority, 1975, p. 89.

*Contributions to government revenue are made up of export duty, producer sales tax and profit.

not readily convert their cocoa, oil palm, or rubber holdings into food crop use, they continued their old practices and were thus exploited by the Marketing Boards.

Cocoa and palm kernels, though having declined in production, are now Nigeria's only major export crops. Once the world's leader in groundnut exportation and a leading exporter of palm oil, Nigeria now even imports some of the oil that it receives from these two crops. Not only is the export market affected, but the local groundnut oil and cottonseed oil milling industries are largely idle, and the country has to import cotton lint to feed its largely idle textile industry (*West Africa, May 12, 1986*). The Marketing Board continually raised producer prices, in the 1970s and 80s, but in vain. It remained more profitable for farmers to sell groundnut or homemade groundnut oil to traders, or not to grow it at all.

Because price increases seemed to have no effect, and production of the export crops experienced absolute decline as did food crops, the Obasanjo government transformed the Marketing Boards and put these newly created boards under Federal control in 1977. The seven boards so created included a board for each of the former five major export commodities (cocoa, groundnut, palm produce, rubber and cotton) along with the newly created Nigerian Grains Board and the Nigerian Roots and Tubers Board. The transformation of the Marketing Board did not produce the intended results. Nor did the export crops or the two newly created food marketing boards get a boost from the internal trade. The food crops trading which was in the hands of private traders still remains that way. This is the main reason Marketing Boards became largely irrelevant to Nigeria's needs, and were subsequently abolished in the country as of June 1986 (*West Africa, May 1986, p. 989*).

Credit and the Nigerian Agricultural and Cooperative Banks

The issue of credit allocation to smallholders will be mentioned quite frequently in sections of the next chapter as well. However, it is appropriate here to make a more elaborate analysis of the issue as it contributed to either improving or stifling agricultural growth in the country. Despite the major transformation the agricultural sector has gone through, basic problems facing governments have remained unchanged in the past two decades. The means of increasing output and keeping rural youth interested in agriculture has been stifled by the practices of the government against the smallholders who, though they have very little money or political power, constitute over 95 percent of all producers. As well, there is a widespread belief that the peasant farmers are incapable of achieving the desired overall increases in output and keeping pace with population growth in food production. Therefore, the mass majority of the farmers receive no monetary assistance from the government.

While the government has sought solutions in green revolution type campaigns (such as "*Operation Feed the Nation*" and the "*Green Revolution Program*" under the civilian regime), farm mechanization, and scale-enlargement, it has injected huge amounts of funds into these programs while excluding smallholder.

It is noteworthy that since 1960 agricultural credit for farmers has been a politically controversial issue. While in the First National Development Plan an allocation of ₦14 million was made for credit purposes, the controversy that mounted from this crippled the entire program, which probably benefited only those regional politicians directly involved in it. Apart from that, agriculture in the country relied — somewhat uncertainly — on traditional sources of lending.

The first attempt by the Federal government to make agricultural credit available was contained in a directive written after the Civil War year that commercial banks set aside 6 percent of their lending capital for farmers. This directive was simply ignored (*Ogbona 1979, p. 129*). Then, during the Second Plan, the Federal government established in 1973 the National Agricultural Credit Bank, headquartered at Kaduna, and this in turn was hampered by regional political pressure. The money allocated during the Second Plan period was again wasted, by a few elitist and political hands.

The formal importance attached to agricultural credit for farmers (despite the government's inconsistency) led, on the advice of the World Bank, to a final establishment of the Nigerian Agricultural and Cooperative Bank (NACB) at Kaduna during the Third National Development Plan, 1975-80. Involving an estimated capital of ₦150 million, over the five year period, this plan supposedly reflects the petroleum sector's contribution to agriculture. In addition, state-owned Agricultural Credit Corporations were established in order to eliminate the problems posed by the lack of adequate collateral of smallholder farmers. The Agricultural Credit Guaranteed Scheme was established to encourage commercial banks to give peasants agricultural loans, loans guaranteed by the federal government through the Central Bank. In this manner the government made an effort to enforce its monetary policy guideline, which stipulated that a minimum of 6 percent of commercial banks' sectoral allocation should go to the agricultural sector.

At the end of the first four years of the Plan the NACB had made a gross disbursement of ₦157.5 million, which by the government's own admission, favored corporations, large-scale farms, and farmers who possessed adequate collateral (*Fourth National Development Plan 1985-85, pp. 78 & 85*). Money loans to small-scale farmers were awarded through cooperatives, which invariably were dominated by city-based tycoons. Since there was inadequate supervision and follow-up of the use of the money, these influential and powerful city-based leaders used the cooperative as another instrument of securing large credits for their private businesses, which in some cases had nothing to do with the intended goal of promoting agricultural productivity. The smallholder, who was supposed to benefit from this, was instead pushed out, due to the cooperative's cumbersome credit requirements. In order to meet the conditions established for securing a loan, a farmer had to be a member of a cooperative society that would "guarantee his credit worthiness," he had to have the *required resources in terms of land, labor and managerial capacity,*" and he had to have an agricultural plan for the future in agreement with the Corporation or its local representative for improved farming methods that would allow him to repay a loan at the first instance of income. Obviously, all of these conditions excluded most smallholders.

The performance of the commercial banks under the Credit Guaranteed Scheme, in spite of the required stipulation that 6 percent of loanable funds go to the agricultural sector, appears to have left much to be desired, as the smallholder farmers who really needed the loans were not given the opportunity to obtain them. In the face of the existing crisis it would not have been practical for private institutions to undertake such a suicidal venture when the government itself had been avoiding the smallholders since Independence. Moreover, agriculture has become the least desired and reliable occupation, making the poor smallholder invariably incapacitated in attempts to meet the requirements for loans from the commercial banks.

The conditions for acquiring credit from the NACB were practically impossible to meet from the point of view of the peasant farmers, who at the same time were up against competition from very powerful rivals. While the bank recognized the individual farmers, cooperatives, partnerships and limited liability companies, along with government-owned companies, state agricultural organizations, and other government bodies as loan beneficiaries, it did not specify that individual peasants should be given preferential consideration since they could not compete on equal terms with others. Instead, substantial collateral in the form of real estate, life insurance policies, and legal mortgages was rigidly required for obtaining credit (*Ogbona 1979, p. 130*).

It is clear that the illiterate farm villagers, for whom things like real estate and insurance have no meaning, were never going to benefit from the Credit Scheme. Why should a peasant on a two or three acre plot be required to produce a feasibility study before securing financial assistance? Peasants in general do not need huge amounts of money to operate their farms. What most of them need is a liberal loan of ₦50, ₦100 or ₦200 for each planting season, and they will utilize it to the utmost. But this consideration was not provided by the government, and instead it wasted hundreds of millions of naira on large-scale schemes that produced less than 5 percent of the total output and even contributed to the present crisis. Meanwhile, the farmers who could afford to do so at all got their loans from private individuals at a 25, 50, or even 100 percent interest rates.

The conditions during the Fourth Plan Period were no better. All indications show that the vast majority of the farming group was pushed out again, although policies on paper seemed to reflect some concern for the smallholder. The first two years of the Plan witnessed the following development in the credit program: whereas total credit disbursement for large-scale orientation institutions amounted to ₦75.7 million and ₦68 million respectively for 1981 and 1982, only ₦603,454 and ₦1,034,384 respectively were disbursed under the smallholder scheme for the two years, to a farming population of over 18 million. While in 1982 the NACB approved 79 loans in the amount of ₦28,714,715 to big corporations and other large-scale farm institutions, only 430 loans were made under the smallholder scheme, to the amount of ₦1,061,356 (*Ministry of Agriculture, Annual Report 1982, p.28*). This clearly reflects the neglect of the majority by the government. Indeed, most of these loans inevitably went to non-farmers for purposes other than agricultural improvement. The truth of the matter is that agricultural credit facilities have been designed for the big capitalistic farmers. Even with the extension to agriculture of industrial fiscal incentives involving accelerated depreciation, import duty relief on tractors, etc. would only benefit the small percentage of capitalist farmers. Peasants do not need depreciation allowance and tariff relief on their crude hoes and cutlasses.

From the analysis of the two main incentives, price and credits, it is apparent that the majority of farmers who produced well over 90 percent of the agricultural products in the country were consistently neglected by the successive governments. Whereas the colonial administration used the peasants to produce essential food products by at least providing markets for their products, the post-colonial Nigerian governments have engaged in a progressive alienation of the peasants in the food production process. The policymakers have ignored the peasants by shunning policies that would enhance domestic food production, and by building institutions and structures that have exploited them, eventually removing them from their nutritional base instead of helping them expand their economic base.

97

There was much the government could have done to alleviate the burden of the poor farmer. If nothing else, it would have made sense to make some effort to utilize some of the oil revenue to remove the tax burden on the agricultural sector, so that the real income of the average farmer could be spent to help him expand his economic base. Instead the government continued to exploit him through such means as heavy direct and indirect tax burdens, and waged a campaign against him to remove him from the land.

Encroachment on the Smallholder

The government has encouraged the dissolution of the land tenure system and communal land ownership, even though they have been the only means by which a vast majority of the country's population can sustain itself. Most farmers have holdings of two or three acres, on which two or more crops are raised simultaneously. Without this system, mass starvation would result. While the government desires to eliminate the rudimentary agricultural techniques still practiced among the majority of farmers — through emphasis on large-scale agriculture, especially for export crops, which brings it huge revenue — it is not making a concurrent effort to provide an alternative job market for the population. Neither has the effort given to large-scale agriculture brought about a significant increase in the production of crops in the country. Meanwhile, the phasing out of the smallholder continues to create chaos.

The phasing out of the smallholder has been an ongoing process since the colonial period. The first such move was made in southern Nigeria in 1917 with the Public "*Land Acquisition Ordinance*," which gave the government the right to acquire land for public purposes either for a minimal fee or lease, and if the land was unoccupied no compensation would be given. This ordinance was followed by the "*Nigerian Town and Country Planning Ordinance*" of 1946, which empowered the planning authority to purchase land for approved schemes either by agreement or compulsion (*Olatunbosun 1968, p. 2*). These ordinances, according to Olatunbosun, were useful only in circumstances in which the government had interest, since land could be acquired only for public purposes. Apart from that, not much was accomplished through these ordinances.

In the north, where the Fulani rulers had allowed everybody including strangers to occupy as much land as was necessary for their support, a different form of oppressive land acquisition was introduced. "*The Land and Native Rights Ordinance*" declared all native lands to be under the control of the governor, and to be held and administered by him for the benefit of the natives of northern Nigeria. This ordinance empowered the governor to grant rights of occupancy to natives as well as aliens, and for the first time natives had to pay rental fees for the land they occupied. This ordinance played a significant role in reducing the land holdings of the communities in the region.

While the colonial government consciously sought to maintain peasant production as opposed to capitalist production, it also set the stage for the enhancing of capitalist penetration of peasant society. The post-colonial leaders who took over didn't change any of the rules, but promoted them to their own advantage, and to the ultimate detriment of the population.

Since Independence, the involvement of the government in removing the peasants from the land has taken different forms, from dire neglect, to oppressive policies, to denial of the benefits peasants earned. Policies that emphasized large-scale production, especially of export crops, were specifically designed to eliminate the smallholder, but the process was delayed because of the discouraging performances of the programs that were designed to accomplish the goal. However, the process continued to hurt the many farmers who were displaced by these programs.

In pursuit of their priority of export crop production, the regional governments of the First Republic, through their Development Corporations, established cocoa, palm oil, rubber, and coconut plantations, especially in the then three southern regions. In addition, farm settlements were founded, the aim of which was not only to increase cash crop production, but also to transform peasant farming into capitalist farming. In the former Eastern Region, six such settlements were established in 1961 alone, each of them between 400 and 600 acres large. In the Western Region, a total of 45 farm settlements came into existence between 1962 and 1968, with a total of 34,000 acres. Some of these establishments are located in Boki and Uzo Uwani in the east and in Okitipupa, Onisere and Ile-Oluyi in the west (*Ake 1985, p. 62*).

The slow conversion of the peasant farm to that of a capitalist mode by the government was perhaps hastened by the food crisis and the great interest shown in agricultural investment by the World Bank from the mid-1970s. Given the ideological bent and the economic orientation of the managers towards large-scale production, it is perhaps understandable that they would sanction the required transformation of "*inadequate*" peasant production to modernized production. This then was the goal of subsequent agricultural policy.

Capitalist cooperatives were another rural institution which peasants were required to join for the purpose of developing a cooperative type of farming. This was an arrangement in which participating farmers brought their plots of land together in such a way as to permit relatively easy mechanization, and to avail themselves of a full range of extension services. This, however, did not meet the basic needs of the peasants, because the true purpose of the cooperatives was transforming the land tenure system. Cooperatives came to be instruments for social manipulation of the peasants by government, run by powerful elitist city politicians who served only their own interests, sometimes acquiring loans for private businesses that had nothing to do with agriculture.

During the Second National Development Plan (1970-74) the government still viewed peasants as a serious hindrance to the agricultural sector's development and persisted in changing the peasants despite their large contribution in previous years. Obviously a government which is so set against small-scale peasant production, in spite of the peasants' integral role in the production of even cash crops, is not going to be responsive to their needs. However, the federal government's persistent attempts to consolidate the farm land were slowed by the politics involved in the land tenure system, and by the varying social and cultural conditions in different parts of the country. The responsibility of system reform was therefore left for the state government. It is not surprising then that the federal government concentrated only on creating facilities for large-scale capital-intensive farm units that would phase out the smallholders, while the state concentrated on their oppressive campaign against them. To this end several agricultural projects and programs were introduced, among which were the different large-scale irrigation schemes, the National Accelerated Food Production Program (NAFPP), the Livestock Development Project, and Agricultural Development Projects (ADP) and Agricultural Development Area (ADA), both of which are under the Integrated Agricultural Development Program.

In its effort to promote large-scale agriculture, the government in the 1970s, through the help of the World Bank and private European firms, initiated the development of three huge irrigation projects. These were the Chad Basin, the Hadejia-Jemaare valley, and the Sokoto-Rima valley projects, which would create an irrigated area of 274,000 hectares by 1991 at a cost of N2.2 billion. The drive for irrigated agriculture is perhaps understandable in terms of drought risk, especially in some areas, but the smallholder was not included in these projects. The government, in its overriding concern for the urban population, concentrated on large-scale farming, and in the process drove the smallholder from his land. Ironically the small holder was the one who could have provided the foodstuffs lacking in the urban market, had he been provided the right incentives.

The NAFPP is an ongoing program started in 1972 involving government, private institutions and selected private farmers, extension services, and research institutes. Its supposed objective was to raise farmers' income through the diffusion of new agricultural technology. In this program too, however, pri-

100

vate estates were favored against the smallholder through an agricultural credit guarantee scheme established by the federal government. Again, during the Third Development Plan 1975-80, emphasis was laid on large-scale mechanized farms, especially those established by public sector enterprises. Such farms were thought to be the quickest and most efficient way to increase output and solve the problem of growing shortage in farm labor. The intended role of the NAFPP of helping the smallholder was abrogated.

The ADP first started in 1975 and was co-sponsored by the Nigerian government and the World Bank, which had become very interested in agricultural development in the country. This program called for the establishment of agricultural development projects in various parts of the country, to promote integrated rural development by providing facilities for intensive agricultural extension services, modern input supply, and up-to-date distribution systems. Consolidation of holdings and farm mechanization were paramount to this program achieving its goal. Eleven such projects were planned, but as of the 1982 season only three were completed.

Despite all the ambitious efforts made by the government, the food crisis worsened; the programs became parasitic institutions which further exacerbate the situation. The deepening food crisis led the Obasanjo administration (1975-79), almost in panic, to launch the propagandistic "*Operation Feed the Nation*" (OFN) program on May 12, 1976. The program was directed at mass motivation and incentives (heavily subsidized, improved seeds and fertilizers). But except for the attempted distribution of fertilizers to farmers, the program lacked any organizational base to mobilize and motivate peasants toward higher agricultural production. Like many other dictatorial military measures, the program ignored the legitimate economic and political aspirations of the masses and excluded them from actual agricultural participation. Instead, urbanized bureaucrats and students were paid to participate in rural production schemes (*Zartman, 1983, p. 124*), and most of the fertilizer wasted in the sun (*Onimode 1982, p. 174*). The program which promised to supply fertilizers abundantly to farmers had, in 1978-79, the third year of the program, seen only 872,000 acres fertilized (Table 5.3), and the following year this acreage decreased to 805,000, to further reflect a lack of concern for smallholders. The table also shows that some states (Bendel, Cross River, Lagos, and Rivers) did not have a single acre fertilized during this period, while other southern states were also badly neglected. However, in connection with the Fourth National Development Plan 1981-85 discussed below (chapter 6), most of the fertilizer actually applied went to improving export crop production — cotton, beniseed and ground

101

nut in particular as much of the land area fertilized was in the northern states of Kaduna, Kano, and Sokoto, the states that produce these crops.

Table 5.3

Land Area Treated with Fertilizer 1978-79 - 1980-81

('000 ha.)

STATE	78/79	79/80	80/81
ANAMBRA	4	0	4
BAUCHI	84	82	139
BENDEL	_	0	4
BENUE	56	111	_
BORNO	90	39	66
C. RIVER	_	0	_
GONGOLA	23	28	149
IMO	2	1	1
KADUNA	228	213	825
KANO	70	104	153
KWARA	6	8	133
LAGOS	_	1	0
NIGER	63	98	16
OGUN	4	2	1
ONDO	5	8	13
OYO	50	33	26
PLATEAU	24	33	12
RIVERS	_	1	_
SOKOTO	162	43	219
NIGERIA	872	805	1,800

Source: Nigerian Ministry of Agriculture, 1982

The nobly conceived OFN did not realize its objective because much of the money was thrown to dishonest public officials without any preplanning or provision for accountability. OFN was a deserved failure, and it was abolished by the Shagari administration in 1979. The program indeed created more problems for the country than it intended to solve. In spite of the formal outburst of enthusiasm that greeted its inauguration, this great idea of agricultural renaissance through heavy subsidies was again lost to the peasants, who now regard the program as "*Operation Fool the Nation*".

The replacement of the program by the Green Revolution was almost unnecessary because the same administration betrayed its original goal with the "*Land Use Decree No. 6*" of 1978. This Land Use Act was the most dramatic reform program promulgated by the government to eliminate those small-farmers who still farmed primarily under the land tenure system. The decree purported to vest all land into the hands of the state governments by 1978. The main objective of the Act was to free the land of the smallholder for the purpose of promoting large-scale mechanized, capital intensive agricultural programs by private, large-scale investors. In addition, the government believed that this would make it easier to attract foreign entrepreneurs and foreign capital to agricultural production. To this end, the government established the Land Allocation Advisory Committees and Land Use Allocation Committees, which were to be instrumental in enforcing the Act in rural and urban areas respectively (*Ake 1985, p. 64*). Agricultural land was to be allocated freely and almost indefinitely. This ostensibly meant that land ceased to be a constraint for agricultural producers, who were once hampered by the land tenure system.

The application of the Act showed a gross disregard of its provisions. A vast majority of the beneficiaries came from the ranks of the dominant class. Civil servants, administrative secretaries, police and military officers, business tycoons, industrialists, contractors, traders, and customs and excise officials were the beneficiaries of the Land Use Act, for these people, because of their positions, acquired land with ease from the government. Meanwhile, the poor people in the country who really needed to farm the land to sustain themselves were forced to become laborers, while others were removed from their farmland.

Furthermore, the Act undoubtedly played an important role in the establishment of huge agricultural projects through the River Basin Development Authorities. In the words of the Shagari Administration, the Act provided the necessary "*boost*" to the sector's involvement in large-scale agricultural activities by encouraging the consolidation of holdings and large-scale production. This obviously was welcomed by the state governments, as it would encourage private sector involvement in large-scale farming (*Ondo State Fourth National Development Plan 1981-85, p. 16*). Meanwhile, some of these River Basin Development Authorities were abandoned after having displaced many farmers in the process. Examples of some of these RBDA are the Benin-Owena, Chad Basin, Ogun-Oshun, and Niger River Basin Development Authorities, which were either abandoned or inadequately utilized after hundreds of millions of naira were spent towards their development.

While the Act encouraged many urban based elites to grasp the best land for themselves and allowed the government to acquire land with ease to establish its large-scale capital intensive agricultural projects, it also resulted in landlessness among the masses. The poor peasants were actually victims, dispossessed of their land with little or no compensation. The rural population was pushed off the land and either became rural proletariat, increasingly dependent on the local petty bourgeoisie, or drifted to urban areas in search of jobs which didn't exist.

The Land Use Act, in fact, set the stage for the ill-conceived and deceptive "*Green Revolution Program*." Launched in May 1980, it promoted the most radical method by which to force the citizens from their land. While its original objective was to redress the apparent deficiencies of the OFN, to create the means to meet the needs of small-farmers, and to spread the benefits of rural development to the local level (*Federal Ministry of Agriculture, Information Bulletin on Nigerian Agriculture, 1984*), the program betrayed its original objective by emphasizing large-scale capital-intensive production, again ignoring the smallholder. In this way the Green Revolution program turned out to be an instrument of the destruction of the peasants.

The term "*Green Revolution*" was coined to describe rapid development strategies for boosting production of agricultural products, but it was not a new concept. Other third world countries who tried the program boosted output only at the cost of enormous problems: above all, increased landlessness, deprivation, and poverty of the rural majority. Consequently, the Nigerian government's adoption of the term might have seemed rash (*West Africa, April 21, 1986, p. 829*). The Nigerian government has always been quick to adopt policies without studying their implications. Such ill-informed moves were made with regard to OFN (1976) and the present second tier currency market (1986), both of which were adopted from the Ghanian Development Strategies. Nigeria's adoption of the popular Green Revolution program was therefore consistent with its performance record. The Green Revolution's high yielding variety (HYVs) seeds, as use in other countries, according to Nzimiro:

> required expensive input — irrigation, fertilizers, pesticides, machinery, and were possible only on large individual or corporate holdings; these have duly spread, ordinary farmers being turned off the land or kept on it, as serfs or laborers. The masses displaced in the process became less able than ever to afford food in the midst of overflowing granaries. In this way India achieved food self-sufficiency with overflowing granaries and the masses were less able than ever to afford food. Nigerians who talk of food self-sufficiency need to know that it could take that form (*West Africa, April 21, 1986, p. 830*).

Critics suspected that Nigeria's Green Revolution could have, in fact, meant replacement of small-scale farming by large estates, agribusiness, and landlordism. These concerns were voiced only by some agricultural experts and academics. Since the press and the public were invariably ill-informed about the program, the Nigerian government had nothing to fear. Moreover, officials made a public pronouncement that the smallholder would be helped in the program through subsidized fertilizer supplies, extension work, etc., on which the agricultural sector placed its hopes because of the promise seen in the new civilian government. But this federal government also continued to promote large-scale agriculture; and, being concerned only about the supply of food for the urban consumer, it directed its attention away from the smallholder and injected huge amounts of money into the irrigation and agricultural projects, some of which were already established. It also promoted large-scale farming by inviting foreign agribusiness to enter into partnerships with both government and private citizens.

Focusing on the urban consumer probably began the downfall of the government's GR program, which has been the cause of many other mistakes in agricultural policies. This was exactly what Nigeria did with its Green Revolution program by encouraging hope that some rapid new agricultural development could ensure abundant food supplies where traditional farming had failed. The population (especially the urban population), being uninformed about the program, did not envision the impossibility of the program or the ensuing social disruption and deprivation of the masses. They simply trusted the government, which got carried away with its wasteful spending on different agricultural projects while the food shortage situation worsened. And in the process thousands of smallholders were deprived of their only means of survival by purchasing land for small amounts of money.

This program, which raised the hopes of the population, turned out to be a political gimmick used by politicians to win support for their corrupt practices. It was therefore not surprising that the GR, whose institutional structure mirrored its predecessor OFN, became an instrument by which peasants were exploited and alienated instead of mobilized. Due to the program some of the most ruthless political bandits in Nigeria's history emerged, in "green revolutionary hunger".

As damaging as these major programs, projects, and schemes were, such schemes presented less potential danger to smallholders than the growth of private landlordism. The Land Use Act, which freed the land from the present land tenure system, was promoted by the Green Revolutionist government to the extent of inviting any foreign or indigenous interest into the sector. This is still occurring rapidly, as many foreign capital establishments have started investing in the country's agriculture. Nineteen joint ventures were already planned by the first two years of the program, by companies from Brazil, Canada, and Europe, and in July, 1980 the U.S. government and Nigeria signed a memorandum to encourage heavy investment by American agribusiness in conjunction with the U.S. Department of Agriculture. One such venture was the Bakalori irrigation project 150 km southeast of Sokoto, which was placed into the hands of an Italian contractor. The total allotment for two contracts to be completed by March 1980 was ₦154 million, but by January of that year ₦350 million had already been wasted and construction was blocked by farmer opposition (*Zartman 1983*). Other establishments have included the Commonwealth Development Corporation for Sugar Project in Gongola State, FIAT, SCOA, and the UAC for supply of agricultural machinery, and the Beatrice Foods of America and Cadbury Schweppes of Britain, which are involved in growing tomatoes (*Ake 1985, p. 65*).

Most damaging of all is that increasing numbers of progressive farmers and urban business tycoons have taken up farming as their business, having acquired the land with ease. Land allocation has become a vehicle for making quick money which the politicians of the Green Revolutionist government of the Second Republic have exploited to the fullest. The Emirs and chiefs of the northern states expressed their concern by stating that:

> *possession of land through allocation by local government, not to talk of state governments, became beyond the reach of the ordinary people. The country watched in silent amazement; ordinary people were dispossessed of their land on payment of meager or no compensation and made landless while these lands were being reallocated to urban elites who had the money to bribe officials (West Africa, November 1986, p. 2312).*

The effect on the poor peasants of the ever-increasing large-scale establishments and government projects is enormous. And it has lasting social consequences, as already noted by Tina Wallace, a stern observer of the situation who sees the smallholder farmers clearly as the victims:

> *These people are definitely losers, and no one pretends they are to benefit. Their housings often worse than before, their (relocated) farm land poorer; they have lost their economic trees for a handful of silver and their nutritional base is thus depleted. The modernization of agriculture is forcing large numbers into non-viable rural situations (Wallace, 1980).*

Despite all efforts made in the promotion of large-scale agriculture — to the detriment of the smallholder agriculture — from the First Republic to the present time, the food crisis has gone from bad to worse. Incapable of mobilizing the masses for development because such an idea is entirely foreign to its economic, political, and ideological conceptions of the development process, the Nigerian government has concentrated instead on mobilizing its elitist and capitalist bourgeoisie from both domestic and foreign sources. This, whether they realize it or not, has continually placed the ordinary Nigerian citizen under heavy deprivation and suffrage.

Conclusion

In principle, the government of Nigeria never saw the smallholder farmer as contributing to the economy of the country and in reality it excluded him from the development of the sector while at the same time exploiting him. The government also seemed to see the smallholder (because of his rudimentary tools, land tenure system, and small-holdings) as the cause of the present crisis and therefore created the facilities and institutions to remove him. The Operation Feed the Nation (1976) and the Green Revolution (1980) programs, promoted by the Land Use Act of 1978, were immediate and deliberate actions taken by the government to remove the smallholder from his land through the institution of large-scale agricultural projects and foreign and private investment in the sector.

Chapter 6

POLITICAL MISMANAGEMENT AND AGRICULTURAL DEVELOPMENT IN NIGERIA

Introduction

The significance of agriculture in Nigeria's life and economy cannot be overemphasized. Approximately seven out of ten people are dependent on agriculture for subsistence living and income. The agricultural sector of the economy had been the backbone of the country's economic development. However, the government's role in agriculture has been that of pure neglect manifested in inconsistent rural policies which at times run counter to even the intention of the government itself.

Prior to the development of the oil industry, over 80 percent of the Nigerian economy depended on agriculture. The two major economic indicators (*Gross Domestic Product and export receipts, see chapter 3*) were a function of the work done in the agricultural sector of the economy. Since the development of the oil industry, there has been a reversal of priority, which has resulted in a complete breakdown of the agricultural sector, the overhauling of which has been a problem since the mid-1970s. Self-sufficient in food production to the extent of exporting surpluses prior to the oil industry, Nigeria is now spending large sums of money importing food that can be produced locally, and the population is paying heavily for it. Basic food prices have skyrocketed to an unprecedented high. With such high prices for basic food items, not many people in the country can live decently. In fact, the average family is worse off now than before and immediately after the Civil War. The lack of well-planned and coordinated policies for the rural sectors makes matters worse for both the urban and rural populations.

The Nigerian government has never been an active supporter of the agricultural sector of the economy, at least in practice. Many successive governmental regimes came up with celebrated agricultural policies and programs designed to bring the country "*back to self-sufficiency*," but they have failed consistently. The failure of these programs calls to attention other

109

factors which repeatedly stifle development, not only of the agricultural sector, but of other sectors as well. Government mismanagement of the national economy, political corruption, greed, nepotism, abuse of power, and tyrannical and oppressive instincts, in addition to a displaced priority in the ruling class, have persistently worked against Nigeria's agricultural development.

Nigeria's self-sufficiency in food production in the 1960s and early 1970s was not a function of government involvement, in a constructive sense. The state of affairs dictated the rather progressive course the sector was taking. People were not necessarily distracted by the circumstances in the government. They, therefore, were productive in spite of government involvement. This condition existed with little or no rural urban income disparities. At the inception of salary hikes recommended by the Udoji and Adebo commissions in the early 1970s, and subsequent salary increases fueled by the rapidly expanding oil revenue, a new set of social class structures was created. While salary increases were granted to both the employees of the private and public sectors in the city's economy, the rural population was not considered. The government which commissioned these salary programs did nothing to salvage the already disquieting plight of the rural population, and no price increase to bridge the gap was recommended for the food farmers produced in the country. Rather, the government exploited the rural population through the marketing boards, which generated huge revenue for the government by running surpluses to keep farmers' prices for export crops down. Yet the rural population had to compete with the big salary earners in the cities to purchase basic necessities. The reaction of many farmers, therefore, was to move to the city. And when food shortages became evident, the government imported food instead of dealing with local farmers to help them produce.

It would not be presumptuous to maintain that the Nigerian government made no effort to plan for its agricultural future, but rather was complacent and focused its attention only on speculative investment strategies. Any country engaging in serious integrated economic planning would not experience the decade-long paradox of one booming sector adjoining one depressed sector. This state of affairs is proof of the lack of internal consistency in planning strategy (planlessness) and priority that has plagued the ruling class since Independence and has led to exploitative policies believed to be handed down from the colonial period. Development strategies followed by Nigeria's leaders not only discriminated against agriculture in revenue allocation, but also were consistently export-crop biased in the allocation of funds. In this respect too, only a few affluent plantation farmers, corporations, and state owned institutions benefited, and the majority of farmers who produced the bulk of the cash export crops were not reached.

In addition, the Nigerian government adopted the strategy of import-substitution industrialization policies practiced in the colonial period (with tariff protection offered to new industries), policies planned to discriminate against the agricultural community. This is because the import duty for protecting import-substituted industries raised the prices of protected manufactured goods to the domestic consumer. In spite of the fact that those countries in Asia and Latin America who adopted import-substitution policies never made any significant progress in their economies, it seems Nigeria did not study the implication of such practices before accepting them. This practice, which discouraged or inhibited agricultural growth, became more apparent in the 1970s and 1980s.

With the booming oil industry, huge foreign exchange earnings, and enormous foreign reserves, Nigerians could have used these funds to develop the country economically. Instead, the country's politicians turned their backs on agriculture and decided over how to share the bigger national product of oil, receiving prodigious contracts with a high percentage kickbacks, and other forms of returns.

This chapter examines both the lower and higher hierarchical activities of the government and how the policies it made consistently worked counter to the benefit of the population, particularly in the agricultural sector, and eventually became detrimental to the entire country.

Historical Roots of Agricultural Development Problems in Nigeria

Contemporary Nigeria cannot be well understood without a brief account of the economic strategies and practices of its past, many of which have been a function of the activities in the rural areas. But always the bulk of the gains from rural activities has been diverted to distant metropolitan centers, creating unusual imbalances between rural and urban sectors. And, with the advent of the oil economy (also developed in the rural areas), exploitation and neglect have become even more acute, and its historical and contemporary dimensions need to be examined.

Today over 75 percent of Nigerians live in the still economically and socially backward rural areas of the country. These areas have and still do, generally, fall victim to exploitation by both colonial and contemporary government officials and policymakers. Past colonial economic policy not only discriminated against rural populations in the matters of social and welfare development, but systematically exploited

111

the natural and fragile resources of the rural people for the benefit of the metropolitan industries and populations (*Olatunbosun 1975*). Peasants, often working fragmented holdings, were mobilized for the production of industrial crops. The colonial powers, without necessarily transforming the peasantry to the modern extensive style, mobilized the peasants to produce export crops, but at the same time allowed them to produce enough food to feed the population. Indeed, Nigeria was self-sufficient in food and was exporting foodstuffs to other nations at and immediately after Independence. As noted in chapter 5, even though the colonial powers tried to consolidate the land in Nigeria, they did not promote extensive agriculture; they settled instead for what the peasants could produce. The colonial policy in Nigeria (and other Anglophone West African countries) restricted plantation development and settlement by white farmers. The opposite was true in East Africa (especially in Kenya and Tanzania), and in the French controlled Ivory Coast, where the colonial powers fully encouraged extensive plantation agriculture and promoted ownership of land by the colonizers, who grasped the best land for themselves (-*Oluwasanmi 1966, and Eicher and Baker 1982*). The colonial powers in Nigeria, therefore, created structures and processes that served, primarily, their own economic and political interests. Their major concern was to establish an export enclave in the colony where resources could be processed and shipped to the home country in Europe. As long as the peasant continued to produce for the economic and political gain of the colonialists, it did not matter what means it took to do so. The bulk of the income derived from such rural economic activities was, therefore, transferred to and consumed in those urban enclaves where the colonial administrators and officials lived in the comfort of modern amenities and social services unavailable to the rural communities. No deliberate and coordinated rural development program was formed to relieve rural distress and upgrade the quality of life for rural people. This was clear from the virtual absence of social facilities in the rural areas. It was, therefore, this regressive pattern of distribution of public expenditure favoring the urban communities that created the inequality and social injustice that had not previously existed.

This development pattern was understandably well taken, since the colonial economic policy was to exploit the helpless rural population for their own economic and political gain, as long as the victims remained passive. It was, therefore, no wonder that the colonial powers made no attempt to provide necessary services to the rural areas. Indeed, colonization disrupted the social, economic, political, and cultural strata, as it would do to any colony.

In spite of the political strength achieved through Independence in 1960, the policies pursued by Nigerians who took control of the government from the colonial administrators continued to mirror in many ways those of the colonialists. This is not surprising, however, since most of the Nigerians who took control of the government were the trusted allies of the colonial administration who carried out the colonial power's "*indirect rule*" policy of exploiting the rural areas. These former colonial officials, therefore, knew nothing but the exploitative practices of the colonial era, and the core-periphery relationships initiated during the colonial period continued to depress rural life by diverting gains from peasant agriculture and other primary activities that took place in rural environments to the cities. The post-colonial leaders, as in Nigeria, not only continued with the exploitative practices of the colonial powers, but went beyond them to encourage a capitalistic mode of production that even the British themselves discouraged in the country. This implies that these leaders, who thought they knew the so-called weaknesses of the colonial powers, had to correct those weaknesses. They introduced what the British shunned immediately upon taking control of the government, hence the introduction of plantation type agriculture in the country, a practice the colonial powers wisely discouraged at least in Nigeria and other populated West African English-speaking countries. The leaders, in other words, knew what they were doing; they probably felt that the colonial powers were keeping something important from them and, having studied in the British and American universities, they were aware of the practices of those nations. They therefore introduced these practices to the country without considering their ramifications in an ecologically fragile society. These practices were promoted to the detriment of the population at large in Ghana and other Anglophone West African nations. In the immediate post-colonial period, little could be done to alter this false start because of inherited technical and financial obstacles. But the promotion of the colonial exploitative practices, and present failures, demands other explanations.

A close look at the Nigerian post-colonial political economy will show that the technocrats who run the affairs of state seldom see peasants as their constituents; as a matter of fact, peasants are not represented in the government. This, of course, is a betrayal of the population for whom independence was gained. After all, the independence of the country was sought to free its people from the exploitative practices of the British powers. The victims of these practices included the rural population, who suffered the most from them. And now in post-colonial government, with competition for government attention, the urban population has always received all of the advantages — the media, the money, and even the function of formulating policy. Its interest inevitably tends to be presented as the national interest. The farmer, on the other hand, has lit-

113

tle political leverage, and although his interests have sometimes been taken into account, they have rarely been a primary consideration. At best, the farmer who worked so hard to provide for the education of these new leaders is now treated no better, under the leadership of his own flesh and blood than he was under the colonial powers. Almost all of the leaders in Nigeria have some connection with the rural area; they should, therefore, understand the almost impossible conditions of the rural population. However, no matter what the motive and reason behind the overnight change of attitude after independence, the African leaders should see fit to treat their own people better than the colonial powers did. But, instead as will be shown in this chapter, the leadership style of the post-colonial leaders was oppressive, neglectful, exploitative, deceitful, and many times abusive.

A common scholarly thesis is that economic policies during the colonial period were an extension of the monopoly interests dominant in the world economy. Their net effect was to incorporate the rural sector into the world economy and into a hierarchical system of administration, which extended down to rural areas. But these policies also resulted in a preoccupation with the production of cash crops, a neglect of food crops, and the creation of exploitative rural/non-rural linkages. Similar patterns have occurred in many other developing countries, which suggests that these policies may have represented a deliberate strategy. This thesis could very well be sustained today in Nigeria, if only the production of food had declined. But this low production extends to the export/cash crops, which almost always received the greatest attention from the colonial governments. Therefore, although there are grounds for this argument, especially in the exploitation of the rural areas, the argument fails if we consider the complete breakdown of the agricultural economy in Nigeria today. Other explanations must be sought.

Nigeria at Independence was self-sufficient in food production. But, since the mid-1970s, this self-sufficiency has been drastically reduced, and today the country is importing a substantial portion of its food need. Export receipts from cash crops cannot pay for even half the food the country is importing. No country should have to emphasize cash crop production when the country is importing food it can produce itself, above its means. Moreover, as indicated above, cash crop production has declined far more than food production, with the only cash crops still on the market being the permanent tree crops (cocoa, rubber and palm produce). Production of cotton and beniseed is now almost non-existent, and groundnut is declining rapidly. Furthermore, Nigeria was still self-sufficient in food production when cash crop production was at its peak. This can be explained by the fact that most farmers practice intercropping,

114

i.e., planting cash crops and food crops simultaneously. However, because the farmers were exploited with regard to their cash crops, the incentive would have been for them to emphasize food crops instead. This was not feasible, especially for farmers in the south, where tree crop holdings could not be easily converted to food crop land. This factor, coupled with the lure of existing jobs in the cities brought on by the oil industry boom, led to the migration of younger, able-bodied farmers from rural to urban areas.

It is obvious from this analysis that colonial exploitative practices cannot, by themselves, explain the present situation in Nigeria's food production. In fact, after 25 years of freedom, it is absurd to attribute our problem today to the colonial era. We are not free if we cannot escape from the practices that caused our suffering. It is not dignified to be controlled by those past practices that forced us to fight for our freedom and eventual independence. A people who have actually freed themselves from oppression would find a way to correct those former ills and work for a better life for all. The fact is that, if Nigeria policy makers were still influenced by past colonial activities, they would not have made some of the radical decisions they did, such as to bring about indigenization of industries just about ten years after independence. And they would not have made a decision to transform the most important sector (agriculture) of the country's economy. Apparently those decisions that were made about the agricultural sector were those neglectful, exploitative, and abusive decisions that were, in most cases, more destructive than those made in the colonial era.

Analysis of the Major Characteristics of Agricultural Policy

Much has been said here about the essential agricultural economy of Nigeria and the neglect of a sector which, before the advent of the oil industry, contributed to the mainstay of the entire economy. The following sections are designed to analyze in detail the major elements and implementation of the agricultural policy in Nigeria.

Objectives and Strategies of the Nigerian Agricultural Policy

The various government regimes in Nigeria have consistently claimed that agriculture (including crops, livestock, fishery and forestry) has occupied the highest position in the priority list of the federal government. Each of these government regimes has invariably shifted blame for the crisis to the previous administration and promised to do better, perhaps bringing the country "*back to self-sufficiency*" and even exporting food to other nations, as well. Therefore, the Federal Ministry of Agriculture, under the ousted civilian government of Alhaji Shehu Shagari, in its "*Outline of Nigerian Agricultural Policy*" (ca 1981/82) identified the following objectives which, for all practical purposes, were consistent with and representative of those of previous and succeeding administrations:

1) *Rapid increase in food production and eliminating imports of food which will release available foreign exchange for the importation of capital, technology, and development of other sectors of the economy. A basic objective in this respect is the attainment of 4 percent growth rate for the sector so as to achieve self-sufficiency in food by the end of the plan period.*

2) *Increase in production of raw materials for the expanding industrial sector, particularly the agro-based industries.*

3) *Increased production and processing of export crops with a view to increasing and further diversifying the country's export base and foreign exchange earnings.*

4) *The expansion of rural employment opportunities so as to productively absorb the increasing labor force.*

5) *The elimination of rapid increases in the prices of food and thus protect the real income of the average Nigerian.*

6) *The evolution of appropriate institutions to facilitate the realization of the country's agricultural potential (Federal Ministry of Agriculture, Outline of Nigerian Agricultural Policy (ca 1981/82))*

Recognizing the problems of the farmers, their poor social condition, and their supposed role in carrying out the above stated objectives, the government developed the following agricultural development strategies:

1) *The establishment of seed, livestock, and fish multiplication farms.*

2) The provision of credit, fertilizers, pesticides, farm tractors, and spraying equipment, etc.

3) The establishment of farm service centers from where farm inputs and services would be made available to farmers and fishermen.

4) The establishment of appropriate marketing and distribution facilities for agricultural produce.

5) The construction and rehabilitation of roads to facilitate access to services, inputs, and markets.

6) The construction of dams, irrigation facilities, and boreholes to provide water for crops, live-stock, and domestic use.

7) The organization of farmers and fishermen into viable cooperative societies (Federal Ministry of Agriculture, _Outline of Nigerian Agricultural Policy_ (ca 1981/82)).

In order to reach the objectives of the agricultural development specified above, the government developed policy measures which will be discussed in the following paragraphs.

Investment in Agriculture

The seriousness of the country's policy in implementing agricultural development can be measured by its monetary allocation toward the sector vis-a-vis other sectors. In Nigeria the commitment to agricultural development can be said to have been merely verbal in that none of the short, medium, and long range plans in the period between 1960 and 1985 were implemented. Moreover, the four National Development Plans the country supposedly implemented not only showed a distinct industrial bias, but the little money allocated to the agricultural sector was in effect large-scale and export-crops biased. Low priority for public investments in agriculture as against import-substitution industries was manifested. An analysis of each of the plans is presented.

First National Development Plan 1962-68

The First National Development Plan 1962-68 (later extended to 1970), drawn up by the politicians who gained control of the government at Independence, was mainly financed by the agricultural sector. However, out of the total capital expenditure of ₦1,353 million for the eight year period, only ₦183.8

million, or 13.6 percent, was allocated to primary production, which included crops, livestock, forestry and fishing. This figure does not reflect the emphasis placed on agricultural innovations in the preamble to the document, and obviously does not mark the beginning of a truly committed indigenous effort to achieve a balanced development of the economy. Out of the ₦183.8 million, ₦78.66 million, or 43 percent, remained unspent, which the Gowon administration interpreted as a reflection of some basic defects in the design and implementation of agricultural plans. This gross underspending, according to the administration, was due partly to the lack of a strong Federal Ministry of Agriculture for effective planning and coordination. The Gowon administration, therefore, planned to remedy this defect.

About 34 percent (or ₦35.74 million) of the remaining ₦105.2 million allocated for primary production in the Plan went to government-directed projects such as farm settlements, plantations, irrigation schemes, etc., all of which were geared toward increased production of export crops. Twenty three percent was allocated to extension, 13.3 percent to credit, 11 percent to research, 2.9 percent to education and training, 7 percent to processing and distribution, and the rest to other unclassified projects (*Second National Development Plan 1970-74, p. 104*).

Although 13.3 percent (or ₦14.0 million) was allocated for credit directly geared to benefit farmers, fishermen, foresters, and husbandmen, small-scale producers including peasant-farmers, gained nothing because of credit problems. As a result, only big estate and plantation farmers, and state institutions that constituted less than 5 percent of the total agricultural sector, benefited from the credit. In the entire program no mention was made of these small-scale producers who contributed over 95 percent of the export crop earnings and food for domestic consumption. It was, therefore, not surprising that the government anticipated a projected growth rate of 2 percent in agricultural production even though the corresponding annual rate of demographic growth was about 3 percent. It is apparent from these facts that the problems of agriculture in Nigeria leading to the present crisis stage have been accruing over several years of neglect, hastening to the present proportion only as a result of the impact of the oil revenues.

Second National Development Plan 1970-74

At the inception of the Second National Development Plan (1970-74) in 1970, agricultural productivity was considered a salient problem, yet no concerted effort was made to correct the situation. Instead, policymakers under the Gowon administration showed a depressingly distinct industrial bias in the allocation of funds. Out of the total capital expenditure of ₦3.272 billion for the Plan period 1970-74 (which was extended to cover the year 1974-75), ₦211.71 million (later revised to read N242.529 million), or 7.4 percent, was allocated to the agricultural sub-sector (*Second Progress Report of the Second National Development Plan 1970-74, pp. 27 and 54*). Out of this revised planned expenditure, the federal government contributed only N69.866 million for the five-year period, with the states contributing the rest (Table 6.1).

As with the First Plan, a great percentage of the allocated funds remained unspent. During the first three years of the Plan (Table 6.1) the federal government's actual capital expenditure for the sector was only ₦34.134 million (and ₦3.653 million for livestock, fisheries and forestry). Out of this, ₦24.93 million, or 73 percent, was given as grants to state governments; ₦1.403 million as grants to Research Councils, National, and International Institutes; ₦2.85 million to different agricultural schemes; and ₦287,057 to meteorological services. The remaining ₦4.66 million obviously did not benefit the local farmers in the form of credit or even input supplies, since the establishment of Agricultural Development Authorities and the newly created Agricultural Bank, both geared toward large-scale cash crops agriculture, were also financed during this period. Of all the project accomplishments made during the three year period, only ₦97,000 was recorded which directly related to food crops research programs, and the entire amount was spent to construct staff quarters in Warri, Birnin Kebbi, and Badeggi. At the same time, research in the development of cocoa, oil palm, and rubber received ₦1.66 million, ₦1.70 million, and ₦1.03 million respectively. The original Plan which, however, detailed the programs of the federal government, retaining the same proportionate assumptions, allocated 55 percent of its budget to federally directed activities and over 25 percent to research and special agricultural schemes, none of which directly benefited the farmer. Less than 20 percent of the original budgetary allocation went to agricultural credit, and this, by all indications, did not benefit the small-farmers as previously stated, because most experienced credit problems. And since it was specifically stated that credit would be made available directly to farmers, particularly in the area of cooperative farming and agricultural marketing cooperatives, credit worthy farmers (big plantation farmers), and state governments, the smallholders cultivating two or three acres of land were apparently excluded. It is apparent then that any money earmarked for this project would not reach individual farmers, since the then twelve state owned plantations were to benefit from all of it. Moreover, these big farm cooperatives were export crop tycoons. Food crop producers were invariably a neglected majority because they did not necessarily generate in-

Table 6.1

Table 6.1

Original, Revised and Actual Public Capital Expenditure for Agricultural Sub-sector, 1970-74

(₦ Million)

Government	Original Planned Expenditure 1970-74	Revised Planned Expenditure 1970-74	Original Planned Expenditure 1970-73	Actual Capital Expenditure			Total Actual Expenditure 1970-73
				1970-71	1971-72	1972-73	
Federal	61.675	69.866	45.134	2.382	10.665	21.087	31.134
Benue-Plateau	5.856	8.527	4.482	0.977	1.660	2.603	5.240
East-Central	20.178	20.321	15.280	1.164	1.419	2.903	5.486
Kano	33.478	47.278	25.300	4.046	5.518	8.028	17.592
Kwara	4.668	4.164	3.722	0.121	0.569	1.126	1.815
Lagos	6.400	7.734	4.200	0.025	0.796	2.240	3.059
Mid-Western	8.630	9.683	6.236	1.089	1.652	1.552	4.293
North-Central	4.657	5.600	4.980	0.711	1.048	1.842	3.601
North-Eastern	6.436	6.223	6.242	0.454	1.558	1.456	3.467
North-Western	7.880	9.358	5.950	0.421	1.565	3.132	5.119
Rivers	8.534	10.177	6.066	0.535	0.715	1.528	2.778
South-Eastern	19.005	19.005	11.270	2.034	3.144	2.198	7.376
Western	24.312	24.593	19.586	2.860	2.950	4.173	9.983
TOTAL	211.709	242.529	158.448	16.819	33.259	53.868	103.946

Source: Federal republic of Nigeria, Second Progress Report of the Second National Development Plan 1970-74.

come for the states. Food production was, therefore, never a priority for the state, at least until the late 1970s, when the food crisis became so widespread.

The 12 state governments, which made an actual capital expenditure of ₦69.8 million over the three year period, were large-scale agriculturally biased as well. It was assumed that the establishment of large-scale production would bring about the desired results of increased production and self-sufficiency in both food and export crops. Within this framework too, there is often a very clear bias for cash/export crops instead of food crops. For example, in the former Western State (Ondo, Oyo and Ogun) only 3,730 acres of rice and maize combined were cultivated through group farming, while 4,583 acres of the same products with cassava were planted under the seed multiplication scheme, costing ₦551,595. During the same period, on the other hand, 15,417 acres (or 95 percent of the planned target) of new planting were established for cocoa, at a cost of ₦2.793 million. And during this period only ₦595,000 was spent by the state for food crops, fruits, and vegetables, while a comfortable ₦5.58 million was spent for export cash crops. A similar bias was observed in Rivers State as well, where 16,000 acres of oil-palm and 24,503 acres of rubber were established, but only 2,000 acres of rice were cultivated under the smallholders' scheme. While ₦1.44 million was actually spent for the production of the export crops (rubber, palm produce), only ₦468,000 was spent for food crops. Out of this ₦468,000, N300,000 went to large-scale rice production including the purchase of three caterpillars that produced only 50 acres of planted rice. From these examples, it is apparent that actual performances did not match the commitment to increased food production. The ₦69.8 million spent by the states seems not to have reached the local farmers, who bore the burden of feeding the population.

At the end of the Plan period, in 1975, ₦173.195 million actual capital expenditure had been made by all governments combined, out of which the federal government contributed ₦64.575 million (Table 6.2). By this time, the food shortage crisis had already become so acute that food importation had more than quadrupled since the beginning of the Plan. Export volume was then running at an all time low as well. It could, therefore, be assumed that government involvement in agriculture had been mere rhetorical, as evidenced by the gross failure of the first two National Development Plans. Planning in the agricultural sector in Nigeria, in practice, in fact discouraged farmers and ruined the morale of the private small-scale farming community in the country.

Table 6.2

Actual Public Capital Expenditure 1970/71-1973/74
(₦ million)

Sector	Total	Federal Govt.	All States
ECONOMIC			
Agriculture	173.195	64.575	108.620
Livestock			
Forestry &			
Fishing	45.363	4.747	40.616
Mining	20.877	20.877	-
Industry	88.523	20.281	68.242
Commerce &			
Finance	56.267	15.673	40.594
Fuel and Power	112.967	103.376	9.591
Transport	516.797	306.726	210.071
Communications	54.178	54.178	-
Resettlement &			
Rehabilitation	30.806	15.580	15.226
Sub-Total	1,098.973	606.013	492.960
SOCIAL			
Education	254.579	99.087	155.492
Health	112.029	39.273	72.756
Labor & Social			
Welfare	28.252	11.174	17.078
Information	41.635	22.320	19.315
Town & Country			
Planning	49.830	16.002	33.828
Water & Sewage	129.098	24.000	105.098
Sub-Total	615.423	211.856	403.567
ADMINISTRATION			
General Admin.	244.666	136.454	108.212
Defense & Security	231.730	231.730	-
Sub-Total	476.396	368.184	108.212
FINANCIAL			
Financial			
Obligation	45.976	45.976	-
Sub-Total	45.976	45.976	-
GRAND TOTAL	2,236.768	1,232.029	1,004.741

Source: Federal Republic of Nigeria, <u>Third National Development Plan</u>
1975-80, p.25.

It was apparent by 1975 that the crisis of agricultural stagnation, and food shortage in particular, had become a very serious threat to the political peace of the military dictatorship; the effects had been felt a few years earlier. With this imminent threat in the minds of the citizens, the government extended fiscal incentives to the agricultural sector. Price incentives, credit facilities, and import-duty relief, etc., as applied to industry, were offered for agricultural production. Recognizing the important role the sector was to play, and seeing that the previous plans had done very little to salvage the sector's activities, the Gowon administration made a misleading gesture in the *Third National Development Plan 1975-80* (1975) by allocating ₦2.2 billion capital expenditure to the sector, out of the total original public sector's capital program of ₦32.9 billion (Table 6.3), which was revised to read ₦43.3 billion. This represents only 5 percent of the intended capital expenditure, compared to 17 percent for transportation and 10 percent for defense. Out of this ₦2.2 billion, the agricultural sub-sector (crops) received ₦1.646 billion, or about 4 percent of the revised program. In terms of sheer magnitude, however, the Third National Development Plan represented a major departure from its predecessors and constituted a real watershed in the country's planning experience. This was evident not only in the multi-billion naira budgeted for the period but also in the introduction of a more efficient management strategy and the ambitious goal of bringing about a permanent improvement of the standard of living for the population. While this allocation was far more comprehensive than the previous two plans combined, this sectoral share in total plan investment was simply inadequate for a sector that had fed some 80 percent of the total population.

Not only was the ₦1.646 billion inadequate to start with, it was further cut by ₦294.476 million to accommodate the newly created Ministry of Water Resources, leaving it with only ₦1.35 billion. This indicates that the ₦612.6 million allocated for water supply projects was directed to the cities, and not to the rural areas that contained over 75 percent of the country's population. Moreover, the ₦1.35 billion was less than 25 percent of the allocation of ₦5.3 billion to manufacturing and was just about 50 percent of the share of mining and quarrying, which were primarily owned by the private sector (Table 6.3).

More fundamentally, most of the overgenerous incentives, as in manufacturing, would be of no benefit whatsoever to the vast majority of the peasantry, who imported nothing, owned no capital to be depreciated, and could not fulfill the bureaucratic and collateral requirements for loans. Consequently, these fiscal incentives for the agricultural sector would remain

Table 6.3

Summary of Public Sector Capital Programs: 1975-80
(₦ million)

Sector	Total	Federal Govt.	All States
ECONOMIC			
Agriculture	1,645.852	750.845	895.007
Livestock	344.046	173.176	170.869
Forestry	109.730	30.014	79.716
Fishery	101.554	58.561	42.993
Minings & Quarrying	2,680.425	2,680.425	–
Manufacturing & Craft	5,315.871	4,907.227	408.644
Power	1,075.238	932.038	143.200
Commerce & Finance	559.355	323.433	235.922
Transport	7,303.068	6,274.342	1,028.726
Communications	1,338.944	1,338.944	–
Sub-Total	20,474.082	17,469.005	3,005.077
SOCIAL			
Education	2,463.822	1,656.193	807.629
Health	759.928	314.160	455.768
Information	380.225	234.341	145.884
Labor	43.187	43.187	–
Social Develop. & Sports	139.603	24.950	114.653
Sub-Total	3,786.765	2,272.831	1,513.934
REG. DEVELOPMENT			
Water Supply	930.038	317.413	612.625
Sewage, Drainage, & Ref. Disposal	428.495	154.499	273.996
Housing	1,837.430	1,650.000	187.430
Town & Country Planning	754.867	250.453	504.414
Co-operative & Comm. Develop.	193.294	16.187	177.107
Sub-Total	4,144.124	2,388.552	1,755.572
ADMINISTRATION			
Defense & Sec.	3,325.517	3,325.517	–
General Admin.	1,124.128	709.210	414.918
Sub-Total	4,449.645	4,034.727	414.918
NOMINAL TOTAL	32,854.616	26,165.115	6,689.501

Source: Federal republic of Nigeria, <u>Third National Development Plan</u> 1975-80, p. 348.

largely nothing but symbolic gestures, except in the cases of a few capitalist farmers.

While there is no available information about how the ₦1.35 billion was spent, many factors that operated within the plan period lead to the assumption that the entire expenditure was a waste. In the first year (1975-1976) of the Plan, only ₦125.689 million and ₦49.186 million (total ₦174.875 million) were spent by the state and federal governments, respectively, out of the estimated expenditure of ₦204.288 (*First Progress Report of the Third National Development Plan 1975-80, p. 30*). These figures combined were more than the actual capital expenditure for the entire five years of the Second Development Plan, the programs of which it was supposed to drastically improve upon. Yet the government itself confessed that no spectacular development was observed in the level of domestic supply and demand, the prices of essential food, or in the volume and value of major traditional export/cash commodities that could be directly attributed to the Plan. All evidence points to continued shortfall in food crops output, increases in foodstuff prices, and diminishing export crop volume. And in fact, this deepening crisis led to the downfall of the military dictatorship of General Yakubu Gowon on his 9th anniversary of power in July, 1975.

It is of critical importance to determine how the money can be accounted for. While the government cited many large-scale production programs, which involved thousands of hectares of new land brought under cultivation and procurement and distribution of thousands of tons of fertilizer and improved seed, etc., they provided no monetary allocation to these programs. The federal government, which allocated ₦49.189 million during the year, spent ₦19.978 million to finance an unidentified 103 projects through the Nigeria Agricultural Bank, ₦6.75 million on oil palm research, and ₦7.12 million on various agricultural schemes and projects, most of which produced no verifiable end results. Additionally, ₦6.255 million went for fertilizer and ₦2.56 million for three crops development that included oil palm, but only ₦2.42 million was allocated to food crops research, out of which ₦1.065 million was spent on fruit and vegetable research, and a demonstration center that produced no results. The rest was basically spent to build quarters and offices for the staff (*First Progress Report of Third National Development Plan, p. 95-101*).

A clear testament to the failure of the different large-scale programs and projects during the Plan period is the case of the unfortunate Peremabiri large-scale rice production scheme in Rivers State. A feasibility study made by the United Nations Food and Agricultural Organization (FAO) experts indicated that this scheme, if fully developed, could produce enough rice to feed the country's population and more. The project at

1975/76 prices would have cost an estimated ₦7.0 million (*First Progress Report of the Third National Development Plan 1 975 - 80, p. 132*) over a five year period (1975-80), which the Nigerian government and the Rivers State government were well able to provide internally from petroleum revenues. But by 1977, the program, which was envisioned to have attained a cultivation level of 1,200 hectares, had witnessed a development of only 20 hectares after having officially absorbed ₦3.0 million. The scheme eventually had to be abandoned for reasons that included bad management, a lack of commitment and cooperation between federal and state agencies, and a shortage of trained manpower (*Ogbona 1979, pp. 125-126*). As foreign exchange became readily available from the oil sector, high quality rice was effortlessly imported from the United States and Asia. This has been identified, according to Ogbona, as responsible not only for the demise of the Peremabiri Scheme but also for driving local smallholder farmers out of work.

A second example is the Mechanized Farm Projects in Bendel State, which were to establish four farms covering 42,000 hectares at the cost of ₦14.0 million between 1976 and 1980. At the end of the first year of the program, 26,000 hectares were acquired and 5,265 hectares were cultivated after having absorbed ₦14.436 million (*First Progress Report of the Third National Development Plan 1975-80, p. 119*). Apparently the money was spent for purposes other than the four projects, since the land could have been acquired in the state with little or no money. In actuality, the entire land, no matter how it was acquired, would have cost less than 10 percent of the allocated funds and could not have warranted a ₦14.436 million expenditure out of the ₦14.0 million allocated for the entire project during the first year alone. Furthermore, the cost of such projects should have been well articulated before plans for such monetary allocation could be made.

As in the Second Plan, even the new land brought under cultivation was export-crop biased towards cocoa, palm oil, and rubber. For example, the former Western State and Bendel State brought 25,859 hectares of new land under cultivation for planting cocoa seeds, but only a mere 1,554.08 hectares were brought under cultivation for rice, cassava, and maize combined. However, the danger of continuing food shortages and the trend towards increasing food importation in a situation of idle abundant local resources forced the Obasanjo government to make major policy changes. This was the main rationale behind the nationwide "*Operation Feed the Nation*" (OFN) campaign which was launched early in 1976. This program, which by all indications was well received, aimed at making the country self-sufficient in staple foodstuff production through increased participation by the masses. Fertilizer and seed distribution was greatly liberalized so as to reach the greatest possible number of farmers who needed them.

A second major policy change was seen in the reform of the Marketing Board system, which sought not only to replace the existing state Marketing Boards with nationwide Commodity Boards, but also to extend for the first time the same principle of institutionalized marketing to food commodities. As of April 1977, the reform would bring into effect seven Commodity Marketing Boards (*First Progress Report, Third National Development Plan 1975-80*). Not only were these two policy changes made during the Plan period, but the government was forced to act on the transformation of peasant farming into capitalist large-scale farming, a change which had always been part of state agricultural policy. To pave the way for this, several steps were taken, the most significant being the *Land Use Act of 1978*, which sought to transform the land tenure system by investing in state government the sole rights of custody of all hitherto unallocated land (Chapter 5). This transformation was designed to attract large, plantation-type farming and foreign capital investment in the sector, which it did until 1983, when the Shagari administration, which promoted the act, was ousted, and Nigeria's agricultural crisis worsened.

However, all the good intentions in the world regarding policy changes could not help the food crisis if there was no action taken to put them into effect. At the end of the Plan period in 1980 only about 27,000 total hectares of cocoa were planted. This is about 1,141 hectares more than the 25,859 hectares planted in the first year of the Plan. In other words, in the remaining four-year period, only 1,141 hectares of cocoa were newly planted in the entire country. In the case of oil palm, which is consumed both domestically and produced for export, only 28,000 ha. were planted over the five year period and only 6,000 new hectare of rubber were planted. Groundnut, once the number one export crop of the country, came up with barely 40 hectares of new planting under the National Grain Company, despite having had an allocation of ₦10.5 million during the 1976 season. Cotton and beniseed, which were among the old export crops, were not mentioned at all, which suggests that little progress was made in the development of these crops during the Plan period.

In its effort to increase food supply, the federal government, during the Plan period, implemented several programs, and the performances of two must be mentioned here for comparative purposes.

The first of the two programs was the National Grain and Root Crops Production Companies. These companies were formed to establish large-scale farms in every state, as applicable. For the entire period, only 1,480 hectares were established for the production of maize, guinea corn and groundnut (720,

720 and 40 hectares respectively) by the Grain Companies, out of the 4,000 ha. (76,000 ha. all together) required from it for each of the nineteen states of the Federation. The Root Crops Production Company established large-scale cassava farms, but the number of hectares cultivated was not recorded.

Rural Integrated Projects was the second program; its activities involved establishment of five projects in five states. These projects, through the direct assistance of the federal government, established large-scale food crop farms. Such assistance resulted in the cultivation of a mere 1,820 ha. of rice. From these two programs, one can see that the government's priority was export crop, biased in that, though the number of hectares cultivated for cocoa, palm oil, etc. was too small, it was still considerably larger than the land actually cultivated for necessary food crops.

In addition, Agricultural Mechanization, which always invariably receives the most attention from the government, received ₦40 million during the period. Much equipment was purchased; mechanical workshops were established in most states; and training in the operation of heavy equipment was established. Under this effort, 44,774 ha. of land was prepared for planting in six states (*Fourth National Development Plan 1981-85, pp. 77-78*). It seemed to have included some of the land prepared for rubber and oil palm in the case of Bendel and Cross River states; however, no mention was made in the plan about what was planted on this land.

While the government reported several accomplishments during the Plan period, only ₦197.45 million (₦40 million for agricultural mechanization and ₦157.45 million for agricultural credit that included all agricultural sub-sectors) was actually accounted for, out of the ₦975.610 million actual capital expenditure (Table 6.4). This leaves us with an unaccounted ₦778.160 million for the Plan period. Allocation of funds for each program was well documented when the Plans were made. How is it possible, then, that at the end of the Plan period in 1980 over 75 percent of the money originally allocated was unaccounted for? It could be that the money was used for purposes other than promoting the local agricultural sub-sector and was justified in this general manner. The disappearance of huge amounts of money through primitive economic practices was a common place phenomenon in the country during the years of the Plan.

Nigeria, in addition to the ₦975.610 million, distributed ₦1,131.4 million among the sub-sectors of irrigation (₦828.175), livestock (₦183.071), forestry (₦85.751), and fishing (₦34.383) as can be seen in Table 6.4. The money expended during this five-year period clearly did not result in a corresponding physical performance. Not only did food importation (averaging over 1 billion naira during the Plan period)

128

Table 6.4

Actual Public Capital Expenditure, 1975/76-1979/80
(N million)

Sector	Total	Federal Govt.	All States
ECONOMIC			
Agriculture	975.610	414.846	560.764
Irrigation	828.175	778.116	50.059
Livestock	183.071	73.910	109.161
Forestry	85.751	27.149	58.602
Fishery	34.383	17.102	17.281
Mining & Quarrying	1,469.959	1,469.959	_
Manuf. & Craft	2,569.667	2,257.212	312.455
Commerce & Fin.	518.863	281.880	236.983
Co-ops.&Supply	207.084	156.678	50.406
Power	1,721.429	1,551.550	169.879
Transport	6,814.135	5,770.807	1,043.328
Communications	1,779.112	1,779.112	_
Sub-Total	17,187.239	14,578.321	2,608.918
SOCIAL SERVICES			
Education	2,994.481	1,731.564	1,262.917
Health	602.940	269.869	333.071
Information	337.407	190.708	146.699
Labor	1.268	1.268	_
Social Develop. Youths & Sports	111.934	22.184	89.750
Sub-Total	4,048.030	2,215.593	1,832.437
REG. DEVELOPMENT			
Water Supply	870.999	81.310	789.689
Sewage, Drainage, & Ref. Disposal	84.064	5.956	78.108
Housing	1,200.166	848.974	351.192
Town & Country Planning	766.458	163.756	602.702
Comm. Develop.	192.699	_	192.699
Sub-Total	3,114.386	1,099.996	2,014.390
ADMINISTRATION			
Defense & Sec.	2,852.406	2,852.406	_
General Admin.	2,231.699	1,585.344	646.355
Sub-Total	5,084.105	4,437.750	646.355
GRAND TOTAL	29,433.760	22,331.660	7,102.100

Source: Federal Republic of Nigeria, <u>Fourth National Development Plan,</u>
1981-85,p. 29.

replace what could be produced locally in the country, food production declined in absolute terms. The government itself was forced to admit that, while all other sectors recorded a very high growth rate during the Plan period 1975-80 (18.1 percent for manufacturing; 17.7 percent for government services, and 13.9 percent for building and construction), agriculture recorded a negative growth rate of 2.1 percent as against the projected 5 percent increase (*Fourth National Development Plan 1980-85, p. 5*). It was also during this period that the agricultural share slumped to less than 20 percent of the GDP from its share of 60 percent in 1964; and agricultural exports fell to the 3-5 percent range from its high share of 70 percent of national exports in 1964.

It can therefore be concluded that no matter how much money a government allocates to the sector, and no matter how well politicians master their programs, agriculture will suffer a sad fate if promises and plans are not put into practice. It seems that the crisis in the agricultural sector in Nigeria, ironic as it is, is directly related to increased expenditure on the part of the government. The ₦975.610 million the country actually spent on the agriculture sub-sector was more than four times the money spent from 1962-1975, yet the situation went from self-sufficiency to food shortage, and then to chronic agricultural crisis. Basic institutional problems, while difficult to pinpoint because of their nature, can be called upon to explain this problem. Mismanagement, gross corruption, and embezzlement are characteristic problems in Nigeria, and the presence of these traits in the ruling class will continue to deprive Nigeria of the development that is long overdue.

When the military government of Obasanjo relinquished power for the civilians to take control, it was welcomed by the citizens. And when the civilians took power under the leadership of Alhaji Shehu Shagari, agriculture was accorded the highest priority in the country's development strategy. From Independence until 1979, when the civilians took control of the government, large-scale export crop farming was favored, again at the expense of the peasantry, who produced over 90 percent of the agricultural output. In May 1980 the new civilian federal government launched the "*Green Revolution Program*", which superceded the OFN Program that had apparently failed due to widespread corruption and gross mismanagement. Its undemocratic nature became apparent when the program totally ignored the legitimate aspirations of the actual agricultural producers and excluded their mass participation. The Green Revolution Program, planned to remove the deficiencies of the OFN, was therefore designed to meet the needs of small-farmers and spread the benefits of rural development to the local level, both of which had been neglected by previous governments with the hope of bringing the country back to self-sufficiency. This new program was under implementation when the Fourth National Development Plan 1981-85 went into effect in 1981. The Green Revolution program was not only intended to deal with the worsening food situation, but also to improve agricultural exports.

Fourth National Development Plan

The performance of the Third National Development Plan, even according to the government, fell short of the high expectations which had prevailed at the outset of the Plan. Therefore, the Fourth National Development Plan 1981-85 was launched to improve upon the former plans, especially the Third Plan, which represented a major departure from the course of the spending and planning history of the country. Certain features made this new plan uniquely different. First, it was the first plan to be formulated by a democratically elected government under a new constitution based on the presidential system of government. Secondly, with its projected capital expenditure of about ₦82 billion, the plan was considerably larger than all of its predecessors combined. And finally, it was the first plan in which local governments participated, following their constitutional position as a distinct level of government with specific responsibilities.

Noting the implication of heavy reliance on imported food as against domestic production, the clear bias for export crops over food crops by former governments as documented in the plans, and the "*good news*" of wealth in untapped natural resources available for the development of all areas of agriculture, the Fourth National Development Plan was set forth to make a drastic change in the sector to bring about the desired standard of living for the citizens. To achieve this goal the governments made a planned public capital investment of ₦8.828 billion to all sub-sectors of agriculture out of the total public capital investment of ₦70.276 billion. The share of the federal government amounted to ₦5.4 million, or 62 percent, the state governments contributed ₦2.988 billion, or 33 percent, and the local governments gave ₦439 million. This figure is at least four times as great as the original allocation of the Third Plan and at least three times that of the previous three plans combined. Table 6.5 shows the sub-sectoral breakdown of the capital program.

The agricultural sub-sector (crops alone) received ₦5.438 billion, or 62 percent of the total. Therefore, a complete turnaround of events should have occurred at the end of the Plan. In fairness, it must be said that ₦5.438 billion was a massive amount of money to spend on a sub-sector, and by all indications, it was more than all of the allocated public capital expenditure for the first two plans combined. And yet, it was still considerably less than the ₦7.8 billion, 10.7 billion, and 6.2 billion allocated for manufacturing, transportation and administration, respectively (Table 6.6). Distribution of funds in this manner was apparently in violation of the priority the government said it would give to agriculture.

Table 6.5

Public Capital Program for Agriculture, 1981-85
(₦)

Crops	₦5.438 billion
Irrigation and Water Resources Development	2.255 billion
Livestock	0.672 billion
Forestry	0.292 billion
Fishery	0.171 billion
TOTAL	8.828 billion

Source: Federal Republic of Nigeria, Fourth National Development Plan 1981-85, p. 88.

However, the issue of whether or not the government fulfilled its commitment in monetary allocation is of little concern here. The overriding concern is the honest implementation of the programs and the management of the money that was allocated to bring about the desired results to the sub-sector. After all, the government admitted that the performance of the sector was unsatisfactory despite the large sums spent by all of its levels. The implications of this statement are far-reaching. It implies that the government spent enough money for the sector but was not seeing a tangible result of the expenditure. In other words, something was wrong with the system which the government was not willing to admit. Instead, the government allocated four times as much money to the sector than it did in the immediately previous plan, thinking that this huge monetary allocation, by itself, questionable as it seems, would bring about the desired results.

The issue of proper management and accountability seemed to be, at least in practice, of little concern to the administration, as was true for the former governments. Nepotistic and partisan assignments of cabinet posts without any formal screening of qualifications was a notorious element of the government's practices. Most of those appointed cabinet members, and even some elected officers, came to government with a "*get-rich*" mentality and, therefore, cared very little about how money was actually spent, as long as they had their own share.

Table 6.6

Summary of Federal, State and Local Governments' Programs: 1981-85
(₦ million)

Sector	Total All Govts.	Federal Govt.	All State Govts.	All Local Govts.
ECONOMIC				
Agriculture	5,434.188	2,962.656	2,188.931	282.601
Irrigation	2,254.803	2,000.000	254.659	9.144
Livestock	674.157	252.784	312.548	108.825
Forestry	292.377	97.230	173.972	21.175
Fisheries	172.006	87.330	63.047	21.629
Mining and Quar.	5,409.000	5,409.000	-	-
Manufacturing	7,811.952	6,368.000	1,355.661	88.291
Power	3,106.259	2,440.000	706.259	-
Commerce and Fin.	1,735.570	586.500	714.207	434.863
Co-operative	184.022	32.500	147.826	3.696
Transport	10,706.616	6,790.500	3,318.695	597.421
Communications	2,000.000	2,000.000	-	-
Science and Tech.	600.000	600.000	-	-
Sub-Total	40,380.950	29,586.500	9,226.805	1,567.645
SOCIAL				
Education	7,703.079	2,450.000	4,253.020	1,000.059
Health	3,043.885	1,200.000	1,573.576	270.309
Information	628.833	300.000	314.964	13.869
Labor	74.500	74.500	-	-
Social Devel.	873.149	150.000	586.882	136.267
Sub-total	12,323.446	4,174.500	6,728.442	1,420.504
ENVIRONMENTAL DEVELOPMENT				
Water Supply	3,116.850	-	2,805.026	311.824
Sewage, etc.	629.259	-	482.139	147.120
Housing	2,686.921	1,592.000	1,033.552	61.369
Town and Ctry. Plan.	4,912.023	2,648.000	2,014.078	249.945
Environmental Prot.	25.000	25.000	-	-
Sub-total	11,370.053	4,265.000	-	-
ADMINISTRATION				
Defense and Sec.	3,940.000	3,940.000	-	-
General Admin.	2,261.776	534.000	1,429.879	297.879
Sub-total	6,201.776	4,474.000	1,429.879	297.879
GRAND TOTAL	70,276.225	42,500.000	23,719.939	4,056.286

Source: Federal Republic of Nigeria, <u>Fourth National Development Plan</u>, 1981-85, p.389.

This was the political climate under which the Fourth National Development Plan was launched and implemented. However, the Shagari administration fervently vowed to change the government's attitude to a more concrete and practical policy towards the development of agricultural self-sufficiency by the end of the Plan period (1985). To achieve this goal, ₦5.438 billion was injected by various tiers of government into the agricultural sub-sector (crops), the problems there being more visible than in the other sub-sectors. The smallholder, who accounted for 95 percent of total output, and who had never previously had any attention from the government, was to benefit from this considerably (*Fourth Development Plan 1981-85, p. 84; Information Bulletin on Nigeria Agriculture 1984, p. 16*). The federal government was to account for ₦2.963 billion, and the state and local governments were to contribute ₦2.197 billion and ₦279 million respectively.

Of the federal capital investment of ₦2.963 billion, only ₦154.608 million was to go to the direct food crop production program. The program was to be implemented through government agencies such as the National Root Crops Production Company, the National Grain Production Company, and the Nigerian Beverages Company Limited. The money was spent to establish processing plants in strategic locations and to establish large-scale farms. While no mention was made of how much land would be involved in the large-scale grain farms by the Grain Production Company, the Root Crops Production Company was to establish a mere 9,676 hectares of large-scale farms in all the cassava producing states during the Plan period. Here, again, ₦154.6 million was directed only to building structures that definitely did not improve the production of food crops as was intended. From this information, it is obvious that it mattered not merely how much money was directed to a program, but how well it was spent to bring about a profitable end.

A breakdown of federal and state government expenditures is presented in Table 6.7. It can be shown that the allocation of ₦248.10 million (in addition to ₦32.4 million for assisting cocoa growing states) for tree crops, cocoa, oil palm, and rubber, three of the export crops, far exceeded that for all of the other food crops combined. This is further reflected in the goal-set of over 447,000 ha. to be established for cocoa in all the cocoa producing states. Another 563,000 ha. (plus nuclear estates costing ₦97 million) was to be established for oil palm production with rubber accounting for another 105,000 ha (*Ibid 1981, p.91-92*). It seems that the federal government still, at this point, cared very little about food crop production in spite of the claim that it would take a leading role in the production of all agricultural crops. It is no wonder, then, that the country spent over ₦2 billion on imported food in the first and second years of the Plan and had to import half of its rice in 1982 (*Annual Report of the Federal Ministry of Agriculture, 1982 p. 5*). Putting the programs on paper seemed to be the only way to deal with the food problem in Nigeria. And interestingly, all the money that was invested in the export crops programs did very little to salvage these crops.

Table 6.7

Public Capital Allocation for Agricultural Sub-sector (Crops), Fourth National Development Plan 1981-85
(N million)

Programs	Federal Government	State Government	Local Government
Food crops production	154.608	152.487	NA
Industrial fiber	NA	NA	NA
Tree crops (Export)	280.500	194.403	NA
Integrated Rural Development	637.580	1,326.000	NA
Production Input			
Fertilizer	469.860	375.000	NA
Credit	379.890	NA	NA
Cooperatives	65.000	NA	NA
Mechanization	240.438	261.000	NA
Infrastructure Development program		28.870	
Grain Storage	206.500		NA
Soil conservation	212.000		NA
other	36.000		NA
Total allocation	2,963.000	2,197.000	279.000

Source: Federal Republic of Nigeria,Fourth National Development Plan
     1981-85, pp. 90-96

A well planned government policy, considering the state of affairs in the country and the alarming food crisis, would make an effort to allocate a great portion of the money on direct production of food crops that would be geared toward the great number of farmers who produce the most food. Instead, the federal government appropriated money to the areas that would directly benefit the export-crop producer or the large-scale capital intensive programs that continued to further depress the situation. In this way, about N1.2 billion was directed to production input that did not benefit the smallholder, who contributed over 90 percent of the output, and another N1.092 billion to integrated rural and infrastructure development. This helped the crisis situation very little and, in fact, this funding was wasted without achieving the goal. The only aspect of the program that would have benefited the smallholders excluded them as well; loans were to be made available only for medium to large scale farmers, for cooperatives, and for government corporations and state owned companies. There was no effort made to accommodate the smallholders in the federal government's credit program. They were again pushed to the states who, by all indication, would do little or nothing to give credit to the smallholder.

The programs of the states and the local governments were similar in nature to those of the federal government. The central government directed the local governments to involve themselves in the establishment of large-scale farms and model farms, and to the implementation of integrated rural development programs, input provision etc., but not in programs designed for the smallholder. While the states allocated ₦152.487 million for direct production of food crops, the smallholder, who was to be assisted through this program, had to compete with the big corporations and large-scale commercial companies, which would be involved in the more favored large-scale mechanized farming programs, that would be further enhanced by the Land Use Decree geared to bring about the desired large-scale production schemes bottle-necked by the land tenure system.

An example of how a state government involved itself in the food production program is presented in Table 6.8 and is sufficient for the argument (see Table 6.9 for details). The Ondo State government, which desired self-sufficiency by the end of the plan period (1985), allocated only ₦24.552 million for the production of 11 different food crops, vegetables, fruits, and processing. Out of this money, ₦23.0 million was allocated to milling and processing industries and facilities. Only a meager ₦1.552 was allocated to different seed multiplication products and to distribution and production of crops. While the state government did not hesitate to allocate ₦3.5 million for purchasing popcorn machinery and processing corn, ₦10.5 million for the gari and starch processing industries, ₦5.0 million for canning, and ₦4.0 million for rice milling (Table 6.9), it deemed acceptable a mere ₦1.55 million allocation to the production of eleven different food crops, vegetables, and fruits that would provide the raw materials to those import-substitution industries. Moreover, this ₦1.55 million was to pay the salaries and allowances, as well as inflated administration costs, of those personnel who would be directly involved in promoting the services.

Once again, the only other program that might have benefited the farmers was the credit program. It was, however, designed so that only the large-scale farmer and export-crops tycoons benefited. The smallholder, who invariably could not produce acceptable credit information, was excluded. More-

136

over, the amount of money (₦5.570 million) involved in the project was too little to include the smallholder. While the federal government seemed to leave the issue of credit to smallholders to the states, in Ondo State at least, the smallholder seemed to be ignored entirely. The fact is that, most of these monetary allocations, and the actual expenditure for various programs and projects, resulted in wasted resources through corruption. For example, a swamp rice milling industry, which was to be established in Agadagba, Ilaje/Ese-Odo, never materialized. The over ₦18 million allocated for the Integrated Rural Development Scheme brought nothing to the citizens. Another ₦8.570 million was wasted on land that was never cleared for cultivation. In 1983 the federal government commented about its good performance since over 50,000 hectares (most of which was in the open grassland savanna) were cleared over a five-year period under the special food production programs (*Information Bulletin on Nigerian Agriculture, 1984, p. 36*). As suspect as this figure is, one can only guess how much money was injected into these programs over the five-year period.

Table 6.8

Ondo State Capital Expenditure on Agricultural Sub-sector
Ondo State Fourth National Development Plan (1981-85)
(₦. million)

	Direct Production	Milling, Canning and processing
Food crops	1.55	23.00
Cash crops	32.87	2.50
Credit	11.00	5.00
Integrated Rural Dev. Scheme	18.37	–
Farm Input	12.96	–
Agric. Education	1.04	–
Total Alloc.	77.78	30.50
Total column 1 & 2	108.28	

Source: Ondo State of Nigeria, Ondo State Component Fourth National Development Plan 1981-85.

Even though very little information is available as to how the entire ₦5.438 billion was spent, certain activities, political, social, and economic, lead us to believe that most of the actual allocation of the ₦5.438 billion was dissipated by politicians through corrupt practices. While the international oil market

Table 6.9

Ondo State Capital Expenditure on Agricultural Sub-sector Ondo State Fourth National Development Plan 1981-85

(₦ million)

Food Crops	Direct Production	Milling, Canning & Proc. Industries
Rice	0.178	4.0
Maize	0.186	3.5
Cassava	0.141	10.5
Yam	0.217	
Cowpea bean	0.310	−
Pineapple	0.056	
Citrus	0.193	5.0*
Tomato	0.134	
Plantain/banana	0.030	
Soyabeans	0.085	−
Sugar cane	0.022	
Sub-total	1.552	23.000
Tree and export crops		
Cocoa	26.800	
Oil Palm	5.713	2.5
Kola	0.072	
Rubber	0.128	−
Coffee	0.025	−
Cotton	0.128	
Sub-total	32.870	2.500
Agricultural Credit		
Cocoa marketing and maintenance	5.000	
Food crops production	5.570	5.000
Yam trade	0.250	
Horticulture and others	0.500	
Sub-total	11.000	
Integrated Rural Dev. Scheme		
Water Supply	3.574	
Farm & rural roads	1.429	
Plant protection	1.429	
Agricultural Dev. projects	11.937	
Sub-total	18.370	
Farm Input		
Land Clearing, services	8.570	
Fertilizer supply	2.860	
Seed Treatment	0.615	
Storage facilities	0.443	
Soil conservation	0.264	
Agro-service centers	0.004	
Pest control and storage	0.200	
Sub-total	12.960	
Agricultural Education	1.036	
Total allocation	77.780	30.500
Total columns 1 and 2	108.28	

Source: Ondo State of Nigeria, Ondo State Component of Fourth National Development Plan 1981-85

*Includes canning of all fruits and vegetables.

138

affected the programs of the plan, it did not stop the politicians from following their unconventional practices. Not only was the budget for the agricultural sub-sector wasted, but the entire original capital expenditure of ₦70.276 billion was at their disposal. Rarely in history have politicians been more ruthless in looting public funds for their personal gain. The image of Nigeria, which is regularly echoed in the international scene, is that of a country drifting hopelessly towards economic collapse. Nigeria is said to have started destroying itself without a nuclear enemy. Corruption and economic squandering are readily available explanations. Official buildings worth millions of naira have been burned down to cover up politicians' corrupt practices (*West Africa, April 11, 1983, p. 882*). Thirty million naira were embezzled in Abuja, the new federal capital in January 1983; and to cover up the crime, the building was burned down (*Daily Times January 9, 1983*). Several other buildings, including the P & T, NET, Ministry of Education, and other state buildings were burned to cover up fraudulent acts (*West Africa, January 9, 1984*). Political opponents readily blame each other for tactics designed to cover white collar robbery. The involvement of high government officials in fraudulent activities amounting to millions of naira has been commonplace (*West Africa, January 24, 1983*). However, it was not until 1984, after the civilian government was overthrown, that it was revealed that some of the politicians had actually embezzled hundreds of millions, and even billions, of naira from the country's purse. The most visible was the case of the former Minister of Transportation, Amaru Dikko (controlling 25 percent of the nation's budget, Table 6.6) who absconded with an estimated ₦2.0 billion, and is now in exile in Britain.

While the record of Nigerian politicians as perpetrators of corrupt practices is well known — it was one of the main reasons for the military takeover of the government in January 1966 and in July 1975 — corruption was more subtle and less pervasive then than during the Second Republic under the Shagari administration. The pattern it took during this administration was radical, oppressive, and extremely pervasive. The destruction was catastrophic, and the country's masses are the ones now paying. The condition, as it existed during the Shagari Administration, is summarized in the words of his immediate successor, General Buhari:

> *While corruption and indiscipline had been associated with our state of underdevelopment, these twin evils in our politics have attained unprecedented heights over the past four years. The corrupt, inept and insensitive leadership in the last four years has been the source of immorality and impropriety in our society since what happens in*

139

any society is largely a reflection of the leadership of that society. With no corruption in all its processes, this government will not tolerate kickback, inflation of contracts and over-invoicing of imports, et cetera. Nor will it condone forgery, fraud, embezzlement, misuse and abuse of profit and illegal dealing in foreign exchange and smuggling... Corruption has become so pervasive and intractable that a whole ministry has been created to tame it (West Africa, January 9, 1984, p. 57).

From very early on in the Second Republic, people, across the board, started to express their dissatisfaction with the politicians who took over the government. There were mounting signs that it was squandering some significant portions of the precious capital that had been so difficult for the government to accumulate in the midst of the oil glut. Now, as in the First Republic, leaders of opinion were becoming disgusted with corruption, extravagance, selfishness, apathy, inefficiency, insensitivity, combativeness, tribalism, and violence among the nation's politicians, particularly its legislators. In the newspaper columns of political commentators, and in the private discussions of ordinary citizens and students, local and abroad, the signs of eroding faith in the political system, the hallmark of political decay, were manifested. The feeling was succinctly summarized by the title of a column, *"Our Legislators are Greedy"* which complained:

Across the discussion of their salaries, accommodations, amenities, order of precedence and other privileges, you find their greed taking over right, left and center. From the disco and booze loving law makers in Lagos to the chicken loving legislators in Calabar, they are a greedy lot (Sunday Tribune, June 14, 1981).

The feeling that the legislators had gone into politics in order to look after themselves, to loot the proverbial *"societal cake"* (The Punch, July 1, 1981) is substantiated by the nagging problems of absenteeism and bad work habits, including lateness, in the National Assembly and by the manner in which issues were deliberated and voted on (West Africa, April 19, 1982, pp. 1050-51). This shows that the legislators have other concerns which must be attended to before the nation's business. Despite threats and warnings issued to them, and despite the constitutional requirement for both Houses to convene 181 days out of the year, they continued with their loose manner of handling national business. This was further compounded by their extravagant display of wealth and expensive overseas spending in the United States, Canada, and Western Europe.

And while the majority party (NPN) opposed a demand by the Nigerian Labor Congress for a ₦300 per month minimum wage as inflationary, a mere handful of the NPN party "*men of timber*" raised ₦5.0 million among themselves in a matter of minutes to dedicate their new headquarters (*Zartman 1983*). Such insensitivity obviously brought about discontentment and uproar to the extent that one representative declared in a House debate on the Minimum Wage Bill:

> *I am haunted by fear of what may happen should things continue as they are now. Seeing this shameless display of wealth and callous show of positions of power and privilege in the midst of miserableness and wretchedness, I am afraid, Mr. Chairman, I am afraid. And only a fool would not be (Fagbamigbe, 1982 in Zartman 1983, p. 71).*

Other global assessments have been even more certain and unforgiving in their judgments of political bankruptcy, betrayal, and rape, as reflected in the commentary of a University of Ife academician:

> *The last eighteen months... have left the average Nigerian baffled and disappointed. All hope in the ability of our politicians to learn and run the nation's affairs along acceptable and reasonable models has been dashed... While our men in the National Assembly fiddle (presumably pursuing their private business... important government functions are held up. Yet they insist on paying themselves in excess of what seems reasonable in comparison to other hard-working Nigerians and collect all forms of allowances under various pretexts... Here are men unwilling to subject themselves to public scrutiny. Who are men such as these, to make laws for the conduct of lesser men? (Sunday Sketch, in Zartman 1983, June 7, 1981).*

This was the atmosphere in which the Fourth National Development Plan was implemented. It is, therefore, no wonder that Nigeria, after spending billions of naira in the agricultural sector, experienced not only the worst food shortage in its history, but a total breakdown of the economy and social order in the form of riots, murders, and moral decay between 1979 and 1983. Never in the history of the country had the people felt the pangs of hunger so much. And yet, this last National Plan experienced the greatest allocation for agriculture under the broad program named "*The Green Revolution*," supposedly to bring the country back to self-sufficiency by 1985 in food, and to export agricultural products in excess of what was exported before the oil boom.

Overtaken by their greed for the country's limited resources and awarding contracts even to themselves, politicians turned their backs on the masses not only in the farming community but also in the cities, who waited for a savior to intervene. While locally-produced food dwindled, the government engaged in the importation of food from other countries with oil money (Chapter 3) to replace domestic production, under the pretense that money could buy everything they needed, and exploited the masses by selling some of this imported food, especially rice, for three times as much as it had paid for it (*West Africa*, *February 27, 1984, p. 424*). When the oil revenue slumped, it made the importation of food increasingly difficult and led to the use of rice in a political game to acquire money to finance the political campaign in 1983, to win votes and elections that cost an estimated ₦2.0 billion and left many bloody scars on a country with so fragile an economy (*West Africa*, *January 9, 1984, p. 54*). For example, a staple food item (rice) which landed in Nigeria in 1983 at a cost of about ₦20 per 50 kg. bag was sold at ₦38 (*another source put it at ₦50 or ₦60, West Africa, February 27, 1984*) instead of ₦24 a bag by the government but reached the consumer at prices that far exceeded ₦100 a bag. A ton of sugar which used to cost £200 sterling in early 1980, cost £1,000 by the end of 1983 (*West Africa*, *August 19, 1984, p. 1685*), while the international market price was £160 a ton. The politicians, it is said, in the ultimate demonstration of their lack of concern, played patronage politics with rice, while consumers suffered (*West Africa*, *March 19, 1984*). This was the manner in which the politicians of the Second Republic underhandedly depleted the public purse and exploited the masses. And because they did not show concern for the citizens, they prodigiously awarded contracts for ill-conceived Green Revolution program to the much criticized new federal capital at Abuja (where almost every contractor had connection with politics), and speedily implemented programs lacking any honest feasibility study.

Many citizens visited with the then president, expressing their concerns, but to no avail. The last visit he received was from the bloodless coup that supplanted his government. Consequently, the Buhari regime, which was heralded with the most popular enthusiasm accorded any new government in the history of the country, had to implement the remaining years of the Plan's programs partly with money borrowed from both internal and external sources; this spree had even started during the civilian government. Ineffective in dealing with the crisis situation, inconsistent policies, suppression, and continued deterioration of the economy, the government had to be overthrown by another military government on August 27, 1985. In effect, the population, which had heralded the new regime witnessed a systematic annihilation of the hope they'd had in Buhari's correcting the mismanagement of the economy; lack of public accountability, insensitivity of the political leadership, and general deterioration in the standard of living had subjected the common man to intolerable suffering. The new government, in effect, was only a prototype of the one it replaced. The reason for its takeover, after only 20 months in office, is summarized in the words of the present leader, General Babangida:

> The initial objectives were betrayed and fundamental changes did not appear on the horizon. Contrary to the expectations, the population was subjected to a steady deterioration in the general standard of living and intolerable sufferings reached unprecedented heights. Prices of goods have risen higher, scarcity of commodities has increased, hospitals still remain mere consulting clinics, while educational institutions are on the brink of total decay. Unemployment has stretched to critical dimensions (West Africa, September 2, 1985, p. 1792).

So, the Fourth National Development Plan was a tragedy, basically characterized by corruption, greed, gross mismanagement, and blatant abuse of power. And, yet, many writers and observers still shift the blame on colonial powers and present Western "imperial" nations to explain the problems of Nigeria and Africa. The Nigerian case is apparently exceptional because of the pervasive manner in which these unconventional vices operated between 1979 and 1983, to turn a relatively rich nation into a poverty stricken one. No country in Africa, especially those in the sub-Sahara, to our knowledge, escapes the vestiges of these practices as described in the last few pages. These practices impede development because they erode the only resources that are available for development.

Conclusion

Several conclusions can be drawn from the spending pattern of the governments as to the agricultural sector. The first conclusion is that the agricultural sector was neglected and industry was favored in total capital allocation, even though the agricultural sector contributed over 70 percent of the government revenue in the 1960s. In addition, in all the four Development Plans, industry, which is necessarily a private sector, has always received great attention from the government in monetary allocation, promotion, and incentives. This should not be so in an agrarian society such as Nigeria. An economically undesirable sector should not bear the burden of all the sectors that contribute very little to the nation's economy and yet suffer the government's inattention. And when the oil industry started to expand, the government literally substituted domestic production, especially food, with imported agricultural products, as money became abundantly available.

Secondly, the little capital allotted to the agricultural sector was export crop biased. This was so because of the huge revenue the government accrued from the producers through the powerful marketing board. By the government's own admission, there was often a very clear bias for cash/export crops as against food crops in fertilizer consumption. The application of improved practices was also restricted to export crops (*Fourth National Development Plan*, *1981-85, p.78*). The Nigeria Agricultural and Cooperative Bank and the state-owned Agricultural Credit Corporations created to give credit to farmers were designed to benefit the big capitalistic farmers who produced export-crops. Even though the capital-intensive food crop producer had recently received some attention from the government, he never benefited as much as the export crop plantation farmers who brought huge revenue to the government. However, despite the formal encouragement given to export crop production and the rehabilitation of the plantations under the first three plans, Nigeria's agricultural exports never produced expected results.

Finally, and probably the most important conclusion to be drawn from this chapter, deals with the deleterious effect of the primitive practices of the various government regimes from Independence to date. We cannot continue to act under the pretense that Western capitalistic influence and exploitative practices are the factors that have deprived us from development. We are not fools, and obviously do not "*feed ourselves through the nose.*" Maybe it is time we shifted blame to ourselves. Our leaders, from the beginning, acted savagely against their own people. It is time that the nations of Africa accepted responsibility for the perilous conditions they find themselves in. While other nations may have taken advantage of our irresponsible policies and underdevelopment, our elites in different generations also betrayed us by exploiting their own people through slavery, the exploitation of natural resources, and the economic exploitation of the masses in the present day. And yet, some of our own people are quick to blame Western capitalism as the source of the problem in Africa, at the same time being among the most capitalistic people in the world. In the case of Nigeria, it has left the rural population virtually helpless and the oil producing communities invariably worse off than before the advent of the oil industry, while the cities and its big politicians grow richer with that same oil money.

144

Therefore, it can be concluded that corruption and mismanagement are the overriding problems in the development of Nigeria. In the face of corruption, individuals cannot always be enlightened as to what an obvious problem or solution may be. Furthermore, in the face of corruption, whether problems are seen accurately or not, policies and strategies cannot, in any way, be effectively administered to carry out their purpose. This is blatantly seen in the way more and more money was allocated to agriculture with each Plan, with seemingly better policies and better intentions, as the sector was growing worse all the while. Mismanagement, deception, and corruption cannot go hand in hand with progress in a country that has such a long way to develop.

Chapter 7

RURAL-URBAN DICHOTOMY AND RURAL-URBAN MIGRATION IN NIGERIA

Implication of the Management Strategy Adopted by the Nigerian Government

It is ironic that the average Nigerian is worse off today than before the petroleum industry expanded. While the expansion of the oil industry has not brought about a worse situation for many Nigerians, its management has set the stage for the acceleration of the crisis which started earlier. The neglect of the rural sector started before the 1970s' decade, and this is evidenced by the distressing condition of public facilities for the rural population vis-a-vis the urban population, even though the bulk of the public fund was generated through the exploitation of the rural population.

Farmers were never content with the treatment they received from the government, being well aware of the abuse they received from the marketing boards. They were also cognizant of the diversion of money they worked for to benefit the urban population while they were neglected. The "*Agbekoya*" uprising mentioned in Chapter 5 was a demonstration of the farmers' rejection of the political suffering they had experienced due to the government, which was only made worse by the heavy taxes imposed by the government in 1969, probably to finance the Civil War which had started two years earlier.

Although the government has been involved in a verbal commitment to raise the standard of living for the rural population, their condition, all the while, has worsened. All the celebrated rural development programs launched during the Third and Fourth National Development Plans did nothing but enrich a few urban bureaucrats, who used the money to multiply their bank accounts.

The development of a country cannot take effect without a great proportion of the population participating in a constructive manner. In Nigeria, where the majority of the population is still in the economically disadvantaged rural setting, such development programs should be directed to those areas. Not only was this not the case, but the rural population was used by the state as a means of generating capital for the development of the urban centers without the rural people themselves benefiting from the fruit of their labor.

This grinding oppression of the rural population, and of farmers in particular, has over the years rendered them hapless victims of the government. Not only have they been effectively refused their nation's fortunes, which they helped generate, but repression and continuous neglect has destroyed their reproductive energies; and the younger generation has responded by moving to the urban centers.

Government disrespect of the rural population has been made evident through the development policies presented in the last chapters. Not only are the farmers increasingly being torn from their only means of caring for their families, but they have been constantly neglected by the government in the national development that has taken place over the years. In light of the various contributions farmers have made toward the growth of the country, one would expect that the amount of services provided for rural areas would be commensurate. But this is clearly not the case in Nigeria.

The physical productivity of any individual in any given society depends, among other things, upon the availability of a social and economic infrastructure. A population which has constantly been plagued by disease without any proper medical attention is obviously subjected to fruitlessness and unproductivity. Under such circumstances, the population would only worry about surviving from one day to the next. Nigeria's development strategy allegedly magnifies such constraints. The provision of health facilities, communication facilities, reliable sources of good water, and a clean environment are some of the items that make up the complex social infrastructure — a deficiency of these will impede development. In addition, the availability of banking services, credit and marketing facilities, and educational and knowledge-oriented facilities is a desirable prerequisite for overall economic and social development.

Considering the sectoral distribution of public funds as presented in the four plans mentioned earlier, it appears that, in absolute terms, there has been an increase in public capital allocation to the agricultural sector. However, if we consider it proportionally, we witness a decreasing involvement. For easy reference, the distribution of public-sector resources in terms of allocations to agriculture and non-agriculture during the four plans periods is presented in Table 7.1.

148

Table 7.1

Distribution of Public Sector investment 1962-1985
(per cent)

	1962-68		1970-74		1975-80		1981-85	
	p	a	p	a	p	a	p	a
Agriculture	13.6	7.7	9.4	9.8	6.7	7.2	12.5	na
Non-agric.	86.4	92.3	90.6	90.2	93.3	92.8	87.5	na

Sources: Federal Republic of Nigeria, <u>National Development Plans of Nigeria</u>
<u>1962-85</u>

p = Plan capital allocation
a = Actual capital allocation

It is not a coincidence that the government puts little importance on the development of agriculture. It is a deliberate action taken against the mass majority whose livelihood depends on the sector's survival, so that the government does not have to worry about providing for their social and welfare needs. A close look at the rural-urban distribution of public-sector investment expenditure (not simply physical performance) along the line of the various development plans reveals a clear picture of neglect of the rural areas, obviously consistent with the rural development policy of the government of Nigeria.

Various studies have examined the distribution pattern of the social and non-agricultural economic activities in the country. None of these studies seems to give a pleasant view of the situation for the rural areas. There is just no other way of explaining the situation. The fact of the matter is that the government has deemed it acceptable to leave over 75 percent of the population, which has very little public representation, in destitution. Olatunbosun, who noted the neglect of the rural areas with regard to the provision of economic, social, and welfare activities, pointed out the importance of these rural non-farm activities, without which the rural sector could not be expected to play the required role of affecting demand. Ake and Uyanga both observed the apparent imbalance in the distribution of social and economic activities in a country where over 75 percent of the population resides in the rural areas. And the government itself admitted its urban bias in the distribution of health care facilities and in the inadequacy of other social services in the rural areas. It seems that the government saw the need for such activities, but it could not see the connection of such facilities to the overall development of the sector. However, it is the provision of these activities that would bring about a balance in overall development.

The planning process in Nigeria does not involve participation of the rural population, especially the peasantry, and, consequently, the peasant has no influence in the allocation of public-sector resources. The resource allocation in development policy is therefore directed by the urban based political class, the civil servants, and the professionals in the mainstream, with the civil servants dominating in the implementation and the exact allocation phase (*Ake, 1985*). This means that the masses who are not represented are given a marginal place in the entire national planning process and implementation.

The calculations of Claude Ake from the first three Development Plans are quite informative and will serve as a base for understanding this rural-urban disparity in the non-agricultural public resource investments. Table 7.2 represents the rural-urban distribution of planned public-sector investment during the First National Development Plan. From the table, it is disappointing to see that rural services such as water, electricity, health, and other social services were given such limited attention, while over 75 percent of the country's labor force was then employed in agriculture. For example, it was quite acceptable for the government to allocate only 3.9 percent of the total allocation for health services to the rural sector that had by then over 80 percent of the country's population. The corresponding physical performance was evidenced by nothing more than paperwork.

Table 7.2

Rural-Urban Distribution of Social Services During the First National Development Plan 1962-68
(percentages)

Activities	Rural	Urban	Category indefinable
Electricity	0.6	97.9	1.5
Communication	0.0	91.4	8.6
Health	3.9	76.2	19.9
Information	0.0	37.8	62.2
Social welfare	9.2	90.8	–
Water supply	39.6	58.5	1.9
Town and country planning	0.0	100.0	–
Average	5.8	89.6	4.6

Source: Ake, C., <u>Political Economy of Nigeria,</u> 1985.

As shown by the table, in three of the items (communication, information, and town and country planning) the rural areas were not given any place in the distribution of resources. In addition, less than one percent of the allocation for electricity went to the rural areas. Water, which is relatively abundant both over and underground in most rural areas, could not be provided safely for the masses. Even though some consideration was accorded to its supply in the budgetary allocation, the physical supply of safe drinking water in the rural areas has been non-existent.

During the Second Plan period, the concentration of public resources in the urban areas at the expense of the rural mass majority was still suggestive. As Table 7.3 shows the percentage share for water fell from its high of about 40 percent during the first plan period to 14.7 percent in this plan period. This was not equitable for a nation whose countryside had been increasingly infected by water-borne diseases. Electricity increased from less than a percentage point to 11 percent, with social welfare increasing to 28.2 percent from its low of 9.2 percent during the first plan. Two of the areas, communication and information, were still unattended to in rural areas by the government.

Table 7.3

Rural-Urban Distribution of Social Services During the Second National Development Plan 1970-74 (percentages)

Activities	Rural	Urban	Category indefinable
Electricity	11.0	89.0	–
Communication	0.0	100.0	–
Health	6.6	43.1	50.3
information	0.0	53.9	46.1
Social welfare	28.2	66.1	5.7
Water supply	14.7	60.8	24.5
Town and country planning	9.1	81.4	9.5
Average	9.3	73.7	17.0

Source: Ake, C., Political Economy of Nigeria, 1985.

Even though there seemed to be some slight increase in the percentage share to the rural areas, a corresponding reduction in investment was accorded the agricultural sector during the period. This possibly shows that the government wanted to spend as little as possible in the rural areas. It was no wonder that the standard of living of the rural people did not change

151

significantly from what it was in the colonial era after 15 years of independence.

Nor did the Third National Development Plan bring an encouraging outcome. The marginality of the peasantry and the rural people in general in the distribution of public sector resources was even more indicative. Even though the Gowon administration rated the bridging of the rural-urban income gap as a critical objective in the plan, its allocation of only 4.1 percent of the non-agricultural public investments (Table 7.4) to

Table 7.4

Rural-Urban Distribution of Social Services During the Third National Development Plan 1975-80
(percentages)

Activities	Rural		Urban		Category indefinable	
	p	a	p	a	p	a
Industry	3.4	8.9	96.7	91.1	0.0	0.0
Commerce &finance	4.9	2.2	86.7	98.8	8.4	1.0
Electricity	21.9	23.9	78.1	76.1	0.0	0.0
Communication	0.1	0.1	97.5	98.4	2.3	1.5
Health	13.3	7.2	50.0	75.7	36.6	17.1
Information	0.0	0.0	67.4	53.2	32.6	46.8
Social welfare	0.4	0.5	68.3	84.8	31.3	14.7
Water supply	23.6	20.0	68.2	70.6	8.2	9.4
Sewage / drainage	0.0	0.0	100.0	100.0	0.0	0.0
Town & country planning	2.5	1.3	88.7	89.3	8.8	9.4
Co-operatives & Supply	9.9	16.4	16.5	9.0	73.6	74.5
Community dev.	74.2	84.3	7.0	15.7	18.7	0.0
Labor	0.0	0.0	100.0	100.0	0.0	0.0
Housing	0.0	0.0	100.0	100.0	0.0	0.0
General Admin.	0.7	0.0	84.5	41.8	14.8	58.2
Defence & Security	0.0	0.0	39.0	9.2	61.0	90.8
Average	4.1	4.6	78.4	58.1	17.5	37.3

Source: Ake, C., Political Economy of Nigeria, 1985.

Note: p = represents plan allocation.
   a = represents actual allocation for the first year of the plan.

the rural areas does not seem to support that claim. Moreover, the supposed emphasis on agriculture investment during this plan on direct government production involves a corresponding reduction in the proportion of public-sector resources allocated to the support of the rural population.

The civilian government under Shagari witnessed a worsening of the crisis situation, not only for the rural population, but for the urban population as well, as the Fourth National Development Plan (1981-85) under this administration continued to follow the same trend of previous plans. A huge amount of capital investment was made, as shown in Table 6.6 in Chapter 6, but the money was dissipated among dishonest politicians who had no concern for the citizens.

Also to be noted in this context is the virtual absence of educational institutions established by the government in the rural areas. Before the takeover of schools in the late 1970s, almost all of the elementary and secondary schools were established by missionaries, except, of course, the schools operated by the Moslems. The few government institutions were all located in the larger cities. This concentration of higher institutions invariably caused the migration of determined students to the cities.

Trends and Changes in Rural-Urban Nigeria

The neglect of the rural sector (agricultural and non-agricultural activities) as discussed above has not only widened the gap between rural and urban incomes, it has also increased rural underemployment as well as unemployment and the desire of Nigeria's youth to move out of the rural areas into the cities in search of a better standard of living. The cities, on the other hand, cannot handle the influx, which results in undesirable living conditions. The government is now preoccupied with how to make the youth within and around the cities of Nigeria interested again in returning to the rural areas.

The implication of the management and development strategy adopted by the policymakers of Nigeria takes its first toll in the replacement of the agricultural economy by the "management" of the oil revenue. That is, it was not the development of the oil that brought about the crisis; instead it was its management or rather mismanagement that brought about the widening of the rural-urban development disparities. People migrated in response to this fact.

Indeed, the management style of Nigeria's politicians gives the impression that to be in politics is the only sure way to success. The shunning of the peasantry and the almost non-existence of non-farming activities (social and economic) in the rural areas supports this belief. It therefore gives the impression that only a person who has no other options will take up farm-

153

ing as a job. While there is still room for Nigeria to shift the concentration of activities in favor of the rural areas, to make a balanced development and stifle this undesirable rural-urban dichotomy, the trend still apparently favors the urban economy, whose growth rate has also been suffocated by the corrupt practices that have become a way of life in the cities.

In general, humans tend to live beyond their means. This is particularly true of people who want to get to the top fast, without assessing the conditions necessary for that advancement. And it is easier for man to live beyond his means than for him to retreat to his former lifestyle. This is especially difficult for those who have seen the rewards of a modern society that perhaps they did not prepare themselves for.

Nigeria, as a nation, has tried to advance too fast and too soon, fueled by oil money, at the expense of the traditionally-based agricultural economy. With little or no consideration for the implication of such an overnight shift of priority, it is quite difficult to salvage what one has neglected. Nigeria supplanted the agricultural economy with the oil industry, and granted imported agricultural goods instead of domestic production. Figure 7.1 and Table 7.5 demonstrate how abruptly Nigeria replaced domestic production with imported foodstuffs, some of which the country was, and can again be, self-sufficient in. Wheat and some processed foodstuffs, such as milk and sugar, were the only foodstuffs of which Nigeria was in the main a net importer; and, as can be seen in the Table, the growth rate of these commodities did not change as much prior to the abandonment which corresponds with the period of the oil boom. This was so because they were being supplemented greatly by domestic production. As a matter of fact, in some instances, importation of these foodstuffs fell, as in the case with wheat flour, cereal, and fish (stock-fish). But in the mid-1970s the import bill for these products started to soar along with the prices of those products that Nigeria was absolutely self-sufficient in. Rice, which later became an instrument of politicking, acquired a commanding lead along with fish and sugar in the import-mania. This corresponded with the exact period (1975/76) during which a drop in domestic production of virtually all agricultural products was first experienced in absolute terms, brought about by the rapidly declining importance of agriculture, and was evidenced by the abandonment of so much of Nigeria's land under cultivation (Chapter 3).

Nigeria, prior to the development of oil, was not importing rice, maize, coffee or tea; in fact, the country was a net exporter of the latter two items. According to our climatic information, the country was not anywhere near drought conditions between 1975 and 1982, even in the two northernmost stations of Sokoto and Kano. The fact that the country's import bill for each of these commodities, plus some of those it was a net ex-

IMPORT OF FOOD COMMODITIES, 1970-1982

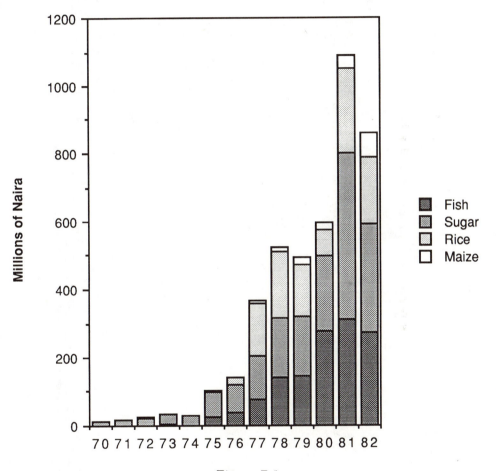

Figure 7.1

Table 7.5

Imports of Major Food Commodities 1965-82
(₦ million)

Commodities	65	66	67	70	71	72	73	74	75	76	77	78	79	80	81	82
Fish	13.4	13.8	9.0	2.0	1.0	1.6	3.7	2.1	24.3	39.6	78.6	141.4	144.2	274.9	310.2	274.2
Sugar	5.2	5.4	6.0	11.4	17.9	21.6	30.9	26.8	74.0	78.6	125.6	173.8	175.0	221.0	490.3	319.1
Milk	7.2	5.8	7.2	13.6	21.8	24.7	22.2	28.3	54.9	63.3	97.8	112.4	134.5	129.4	199.4	241.8
Other dairy products	0.6	0.6	0.6	0.4	0.8	0.9	1.1	1.1	-	-	3.4	4.9	2.3	4.0	3.3	14.2
Wheat flour	0.2	0.4	0.2	0.6	3.2	1.1	1.8	1.0	-	-	4.2	55.1	17.8	9.6	40.5	9.3
Wheat & spelt meslin	-	-	-	15.4	20.6	22.0	37.3	50.7	97.8	97.8	96.4	76.9	124.6	92.4	159.4	179.6
Other cereals	10.2	15.0	12.6	3.0	4.7	3.2	3.1	7.3	-	-	26.9	28.2	12.5	14.2	28.5	19.9
Malt	-	-	-	3.0	4.7	4.7	7.0	10.8	-	-	39.1	33.4	31.5	32.1	49.3	60.5
Meat	-	-	-	-	-	-	-	-	-	-	21.2	43.9	3.9	25.7	15.1	30.3
Live animals	-	-	-	-	-	-	-	-	-	-	2.7	4.0	22.0	19.2	25.0	16.3
Animal feeds	-	-	-	-	-	-	-	-	-	-	4.2	11.6	9.5	15.4	12.6	15.1
Rice	-	-	-	-	-	1.0	0.3	1.5	2.4	20.1	154.9	194.8	152.9	79.4	250.2	195.3
Maize	-	-	-	-	-	-	-	-	-	-	7.6	14.5	22.9	20.9	38.9	69.1
Tomato	-	-	-	-	-	-	-	-	-	-	14.4	25.5	1.9	6.4	4.4	9.4
Coffee & tea	-	-	-	-	-	-	-	-	-	-	5.2	15.2	10.7	14.9	10.6	9.5
Others	9.2	10.6	7.0	8.2	13.2	15.1	19.2	26.7	-	-	53.7	91.5	86.2	89.5	182.5	178.6
TOTAL	46.0	51.6	42.6	57.6	87.9	95.1	126.3	154.8	254.4	299.4	736.4	1027.1	952.4	1049.0	1820.2	1642.2

Sources: Federal Office of Statistics, Annual Abstract of Statistics, (various issues).
Federal Office of Statistics, Review of External Trade, (various issues).

156

porter of, rose beyond all imagination indicates a badly neglected sector whose products the country replaced with an import spree. The fact that Nigeria's problem was not money but how to spend it, as alleged by some complacent and unimaginative cabinet members (*Onimode, 1982*) during this same period, clearly indicates that the country's politicians would not concern themselves with a tedious and undesirable agricultural sector. Instead they turned their backs on the sector by substituting domestic production with effortlessly acquired imported foodstuffs. This explains the failure, or rather the abandonment, of the Peremabiri Rice Project, which was to have supplied all the rice the country needed, a project which would have cost only N7.0 million. Instead the country spent hundreds of millions of naira on importing rice to feed the population.

The migration of the younger generation to the urban areas in large numbers shows the neglect of the rural sector in response to the less tedious oil economy whose excess revenue, the country's politicians believed, would supply the every need of the country. In a state of such a thriving oil industry, even the private producer did not concern himself with the wearisome, undesirable, and unprofitable agricultural sector.

The expanding urban economy, and the creation of more states (1976), meant more labor to be absorbed. On the government side it meant more than a doubling of the labor needs, as more ministries were being created as a result. Government services and construction took the lead in the boom (*Fourth National Development Plan 1981-85*), as new Secretariats and roads leading to these government functionaries had to be constructed almost overnight in the newly created state capitals. Public housing, highways, and expressway construction in major cities, and the new federal capital all demanded enormous labor. The 18 percent growth rate of the manufacturing sector during this period demanded abundant labor as well. This was further boosted by the service industry and distribution, which involved less educational and technical requirements. However, in the face of a labor shortage, not many employers dared to look into the qualification requirements necessary for such services. People from the farms took advantage of this boom by moving to the cities for more lucrative employment in the modern sectors. And this was taking place at the expense of the rural sector. The overwhelming response Linda Lacey received in her field study about the migration of people to the three major urban centers of Nigeria was a demonstration of the compelling push-pull factors that operated during this period. In fact, according to Lacey, the male migrant (age 20-49) made more major contributions to the working ranks than any other group of people, with the greater number of these migrants moving to the cities to obtain what they considered their first modern occupation (*Lacey, 1981*). This leads us to highlight two interrelated factors, economic and social, contributing to rural-urban migration in the country. These, of course, are related to the politics of the oil economy discussed above.

The predominant motive behind most decisions to migrate is economic. People do not relocate if their desires and needs are met where they are. If enough needs are not met in the present environment, people try to relocate in a place where they can expect to meet those needs. For a migrant to make up his mind to relocate, he must perceive differences in opportunities between places. He has to believe that his needs and desires will be better satisfied in the place the movement is directed to than in the place of origin. In Nigeria there were originally no such striking differences between the rural and urban areas, even though there was always a recognition of the low return on human effort, and the very low income, of most rural people. While such push factors have been long recognized, there was no compelling urge to move among Nigerians; apparently the economic conditions in the cities were not much better than in the rural areas for people to take such a risk.

However, the disproportionate development strategy and distribution of economic activities, along with the dissipation of the oil money to salaried employees in the cities, brought about an ever-widening gap between the rural and urban areas. This was further complicated by the rapidly rising standard of living and runaway inflation which the rural population, with its average minimal income, was not prepared for. Greater earnings in cash and/or in kind were needed for a variety of purposes, just as in any urban population. The peasant, with his small holdings, was further incapacitated by the gross neglect and exploitative practices of the government. He responded by moving to the cities in large numbers to fill positions in the expanding industrial and commercial sectors where his salary was guaranteed, and in most cases was 10 times as much as he was earning in the farming business. It was, therefore, no wonder that the cities grew at the expense of the rural economy. While the country's annual population growth rate is estimated at about 2.7 percent, most of the cities have experienced over 15 percent annual growth rates. Ado Ekiti in Ondo State had a 20.2 percent average annual increase between 1970 and 1980. Ilorin, a state capital, experienced a 17.6 percent average annual increase (*Onyemelukwe, in Barrbour et al 1982*), while Lagos, the capital and largest city of the country, witnessed a doubling of its population almost every five years (Table 7.6). Warri and Port Harcourt, as a result of the new development in the oil industry, have also been growing at a phenomenal rate. And within this framework, the capital cities tend to grow faster than the other major cities. Unfortunately, accurate data are not available to reflect these growth rates.

Apart from the economic factors, there are social factors (sometimes intertwined with economic) that may support perceived beliefs about a place and the consequent movement to it. Though these factors may be marginal in their contribution to migration streams, they have paved the way for many individuals to resettle, especially students, who after graduation most likely will not go back to the farm from where they came. Both voluntary and family or peer pressure movements are apparent here. While young adults can move freely to urban centers where their social desires may be fulfilled, family members or friends may pressure them to make such a movement because of the unattractiveness of the farm economy. A characteristic of this socially motivated movement is the tendency of migrants to maintain two homes; one where their daily needs are met economically and socially, and the other where they assemble as a family.

Table 7.6

Estimates of the Population Growth of Lagos 1871-1985

Date	Population	Increase	Growth Rate
1871	28,518	–	–
1881	37,452	8,934	3.13
1891	32,508	4,944	1.32
1901	39,387	6,879	2.12
1911	73,766	34,379	8.73
1921	99,690	25,924	3.51
1931	126,108	26,418	2.65
1952	267,407	141,299	5.34
1963	665,246	397,839	13.52
1970	875,417	210,171	4.51
1975	2,064,000	1,188,583	27.15
1977	3,500,000	1,436,000	34.79
1980	4,000,000	500,000	4.76
1985	4,500,000	500,000	2.50

Sources: Mabogunje, 1968, p. 257.
U.N. Demographic Yearbook, 1970-76 estimates.Abate, 1978, p. 28
Federal Republic of Nigeria, Embassy of Nigeria,
Washington D.C., Volume 4, NO. 1, July -September,1977, p. 17.
The 1986 Almanac, page 242.

Note: Increase and percentage rates of growth were computed from the estimate obtained from sources listed above. The percentage rate was based on the estimated population of the preceding period.

Differences in the standard of living between the rural and urban areas are quite striking. While this has been true for many decades, the situation has become even worse since Independence. People generally have better access to basic social amenities in the cities than in the rural areas. The oil revenue, which could have been used to bridge this wide gap and to improve conditions for the entire population, was concentrated in the cities, and even contributed to making the situation worse for some rural communities, especially in places where the petroleum was extracted. Such basic amenities as hospitals, water supply (Chapter 2), electricity, and institutions of higher learning were, therefore, absent in rural areas. This may have contributed to the movement of people to places where these things could be supplied. In this category, education is a major factor in the relocation process of the younger population. Students, after having acquired an education, resisted going back to the farm, where there were little or no prospects for them.

It is, therefore, not a coincidence that Nigerians responded to the oil economy through mass migration. No matter what reason or reasons motivated migrants to move — political, social or economic — the general belief was that the migrants' desires, needs, and well-being could be better had in the cities than in the rural areas, which were considered marginal places in the management of the oil economy and the development that took place in the process.

Impact of Migration in the Development Process

The management of oil and the neglect of the rural sector, which brought about mass migration into the cities, did have its consequences. During the initial stage, the migration of many people did supply the labor needed by the growing urban sectors. It also benefited the migrants, who accepted better paying jobs and consequently enjoyed a better standard of living. Countries from which Nigeria imported foodstuffs also benefited, as a brand new market for their surpluses was created through Nigeria's development strategy. The only loser seemed to be the rural sector, which obviously was of no concern to the government as long as food to feed the urban elite, whose interest seemed be the national priority in the country's development strategy, was made available through heavy reliance on outside sources.

But the migration of people into cities which were not concurrently expanding their industrial bases seemed extremely perilous and, of course, it was risky. The woes brought about by this shift of priority were far-reaching. Not only did Nigeria deny itself the food it could produce locally and thereby start an import spree, it even relied on outside sources for raw materials that could be produced locally for its industries. But the weak

160

urban economy could not handle the influx of people from the rural areas which started the days of reckoning for the country's development strategy.

The level of migration has risen so high that it has resulted in enormous unemployment in the cities and underemployment in the rural areas. Documentation of unemployment is virtually impossible to obtain in Nigeria. However, if a young country like Nigeria has started to experience unemployment among college and university graduates, as well as high school graduates, it makes one wonder what actually went wrong in a relatively rich country. It is nevertheless the truth that is echoed in the streets of the urban centers and in the headlines of the country's major newspapers: *"Unemployment Among University Graduates"*.

In the rural areas, underemployment is the overriding problem. Many farmers literally abandoned their farms and moved to the cities; others became absentee landlords, especially in the southern cocoa, rubber, and oil palm producing states. After all, they were made to believe that influence and power resided in the cities. Moreover, the management style of the country's politicians made the urban population the beneficiaries of the rural labor, thereby distributing income from the poor to the rich. Apparently this urban-elite bias strategy in terms of efficiency involved the pulverization of incentives for private investment in the rural sector. It encouraged rural-urban migration by draining labor from the rural to the urban areas and creating underemployment in the rural areas, while at the same time creating urban unemployment. This development strategy is a clear case of underutilization of labor resources and, hence, inefficient allocation of labor resulting from gross mismanagement and dire neglect.

The social cost of the government's management style is phenomenal. The high unemployment rate in the cities has brought with it human suffering, and has placed an unbearable load on the local and national governments, and may have contributed to several military takeovers in the country. It can therefore be said that the food shortages, which caused so much human suffering, could explain some of the recent military coups in the country. Apparently the country is not all that stable. This has been compounded by the more pervasive corrupt and undisciplined practices of the country's politicians and government workers. According to the Minister of Communication, Mr. Audu Ogbeh, *"the Federal Government is losing ₦50 million every month as salaries to non-existent workers"* (<u>The Guardian,</u> *September 18, 1983*). In the course of one year, then, Nigeria lost ₦600 million (over one billion dollars) in this particular racket. This money could be spent to construct a dual expressway from Lagos to Kaduna (a distance of about 450 miles); and yet the country has no single expressway that connects the north to the south. It could also be spent to pay the salaries of 200,000 well-qualified Grade II teachers earning ₦3,000 each.

The minister is apparently not informing the press as to the fraud being perpetrated in his ministry, (and he was not, moreover, in the position to inform the public about fraud in other Federal Ministries and parastatals, let alone the nineteen state functionaries), but only as to one particular incident, in the Posts and Telegraphs Department (P & T), which had come to light — payment of salaries to ghost or fictitious workers. It would boggle the imagination if one could reckon the staggering sum of all the fraud committed against the people of Nigeria in the public and private services. And, according to the Guardian, as much as 60 percent of the country's wealth is regularly consumed by corruption, as even the most conservative defender of the system would agree. In addition, other more conventional criminal activities, such as burglary, armed robbery, and more recently, drug trafficking, have been on the increase as a result of the uncontrolled influx of people to the cities.

Even though Nigeria does not have any provision for the unemployed in the form of a social welfare system, it has recently been forced to invest huge sums of money in government housing projects in the big cities to accommodate the ever increasing migrants. Funding for other social services has also increased by hundreds of millions of naira. Police personnel have had to be stationed in places where they were not needed 15 years before.

The concentration of people in the large cities, especially in the national and state capitals, has also created enormous sanitary problems, particularly in sewage disposal, water shortages, and poor drainage, which has caused much disease. In addition, traffic congestion, pollution, and slum conditions plague the cities as the population increases uncontrollably.

This strategy of development by migration has also contributed to inflationary pressures caused by the resulting food scarcities and an increased dependency on foreign goods and know-how, a process which has imposed constraints on the growth of the country's economy. In fact, the country's economy was drastically affected with the creation of many idle industries, especially those which depended on domestic agricultural raw materials. And, since foreign exchange was restricted, it extended to industries which relied on imported raw materials as well. Many workers laid off both in the public and private sectors joined the unemployed.

Government efforts to divert the situation and to stop rural urban migration have been circumscribed by first-class mismanagement, corruption, and a lack of the population's technical skills. The rural areas, in addition, have rather impelling push factors for the young people, which have been compounded by poor living conditions and the near absence of expendable income. In effect, the development of oil and its management that brought about the unconstrained rural-urban migration came with unintended social, economic, and political ramifications the country has not been able to arrest. Both the migrants and the non-migrants are paying the price for the uncontrolled movement of people, and it has been a costly one.

Chapter 8

FIELD STUDY ANALYSIS: THE VOICE OF THE PEOPLE

Introduction

Several issues have been raised in the last few chapters with respect to the agricultural economy and the neglected rural majority. In this chapter a thorough in situ investigation is made regarding the general characteristics of Nigerian farmers, the nature of the problems farmers face, and the avenues that are available for them to deal with those problems. It has been shown so far that the city-based government, whose interests and concerns have mainly been for the city's population, has not properly understood the problems of the rural population and has almost invariably not represented them. This has been demonstrated by the meager support the government has offered to the rural population, as exemplified by the lack of physical development in the rural areas after over 25 years of political independence. Furthermore, the government has not deemed it right to see to the plight of the rural population whose economic activities, in the main, support the country. Instead of compensating the rural population for their labor by distributing the national wealth fairly to accommodate them, the government has helped fuel the already compounded problems for the rural population by incapacitating some areas in the countryside (especially in Bendel and Rivers State where the oil is drilled) and creating facilities to remove them from the land.

As pointed out in Chapter 1, it was appropriate that a study of this sort should be conducted at the level of the local farmers, who are directly involved in the agricultural problems of the country. This in situ investigation is necessary because it helps us better understand the nature of the agricultural problem in the country, as the local farmers themselves are the ones who are directly affected by the sector's problems.

Two states were selected for the field study: Sokoto State in the Northwest and Ondo State in the Southwest. These two states represent the northern and southern limits of the

165

agricultural and climatic zones of the country, respectively. A questionnaire was prepared to conduct the field study (Appendix). However, the questionnaire had to be interpreted to the audience, as over 90 percent of them could not speak English and could neither read nor write. And, in fact, for those who could read and write (police officers, teachers, government workers, etc.), it was not as easy to interpret the questionnaire as expected. As a result, each respondent had to be interviewed personally. Six hundred and twenty-eight local farmers were randomly selected and interviewed from two local government areas in the two states selected.

Selection of the Farm Interviewees

The rural population of most African nations is probably one of the least understood populations in the world. Because most Africans live in remote areas, there has been little interest, if any, in them among urban researchers who would endeavor to go to these remote areas to study them. As a result, most of the studies made about them have been urban based. Foreign researchers who set out to conduct studies on these populations were faced with a language barrier, great suspicion, and discontent on the part of the natives, and, at times, great hostility. As a result, little or no accurate data could be gathered by these researchers. It has therefore been suggested that indigenous researchers with a keen interest in the group could bring about a more practical understanding of the rural population and the problems they encounter.

There is not any accurate information as to the approximate population of the two local government areas in which the research was conducted. However, recent government documents show that there are over 4.8 million and 7 million people in Ondo and Sokoto States respectively, and in each case over 70 percent of the working population is engaged in some form of farming for subsistence and income.

Simple random sampling was employed in preference to other probabilistic selection procedures since so very little was known about the farming populations of Nigeria, their numbers, or their economic characteristics. The lack of data, it was felt, did not justify more elaborate sampling techniques. The sample was taken from farmers who lived on their farms and/or worked within a one-day walking distance from their farms in nearby towns and villages. Several village communities were randomly selected from each local government area. The chief or king of each village was formally contacted if available and was made aware of the project and what it entailed. In most cases, the chief or king of the village, himself, was a farmer and was interviewed, since he would invariably have knowledge of what was going on in his village. However, it was scrupulously designed that no other person who lived in the chieftaincy residential area was interviewed; this would avoid a response influenced by or copied from the chief's response. A sample of the questionnaire is presented in the Appendix.

Local Farmers and their Characteristics

It is now appropriate to take a look at the local farmers of the study areas. For convenience and comparison, we shall analyze the farmers from the two states separately. Sections will be presented on the characteristics of the farmers as summarized in Table 8.1, and the nature and problems of food production, along with an analysis of how the problems are solved, and how involved the different government regimes have been in improving the problems for local farmers. In the following sections, Ondo State will be discussed first, followed by a similar discussion of Sokoto State, and finally the opinion of farmers with regard to how the government functioned in both states will be projected.

Study I: Characteristics of Local Farmers in Ondo State

One of the purposes of this research has been to determine the characteristics of the local farmers. The dominant ethnic group of the Ondo State study area is Yoruba-speaking. Over 93 percent of the sample was from this group. Most lived in small towns or villages of several hundred or several thousand people (Fig. 8.1). A typical house in the study area, as in any part of the state, is built of red mud, sticks, and bamboo with a thatched roof or, at times, a corrugated iron roof. Some homes have been built from cement blocks. A small percentage (6.6 percent) of migrant workers, especially from the Ibo tribe, was encountered. Most of these non-ethnic workers took farming as a second job, and they were mostly elementary school teachers or small shop owners who supplemented their income with subsistence farming.

The average age of a typical farmer in the sample was 48.7 years (Table 8.1). Of the total number of 326 persons interviewed, 64 percent were over 40 years of age. In fact, 36 percent of the sample was 50 years or older, and only 3 percent was 25 years or younger.

The relatively high average age of farmers in the study area left the average farmer with 22.2 years of farming experience. In fact, 46 percent of the farmers interviewed had at least 20 years of farming experience, with only 13 percent having less than 10 years of experience. This relative maturity of the farming population is a reflection of the emigration of the younger population from rural areas to urban areas, as discussed in Chapter 7.

167

Table 8.1

Characteristics of Farmers in Ondo and Sokoto States, Nigeria

	Ondo	Sokoto
Average age of farmer	48.7 yrs.	36.7 yrs.
Under 25 years	3.0%	22.0%
25 to 30 years	7.0%	21.0%
30 to 40 years	26.0%	29.0%
40 to 50 years	28.0%	13.0%
50 to 60 years	19.0%	9.0%
Over 60 years	17.0%	6.0%
Average family size*	10.7 pers.	7.0 pers.
Average number of wives	2.0	1.95
Average number of children	7.4	3.8
Average dependents not home	2.6	0.6
Total average family size	13.0	7.6
Average years in farming	22.2 yrs.	17.4 yrs.
Under 5 years experience	4.0%	14.0%
5 to 10 years experience	17.0%	22.0%
10 to 20 years experience	33.0%	36.0%
20 to 30 years experience	28.0%	18.0%
30 to 40 years experience	12.0%	6.0%
Over 40 years experience	6.0%	4.0
Average land farmed	9.1 acres	13.2 acres
Under 5 acres	41.0%	29.0%
5 to 10 acres	33.0%	31.0%
10 to 20 acres	19.0%	23.0%
20 to 30 acres	5.0%	8.0%
30 to 40 acres	2.0%	4.0%
Over 40 acres	0.3%	5.0%
Average number of workers	7.6 pers.	6.7 pers.
Owner working in farm	97.0%	91.1%
Wives working with husband	90.0%	1.7%
Children working in farm	37.4%	27.5%
Hired laborers working	83.3%	82.0%
Others and relatives	3.1%	-
Materials used in farm		
Hoes	98.5%	96.0%
Machetes	97.2%	14.6%
Tractors	1.8%	11.6%
Axes	79.1%	25.5%
Other materials	15.0%	3.3%

* Family members living at home. These do not include dependents who moved out.

168

Figure 8.1

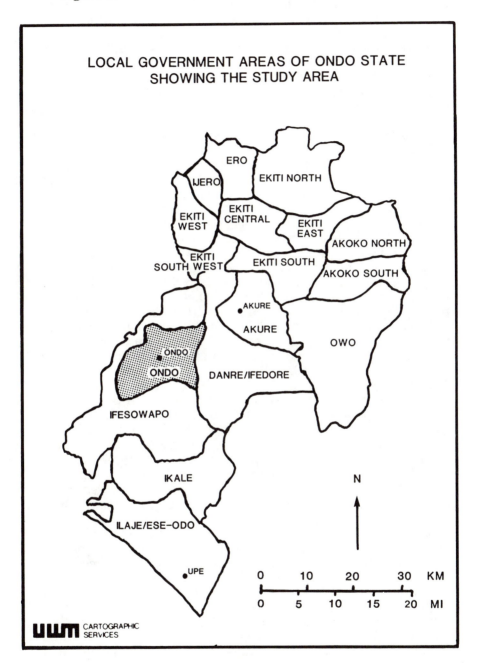

FIGURE 8.1

169

A typical household was composed of 10.7 members including the farmer, with an average of 2.0 wives and 7.4 living children who lived at home and were dependent on the farmer. And of the family members who had moved out, an average of 2.6 members still depended on the farmer for income and existence, and children accounted for 2.3 persons. This brought the total average dependents of a typical farmer to thirteen including himself. An overwhelming 76 percent of the children who had moved out lived in major towns and cities. Of the total number of children who had moved out, about 69 percent moved either to go to school or to obtain a job in the cities. Only 3 percent or so moved due to marriage.

On the average, a farmer farmed 9.1 acres of land. This figure is high for farmers who depend on hoes and other hand tools for their farming. When broken up, it is observed that over 40 percent of the sample farmed less than 5 acres of land, 74 percent 10 acres or less, 93 percent 20 acres or less, and only 1 percent farmed 40 acres or more. (This relatively high average piece of land cultivated in the study area could be attributed to the very few farmers who owned over 100 acres of land).

An average of 7.4 persons worked on a farm. Ninety-seven percent of the sample worked on their own farm. Ninety percent had their wives working with them on the farm, 83.3 percent had some form of laborers helping them, and 37.4 percent responded that their children worked with them on the farm; most of these children worked after school and for only few hours a week. A relatively mature farming population with only 37 percent engaging their children in their farm business reflects the effect of migration of young people in the country, and shows what has transpired over the years since the mid-1970s, as to the importance of agriculture in the country.

The majority of farmers use rudimentary farm implements. Of the total number of farmers interviewed, 98.5 percent responded that they used crude hoes for cultivating their land, 97.2 percent used a cutlass or machete, and 79.1 percent used axes. Despite the supposed claims of the government (since 1975) to have modernized the sector's activities through heavy investment in tractors and other farm machines as rental units at subsidized prices to farmers, only 1.8 percent (out of 326 farmers interviewed) of this relatively affluent farm community used tractors of some form in their farming. Obviously farmers with holdings of only a few acres would not benefit from this supposed program. Probably only those farmers who were connected with some cooperative societies and had substantial holdings would gain from such services. As indicated in Chapter 5, the vast majority of the farmers were excluded from these cooperative societies because of the requirements imposed in order to belong to such societies.

Table 8.2 represents the land ownership of each farmer. Over 80 percent indicated owning some form of land, of which 69 percent of the respondents farmed land that belonged entirely to them; 9.8 percent indicated owning most but not all of the land. Only 15.3 percent owned no land of their own, but used land that belonged to other categories as presented in the Table. Some 4.9 percent rented the entire land for farming, another 3.7 percent used land with permission from owners, and 2.1 percent shared proceeds from land with owners to farm the land. This high percentage of personal land owned becomes significant in food production, as indicated by the farmers' willingness to cultivate more land. We will see later in the discussion that availability of land was not at all a deterrent in farming more land in this part of the country.

Table 8.2

Land Ownership in Ondo State

	All	Most	Half	Some	None
Land owned by					
farmer	69.0	9.8	3.1	2.8	15.3
family	0.6	1.5	1.8	6.4	89.6
Land rented by farmer	4.9	1.5	1.2	6.7	85.6
Land used					
without permission	0.6	0.3	-	-	99.1
with permission	3.7	1.2	1.8	1.5	91.7
Land shared with owner	2.1	0.6	0.3	0.9	96.0
Other types of ownership	-	-	-	0.6	99.4

It is quite difficult to assess in detail individual crops grown on the land, since intercropping is generally practiced in the state. However, the following general statements can be made from the results gathered from the farmers, as presented in Table 8.3. Of the total sample, 89.8 percent indicated using part of their land for growing cassava, one of the most staple food crops in the country. A little over 2 percent of the respondents devoted all of their land for raising cassava, with another 6.1 percent using most of it for this particular crop. On the average, cocoa was the most important cash crop grown widely. Some 3.7 percent used their land exclusively for cocoa trees, and an overwhelming 53.4 percent used most of their land for cocoa. In total, over 87 percent allotted all or part of their land for raising cocoa, with only 12.5 percent not using their land for this crop. The importance of cocoa in this part of the country has been noted for decades. It is presently the most economically viable crop in Nigeria, especially for export earnings. It contributes to over 80 percent of the country's export earnings in the agricultural sector. Corn, yam, cocoyam, plantain/banana and vegetables are widely grown and are accorded a significant place by most farmers. (Refer to the Table 8.3 to see the importance of each crop in the study area).

Table 8.3

Land Used for growing:in Ondo State

	All	Most	Half	Little	None
Cassava	2.1	6.1	3.1	78.5	10.2
Rice	0.3	0.0	0.6	3.4	95.7
Millet	0.0	0.3	0.0	0.6	99.1
Cocoa	3.7	53.4	17.2	13.2	12.5
Cotton	0.0	0.0	0.0	4.9	95.1
Groundnut	0.0	0.0	0.0	18.1	81.9
Soyabeans	0.0	0.0	0.0	0.9	99.1
Maize/corn	0.3	1.2	0.6	81.9	16.0
Guineacorn	0.0	0.0	0.0	0.9	99.1
Oilpalm	0.0	0.0	0.0	20.9	79.1
Cocoyam	0.0	0.6	0.0	81.3	18.1
Yam	0.0	0.6	0.3	88.6	10.5
Rubber	0.0	0.0	0.0	4.6	95.4
Wheat	0.0	0.0	0.0	0.6	99.4
Plantain/banana	0.0	0.6	0.0	76.1	23.3
Cowpeas	0.0	0.0	0.0	15.3	84.7
Vegetables	0.0	0.0	0.0	50.9	49.1
Livestock	0.0	0.0	0.0	10.1	89.9
Other	0.0	4.3	0.3	32.8	62.8

Respondents were also asked how much of their crop they sold. With the exception of those respondents who grew cocoa (which of course is an export crop) and less important cash crops, only very little of their crop was sold for income, as shown in Table 8.4; and the majority who responded that they sold their crops, sold them to cooperatives; few sold them to individuals or in the open markets (Table 8.5).

Finances and Seed Provisions

Different government units in the country have often claimed to allocate huge amounts of money for agriculture and related activities. During the Second National Development Plan (1970-1974), the Federal government established a Nation-

Table 8.4

Proportion of Farm Products Sold in Ondo State

	All	Most	Half	Little	None
Cassava	0.6	4.6	7.4	52.8	25.5
Rice	0.0	0.0	0.6	2.5	9.5
Millet	0.6	0.0	0.0	0.0	10.7
Cocoa	84.0	1.8	0.3	0.6	0.9
Cotton	2.5	0.3	0.6	0.9	8.0
Groundnut	1.2	2.5	2.8	8.6	8.6
Soyabeans	0.0	0.0	0.0	1.2	10.4
Maize/corn	0.6	7.1	5.2	51.2	19.0
Guineacorn	0.0	0.0	0.0	0.6	10.7
Oilpalm	0.9	1.2	4.0	12.3	8.3
Cocoyam	0.9	0.6	3.1	48.5	31.9
Yam	0.3	1.5	3.4	52.1	33.7
Rubber	2.8	0.9	0.3	0.3	9.2
Wheat	0.0	0.0	0.0	0.6	10.7
Plantain/banana	0.6	2.8	2.5	50.9	20.9
Cowpeas	0.0	0.3	0.3	8.6	14.1
Vegetables	1.2	0.9	1.2	33.7	16.6
Livestock	0.3	0.0	0.3	7.7	8.9
Other	19.9	12.0	0.3	4.6	11.3

Table 8.5

Quantity of Products Sold in Different Markets in Ondo State

	All	Most	Half	Little	None
In the markets	4.0	16.6	6.4	59.2	2.1
To cooperatives	5.8	42.0	7.4	20.9	2.5
To individuals	2.8	7.7	4.0	43.2	8.9
Other (specify)	0.3	0.3	0.0	0.6	12.3

al Agricultural Credit Bank to ensure the maintenance of sound credit resources to various subsectors of agriculture in the country. The Plan mentioned no monetary allocation to ensure the credit resources to the local farmers. On the other hand, the sum of ₦242.529 million was allocated to the agricultural subsector during the Plan period, out of which a total actual expenditure of ₦103.946 million was incurred in the first four years of the Plan. However, it was reported that only ₦20 million capital disbursement was made by the National Agricultural Credit Bank from 1973-1975 (*Third National Devel-*

opment Plan 1975-80). This figure is very small for a three year period, for a country with over 18 million farmers.

Subsequent plans of 1975-1980 and 1981-1985 allotted ₦150 million and ₦157.45 million, respectively, to agricultural credit for individual farmers and private companies. However, the actual disbursement was not recorded for the two plan periods. As little as the money (₦307 million) was for the 10 year period, it could still be expected to make an impact on some farmers since the program was specifically designed for them. It was quite apparent that farmers in Ondo State (a state that produces over 40 percent of the country's cocoa for export) was little recognized. The major source of capital for the farmers was the sale of crops and accrued savings (Table 8.6). Over 72 percent of the sample indicated using their own accrued savings to buy their needed materials for farm business. Another 23.3 percent financed most of their farm business from personal savings. On the other hand, both the cooperative societies (who buy most of their cocoa on credit) and the government gave no heed to the farmers' finances. Only two farmers (0.6 percent) out of the 326 sample interviewees indicated that the government gave little aid to them. This strong response does not support the claim of the government. It is obvious from this study that local farmers in Ondo State's study area were left to deal with their problems, even though over 40 percent of the export earnings from agriculture came from this part of the country.

Table 8.6
How Farmers Obtained Finances for Farming in Ondo State

	All	Most	Half	Little
Personal savings	72.7	23.3	2.5	1.2
Family/friends	0.0	0.3	0.6	20.2
Cooperative society	0.0	0.6	1.5	6.1
Government aids	0.0	0.0	0.0	0.6
Other	0.0	0.0	0.0	1.2

In response to a question asking how they obtained their seeds, well over 95 percent of the farmers said that they either bought their seeds in the open market or provided them locally from previous years. Seed provision, however, was one of the most successful projects the government claimed to have accomplished. Table 8.7 shows the contradiction in this study area, and, in fact, only 1.2 percent of the farmers responded favorably for the government. This supports the notion that the traditional farmer was left almost exclusively to deal with his own farming problems, including the provision of quality seeds.

Table 8.7

How Farmers Obtained their Seeds for Farming in Ondo State

	All	Most	Half	Little
In the market	19.3	20.2	6.4	39.0
From previous years	14.4	37.1	7.7	21.2
Provided by Government	0.0	1.2	0.0	0.0
Provided by cooperatives	0.0	0.6	0.3	0.3
Other	0.0	0.0	0.0	0.0

Problems Farmers Face in Ondo State

Nigeria's agricultural economy has most of the necessary ingredients for a favorable future and growth, but it also has significant weaknesses, mainly due to human errors, that will continue to impede growth if they are not radically moderated. Certain naturally induced conditions are beyond man's control. Natural hazards such as tropical cyclones, hurricanes, and heavy thunderstorms generally occur without warning, and then there is often little we can do about them. On the other hand, other natural hazards such as drought and desert conditions have been accommodated in some parts of the globe, bringing about a bountiful living. Eleven possible problems were presented to the farmer interviewees to seek their opinion about the seriousness of each. Though three of these problems have some natural ramifications, they could be contained. But the others depend entirely on human intuition.

Table 8.8 presents the farmers' opinions as to how serious each of these problems were in the farm business in Ondo State. Two of the three naturally related hazards — soil fertility and pest and weed problems — rank very high among the problems farmers had to deal with. The problem of water seems to be moderate, and, in fact, over 35 percent of the sample did not look at water as a problem in farming. On the other hand, soil fertility and pest and weed control problems are rated 73 and 75 percent, respectively, as serious to very serious problems in farming. Provision of the right chemical in each case would improve each of these problems. But the prices of these fertilizers and chemicals (insecticides and weed control treatments) were so high that small-scale farmers could not afford to pay for them. In fact, one farmer declared that "*insecticides which*

175

used to cost ₦1.50 per unit two years ago had risen to ₦12.0 per unit today." That is over a 700 percent increase.

With regard to the human related factors, the problem of money seemed to be the most deterring factor in farming. Almost 75 percent of the sample said that the availability of money was a very serious problem in their farming activities. Another 19.0 percent looked at money as a serious problem. Only 1.5 percent of the sample said money was not a problem in farming. The role of money in the farming business cannot be overstated. A better management and harnessing of finances could help control most of the problems presented in the Table, including the naturally related problems.

Table 8.8

Seriousness of Certain Problems in Farming in Ondo State

	Very Serious	Serious	Somewhat Serious	No problem
Water supply	10.4	29.1	25.2	35.3
Transportation	16.3	43.6	33.7	6.4
Marketing	5.8	43.6	35.0	15.6
Storage	35.0	46.6	12.6	5.8
Price	15.0	50.3	30.4	4.3
Labor supply	19.0	41.4	31.3	8.3
Planting/harvesting	20.2	46.0	27.3	6.4
Soil fertility	36.5	36.8	16.6	10.1
Credit/money	74.8	19.0	4.6	1.5
Pest/weed control	28.5	46.9	23.0	1.5
Quality seed	6.4	42.3	40.5	9.8

Lack of storage facilities and the centralization of stocks in urban centers have also aggravated food insecurity for farmers, especially storage space for perishable farm products. Farmers felt that having inadequate storage facilities was a very serious deterrent to farm expansion. In fact, the second most frequently stated problem among farmers in Ondo State was the lack of adequate storage facilities. Thirty-five percent of the sample perceived storage as a very serious problem, with 46.6 percent seeing it as a serious problem. Only 5.8 percent of the sample found inadequate storage to be no threat to their business.

Planting and harvesting, which demand labor, were looked at as very serious problems by 20.2 percent of the sample. Another 46.0 percent saw this back-breaking aspect of the business as a serious problem. Labor, which is directly related to planting and harvesting, also ranked quite high among the problems. Some 60 percent perceived labor supply as a serious to very serious problem, and another 31.3 percent said that availability of labor was a somewhat serious problem. On the other hand, only 8.3 percent perceived inadequate labor as no threat to their farm expansion and development.

Price is another problem in farming in Nigeria. The farmers' getting a fair price for their goods has been directly or indirectly stifled by the encouragement of importation of similar goods by the government. Farm prices below production costs, overvalued exchange rates favoring imported foods, and direct taxation have done much to erode the economic basis of rural areas and to increase national food-import dependency. Farmers generally do not get a fair price for the goods they produce due to heavy dependence on foreign imports. This, of course, translates into depressing the farmers' ability to produce more at a reasonable price. Of the 326 sample interviewees only 4.3 percent acknowledged that price was not a problem. A little over half (50.3 percent) of the sample saw price as a serious problem, and 15.0 percent perceived it as a very serious impediment to farming, with some 30 percent perceiving it as a somewhat serious problem.

Transportation has been another important issue in the country, especially for rural people. Rural infrastructure in the form of roads has never been given serious attention, at least in practice. Roads are limited mainly to small paths, which at times are not even accessible to simple bicycles and mopeds. The significance of this lack of accessible roads, or any transportation network in the development of agriculture, becomes more evident when one considers the limitation it poses for farmers in hauling their products to and from the marketplaces. Just the fact that the problem of transportation is there sets limits on how much marketable goods farmers are willing to produce. The majority of them resort to producing just enough food to be consumed by their immediate families. The market, per se, is not that much of a problem, but the means of getting the goods to the market is an issue. As one farmer put it: "*You can only carry what your head can carry. They have the money and the Mercedes cars. I have even no bicycle after having worked for over forty years.*" Some 60 percent of the sample pointed out that transportation was either a serious or very serious problem in their farming business, with another 33.7 percent seeing it as a somewhat serious problem. Only a meager 6.4 percent indicated that transportation was not a problem.

The climatic factor, which has been used widely by many government agencies and researchers to explain agricultural underdevelopment in many a developing country, was posed; their response is summarized in Table 8.9 below. Since it was difficult for an average farmer, with little or no formal education, to remember the climatic conditions of each year over a long period, a general question was asked as to how farmers would rank the weather conditions in relation to their agricultural activities. Well over 90 percent of the sample rated weather as generally fair to very good, and said that weather was not a serious problem for them. This, of course, supports the weather statistics for the exact local government area in Chapter 4, Table 4.8.

Table 8.9

Weather Condition in Ondo State

	Very good	Good	Fair	Bad	Very Bad	Don't Know
General	3.4	44.8	49.7	0.9	0.0	0.0
1980	1.5	38.0	48.8	8.0	0.3	1.8
1981	2.1	16.9	62.0	16.6	0.3	0.6
1982	1.8	12.6	43.9	33.4	6.4	0.3
1983	2.5	8.3	16.3	42.9	28.2	0.3
1984	24.2	42.0	27.3	1.5	0.3	3.4

However, the same question was asked of them for the past five years, which obviously, they could only answer if they had been farming during these years. With the exception of the 1982/83 seasons, all other years received a favorable rating of at least 80 percent. Even though the 1982 season was not as bad as that of 1983, a 40 percent negative rating was quite high for this part of the country, which is not in the drought-threatened zone. However, several farmers were quick to point out that it was not related to a drought condition, but was due to lack of sunshine which was needed to dry the cocoa beans. This, obviously, is in support of the rainfall table in Chapter 4. Moreover, the more drought-prone Sokoto study area in the north gave a far more favorable report for the same period as well. In general, farmers do dry their cocoa beans in the sun, as can be observed in the front and back yards of every cocoa producer. Since over 80 percent of the farmers interviewed raised cocoa, it should be expected that they would respond the way they did.

The fact that farmers in Ondo State generally believe that neither the state nor the country produces enough food to feed the population is attested to by their almost unanimous response. In fact, only 1.8 percent of the sample population actually believed that Nigeria was producing enough food. Another 7.7 percent thought that the country was probably producing enough food. On the other hand 90.5 percent of the sample categorically declared that the country was not producing enough food, which 89 percent of the sample thought was due partly to inadequate manpower, along with the paucity of finances and underutilization of land area in the country, as implied in Tables 8.10 and 8.11 below.

Table 8.10

Importance of Certain Factors in Producing More food in Ondo State

	Very import.	Import.	Somewhat import.	Not import.
Farm expansion by individual	44.5	47.2	6.4	1.5
More people farming	54.0	33.1	9.2	3.4
Modern methods of farming	52.4	44.2	2.5	0.3
Providing improved seeds	31.6	57.4	9.2	1.2
Providing fertilizer	49.1	47.2	1.8	1.2

According to Table 8.10, some 87 percent of the sample favored the idea of having more people farming, and over 90 percent saw the need for an individual to expand his farm. These parameters obviously imply that availability of land was not a deterrence in farming, which was only restricted by inadequate means of clearing the land and labor shortage, both of which, of course, are related to the limited financial resources available to farmers, and, to a smaller extent, to government restriction (Table 8.11). The government factor, even though still significant, may have been influenced by the farmers' unwillingness to leave their land, and the slow rate at which the sector has been developing in the southern part of the country.

In light of the problems identified above, the individual farmer was asked who was responsible for solving those problems. The vast majority of the sample, as can be seen in Table 8.12, indicated that they alone had been responsible to a very great extent for solving their farm problems. The government and the research institutions supported by the government were not helpful enough in dealing with the problems farmers faced, and this was not fair to people who contributed a great portion of the government revenue.

Table 8.11

Limiting Factors in Obtaining More Land for Farming in Ondo State

	Very great extent	Great extent	Some extent	Not at all
Government restriction	6.7	16.9	18.1	58.3
No means to clear bush	23.3	48.5	27.3	0.9
No land to obtain	4.3	19.6	33.7	42.9
Money/credit	70.2	20.9	7.7	0.9
Labor shortage	15.0	43.9	35.3	4.9

Table 8.12

Who is Responsible for Solving Farm Problems in Ondo State

	Very Great extent	Great extent	Some extent	Not at all
Government	4.6	4.0	7.4	83.4
Extension Service	1.2	4.6	5.8	88.0
Oneself	76.4	18.4	4.9	0.3

It is demonstrated and confirmed so far in this chapter that there are phenomenal problems confronting the local farmers in general. These problems, mainly, are beyond the control of the local farmer, who has only rudimentary means and inadequate finances to solve them. Unfortunately, very little has been done on the part of the government, despite its claims, to help the farmers deal with these problems, even in areas that the government should be directly involved in.

The pages that follow highlight in a similar fashion the general characteristics of the local farmers and their problems in the more drought-prone Sokoto State. Some comparative analysis will be made as the discussion progresses.

Study II: Characteristics of Local Farmers in Sokoto State

The general characteristics of the local farmers in Sokoto State are quite different from those of Ondo State, described earlier. Figure 8.2 represents the study area. The Hausas constitute the majority of people in the state, making up 90.1 percent of the sample interviewees. Another group that is relatively numerous in the north is the Fulani-speaking people.

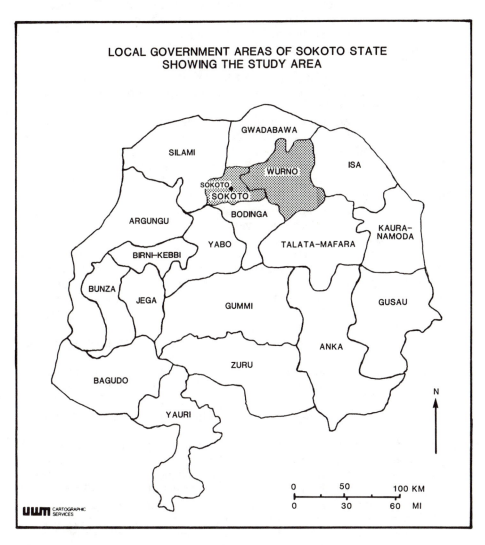

LOCAL GOVERNMENT AREAS OF SOKOTO STATE
SHOWING THE STUDY AREA

FIGURE 8.2

This group, however, represents only 6.0 percent of the sample. The 6 percent is not representative of the group because in actuality its members are the second biggest ethnic group in the North, and Sokoto State has been a residence for a large number of them. The low turnout rate may be explained by the more nomadic life-style of the Fulani people, who make up the majority of the animal husbandmen in the country. In addition, a small percentage (2.0) of Yorubas was encountered, and the rest were from other ethnic groups.

Dome-shaped huts built of bamboo materials and leaves are customary in this part of the country. However, homes built of red brick and cement blocks are quite common in the larger towns as well. Farmers in the Sokoto State study area are quite younger than the farmers in Ondo State. The average age of a farmer in this area was 36.7 years, compared to the 48.7 for Ondo State (Table 8.1). Of the total number of 302 farmers interviewed, 43 percent were 30 years or younger, and 29 percent were between the ages of 30 and 40. Only 15 percent, compared to 36 percent, was older than 50 years. This relatively younger population in the farming sector is reflective of the very high illiteracy rate in the state compared to Ondo State. In fact, only a very small number of the interviewees communicated with the researcher personally in the locally spoken English, commonly called "*pidgin English.*"

The farmers were asked how long they had been farming on their own. An average of 17.4 years was recorded, with 28 percent of the respondents having over 20 years of farming experience compared to the 46 percent in Ondo State for that category. On the other hand, a high percentage of 36 percent had only 10 years or less of farming compared to the 21 percent reported for Ondo State.

An average family size in the Sokoto State study area was 7.0 members, with an average of 1.95 wives and 3.8 children who lived at home and depended on the farmer. And of the family members who had moved out, an average of only 0.55 members still depended on the farmer for income and existence. Children alone accounted for 96 percent of this figure, with the rest from other family members. However, 66.6 percent of the respondents had no children or had children who were old enough to move to other cities. In fact, 18.9 percent of the farmers had no children at all. And since over 50 percent of the farmers were less than 35 years old, it was quite apparent that the majority of their children were still living at home with them. Thus the average dependents of a typical farmer in the Sokoto State study area was 7.55 including the farmer. This figure is quite low compared to the relatively high thirteen members that was recorded in Ondo State.

An average farmer cultivates 13.2 acres of land. This is substantially higher than the 9.1 acres average for Ondo State. And when this figure is broken up, it is observed that 29 percent of the farmers cultivated less than 5 acres or less, 31 percent 5-10 acres, 23 percent 10-20 acres, and only 5 percent 40 acres or more. This relatively high average of land under cultivation can be attributed to the physical conditions that exist in the study area. Here the land is open grassland, which is much easier to cultivate than the dense forest condition of the southern states. In addition, the significantly younger age bracket of the farmers could contribute to a more energetic farming group than that of older farmers in Ondo State.

An average of 6.7 persons of the sample work on a farm in Sokoto State. Ninety-one percent of the respondents indicated working on their own farms. However, only 1.7 percent responded that their wives worked with them on the farm, compared to the 90 percent for Ondo State. The very low percentage of wives working with their husbands can be attributed to the religious affiliation of this particular ethnic group (Islamic), which does not allow wives to work outside of the house. As a matter of fact, the researcher saw very few women outside, and the majority of them he did see were outside of the Hausa-Fulani ethnic groups. It is quite probable that the 1.7 percent were from farmers of other ethnic groups, as mentioned above. A little over 82 percent responded having some form of laborers working for them, and only 27.5 percent said that their children worked for them.

Ninety-six percent of the sample indicated using crude hoes for cultivating their land, 14.6 percent used a cutlass or machete, and 25.5 percent used axes. However, a relatively high 11.6 percent indicated using tractors, mostly through rental services, on their farms. This is over 10 times more frequently as in Ondo State. The open physical condition that exists in this part of the country may have contributed to the more frequent use of tractors.

Table 8.13 represents the land ownership of each farmer in the local government area. Of the total sample, 89.1 percent owned some form of land, of which 75.2 percent indicated farming a land that belonged entirely to them; another 9.6 percent owned most of the land. Only 10.9 percent owned no land of their own but used land that belonged to other categories, as detailed in the Table. Of those who did not have land of their own 7.6 percent used family land for their entire farming business. Another 2.3 rented the entire land. This left less than 15 percent of the farmers using fragmented holdings that belonged to two or more categories of land ownership.

In Sokoto State two grain crops (millet and guinea corn) stand out as the major crops having been accorded great importance in land use. Over 50 percent of the respondents devoted most or all of their land for the production of millet. Another 20.5 percent used half the land for this particular crop. About

70 percent of the farmers were raising guinea corn on their land, and over 90 percent interplanted these major staples with vegetables and other crops. Rice, cowpea beans, and cassava were to a smaller extent grown in the study area as well, and were also interplanted with other crops. Two export crops, cotton and groundnut, were raised as well, but their importance is now waning. Table 8.14 represents the distribution of the vari-

Table 8.13

Land Ownership in Sokoto State

	All	Most	Half	Some	None
Land owned					
by farmer	75.2	9.6	2.3	2.0	10.9
by family	7.6	2.3	1.0	5.6	83.5
Land rented by farmer	2.3	-	1.0	3.3	93.4
Land use					
without permission	-	-	0.3	0.3	99.4
with permission	-	-	0.3	0.7	99.0
Land shared with owner	0.3	0.3	-	0.3	99.0
Other types of ownership	-	-	-	-	100.0

Table 8.14

Land Used for Growing in Sokoto State

	All	Most	Half	Little	None
Cassava	3.6	0.7	0.3	14.9	80.1
Rice	1.7	2.3	2.6	19.2	74.2
Millet	4.3	49.3	20.5	13.6	12.3
Cocoa	0.0	0.3	0.3	0.0	99.3
Cotton	0.0	0.0	0.3	9.9	89.3
Groundnut	0.3	0.3	2.3	24.8	71.9
Soyabeans	0.0	0.3	0.3	5.0	94.4
Maize/corn	0.0	0.0	0.3	16.9	82.8
Guinea corn	0.3	3.0	4.6	61.9	30.1
Oil palm	-	-	-	-	100.0
Cocoyam	-	-	-	-	100.0
Yam	-	-	-	-	100.0
Rubber	-	-	-	-	100.0
Wheat	-	-	0.3	0.3	99.3
Plantain/banana	-	-	-	1.3	98.7
Cowpeas	0.7	0.0	3.3	39.7	56.0
Vegetables	0.3	0.3	0.3	12.6	86.8
Livestock	-	-	-	14.9	85.1

ous crops as indicated by the farmers interviewed. As can be seen in Table 8.15, quite a large number of interviewees sold their cash crops (cotton and groundnut) in the open market and to individuals (Table 8.16). However, as indicated in Table 8.15, very little was sold from the more widely grown crops such as millet, guinea corn, and rice. This suggests that the majority of the farmers and their immediate families consumed most of the proceeds from their farming. Considering the relatively large piece of land that farmers, on the average, cultivate, their moderate family size compared to that in other parts of the country, and the relatively high yield per acre from some of these crops, we should expect a higher selling return from the farmers. But this is not the case. Generally, farmers in this study area believe that they produced enough food to feed themselves, but not enough to sell to others. This last point is reflective of their somewhat high response compared to Ondo State's, in favor of the state producing enough food to feed its population.

Table 8.15

Proportion of Farm Products Sold in Sokoto State

	All	Most	Half	Little	None
Cassava	2.6	4.0	1.3	4.6	7.0
Rice	1.7	2.3	1.7	4.6	13.6
Millet	0	1.7	2.0	12.9	68.2
Cocoa	-	-	-	-	-
Cotton	5.6	3.0	0.3	0.3	1.7
Groundnut	10.3	7.0	0.7	3.6	5.6
Soyabeans	0	1.3	0	2.0	2.3
Maize/corn	2.6	3.0	1.3	2.6	7.9
Guinea corn	0	1.7	1.7	11.9	52.9
Oil palm	-	-	-	-	-
Cocoyam	-	-	-	-	-
Yam	-	-	-	-	-
Rubber	-	-	-	-	-
Wheat	0.3	0.3	-	-	0.3
Plantain/banana	0.3	0.3	0.3	0.3	0.7
Cowpeas	8.3	10.6	3.0	3.0	18.9
Vegetables	1.7	7.6	0	1.7	3.0
Livestock	1.3	7.3	0.3	0.7	4.3
Other	0.3	0	0.3	0	0.3

Table 8.16

Quantity of Products Sold in Different Markets in Sokoto State

	All	Most	Half	Little	None
In the markets	42.1	14.2	3.3	3.6	26.5
To cooperatives	2.6	-	0.7	0.3	28.5
To individuals	6.3	3.0	3.3	14.6	25.5
Other (specify)	0.0	0.3	0.3	0.3	16.2

Finances and Seed Provision

Tables 8.17 and 8.18 represent how the local farmer receives his finances and seeds from various possible sources. Again the local farmer is left to provide for his farm needs. In the 1975-80 plan it was claimed that in 1980 alone over 2,130 bags of improved seeds of rice,wheat, maize, and guinea corn were dis-

Table 8.17
How Farmers Obtained Finances for Farming in Sokoto State

	All	Most	Half	Little
Personal savings	64.0	19.5	2.0	2.0
Family/friends	11.9	1.7	1.0	13.6
Cooperative society	0.0	0.0	0.3	1.0
Government aids	0.0	0.3	0.7	4.3
Other	0.3	0.0	0.0	2.0

tributed to farmers in Sokoto State. Financial aid (over ₦4.0 million) in the form of credit was supposedly given to farmers to purchase agricultural machinery and other tools and implements. In addition, 23,800 tons of assorted fertilizer were distributed to farmers during the period 1975-79 (*Sokoto State Fourth National Development Plan* 1981-85). Obviously, the data in the tables do not support the claims of the government. Sixty-four percent of the sample indicated that they provided all of the finances from their own savings for their farm needs. An additional 19.5 percent responded that they provided most of the money for their farm needs. Families and friends play a more crucial role in Sokoto State than in Ondo State. Here 11.9 percent of the respondents received all of their money from families or friends, and some 16 percent indicated receiving some help from families and friends. On the other hand, only 5 percent of the sample received any aid from the government at all.

186

The case in Sokoto State is disturbing in that the study area happened to be close to the seat of the state government, which for all practical purposes received the lion's share of many government funded activities. If farm communities only 10 to 20 miles away from the state capital, with 70 percent of its land under cultivation, do not benefit much from the government, it is doubtful that communities much less accessible to the government, with an underutilized land area of 70, 80 and, at times, up to 90 percent (*Ibid*), will receive any financial aid from the government. Farmers who live close to big cities normally have far more influence and access to city-base government services than those further removed from the cities, who, generally, do not know their rights and privileges. Furthermore, these people can be easily intimidated and brushed aside by the city-based politicians, if they come at all to demand that their rights be protected.

With regard to seed, almost 65 percent of the sample claimed to provide all of their seeds from previous years, with another 23.5 percent providing most of their seeds from previous years. A smaller percentage of the interviewees bought their seeds from the open market. The government, along with the cooperatives who claimed to have helped the farmers in seed provision, seemed to have contributed nothing in seed provision to farmers. Only a meager 3.6 percent of the sample received some form of seed provision from either the government or cooperatives.

Table 8.18

How Farmers Obtained Seeds for Farming in Sokoto State

	All	Most	Half	Little
In the market	7.9	1.0	2.0	21.2
From previous years	64.9	23.5	2.3	1.0
Provided by government	0.0	0.0	0.7	2.3
Provided by cooperatives	0.0	0.0	0.3	0.3
other	-	-	-	-

Problems Farmers Face in Sokoto State

Sokoto is one of four most likely states to be drought-stricken in the entire country. As a result, weather related problems should be more often felt here than in the southern states. But not all of the state falls within the drought zone. The southern portion receives an average rainfall of over 50 inches and this decreases progressively to about 20 inches in the extreme north. The Sokoto station (lat. 13° 1'N), the north-ernmost station with available rainfall data (Table 4.2), receives an average rainfall of over 25 inches, with a 55 year average of 29 inches (*Federal Office of Statistics, Annual Abstract of Statistics , 1971 p. 4*). The average rainfall here should be very close to the minimum of any station in the country, except probably in the very northern tip of Borno State, where average rainfall is about 20 inches.

Farmers in the Sokoto State study area were presented with the same eleven possible questionnaire problems as in Ondo State. Table 8.19 represents the results of the response of the farmers. The three naturally related problems (water supply, soil fertility, and weed and pest control) ranked high among the problems farmers face in this part of the state. In fact, water supply, next to the problem of money, is the most serious problem, rated at over 80 percent. However, the problem of water is not necessarily related to climatic factors such as drought and inadequate rainfall. It is probably more a problem of a technical know-how than climate.

Table 8.19

Seriousness of Certain Problems in Farming in Sokoto State

	Very Serious problem	Somewhat Serious	Serious	No
Water supply	57.3	27.5	12.9	2.3
Transportation	22.5	17.9	21.2	38.4
Marketing	17.5	14.6	24.5	43.4
Storage	16.6	5.0	7.9	70.5
Price	29.5	12.3	20.5	37.4
Labor supply	20.9	11.3	13.6	54.0
Planting/harvesting	25.2	12.3	17.5	44.7
Soil fertility	39.4	14.9	27.2	17.5
Credit/money	66.6	18.5	9.3	4.6
Pest/weed control	35.8	17.9	27.8	17.9
Quality seed	27.2	7.9	25.8	38.4

The response of the farmers with regard to climate (Table 8.20) obviously rules out climate as the cause of the problem of water supply in this part of the state. While the problems of soil, pests, and weeds are not as serious as they are in the southern state, they are still very expensive to deal with for farmers with very limited income.

188

In regard to the human related problem, the money factor is the most often mentioned enigma in agricultural development. In fact, some 85 percent of the sample (302 farmers) said that availability of money was a serious problem to farming. Only 4.6 percent did not see money as a serious problem in their farming business.

It is interesting to note that the three infrastructurally related factors (transportation, marketing, and storage facilities) ranked low among the problems. Indeed, over 70 percent of the sample said that storage was not a problem for them. This should not be surprising, given the fact that most of the products are consumed by the farmers' immediate families, with little or no marketable leftovers. Moreover, most of the grains produced are not as perishable as those crops raised in the southern states.

The little or no marketable agricultural foodstuffs also explain the somewhat high response (43.4 percent) that marketing was not a big threat to agricultural development. The market, by itself, is not a problem in Nigeria, but if large quantities of foodstuffs had to be hauled to the nearest marketplaces, where there were inadequate storage facilities, then a complex problem would arise. For those who produce more than they can consume at home, storage and marketing are very serious considerations in agriculture, as is a reliable transportation network. The problem of transportation, even though not as pronounced as in the south, still sets limits on how much farmers are willing to produce. While a large number of the farmers rely heavily on animals (donkeys and horses in particular) for transporting their goods to the market, which might have influenced the result, accessible roads are still in their seminal stages, even though the study area was in the vicinity of the state capital.

Nowhere did the problems based on human intuition pose as much threat as they did in the southern study area. There, even the provision of seed, price, and harvesting and planting were all rated as less threatening in agriculture than in the other state, as can be seen in Tables 8.8 and 8.19. As low as these results are compared to those of Ondo State, they are still significant because, overall, some 55 to 60 percent still perceived these as a threat to agricultural development. And these figures are very high for a country whose development strategy has been capital-city biased.

In response to a question asked about the weather conditions for the years they could remember, farmers in general thought that weather has been no serious threat to them (Table 8.20). In fact, over 90 percent of the sample rated weather as generally fair to very good. This, again, supports the weather statistics for the study area in Chapter 4, Table 4.2. When the same question was asked for the past five years, the response was even more positive than in the more humid southern state. Indeed, over 85 percent of the sample said that the weather conditions from 1980 to 1983 had been favorable, but, of course, in 1984 they were still waiting for the rain to come, and it began during the last two days of the field study. As indicated in Chapter 4, the rainy season in this part of the country runs from mid-May to about mid-September. The respondents, therefore, had no way of knowing what the weather would be like for about half of the season when the interview was made. However, the southern state, which had already received much of its rain, responded differently for this same year, with over 90 percent thinking the weather conditions in the state were favorable.

Table 8.20

Weather Condition in Sokoto State

	Very Good	Good	Fair	Bad	Very Bad	Don't Know
General	7.9	45.7	37.4	3.4	3.6	1.3
1980	28.8	32.8	27.8	3.6	2.0	0.7
1981	29.1	30.8	31.5	2.3	2.0	0.0
1982	26.8	25.2	36.8	5.6	1.3	0.3
1983	12.3	29.1	41.4	8.9	4.3	0.3
1984	4.3	13.2	26.5	23.5	8.6	20.2

Most farmers in Sokoto state believed that the state was producing enough food to feed its population. Some 51 percent said that the state was producing either enough or more than enough food. Another 21 percent also indicated that the state was probably producing enough food to feed the population, and only about 28 percent believed that the state was not producing enough food to feed the population. On the other hand, over 43 percent of the sample believed that the country, as a whole, was not producing enough food. This figure is much lower than the more than 90 percent response from the southern state that the country did not produce enough food to feed its population. Apparently, most of the farmers in the Sokoto State study area did not know what was going on in other parts of the country. While their response seemed to be consistent with the question, with regard to the number of farmers in the state and of the country, they also believed that there was a need that more people farm in the country as a whole. In fact, over 95 percent believed that more people should be involved in farming in order for the country to produce more food for the population (Table 8.21).

According to Table 8.21, some 97 percent of the sample saw the need for individual farmers to expand their land for the production of more food. Indeed, fewer than one percent saw no need for an individual farmer to expand his land area under cultivation. This, obviously, shows why the majority (99 percent) of them were actually willing to farm more land if they were given the right incentives. Without exception, all the other variables were accorded a very important place in curtailing the food deficits. Apparently, availability of land is not the problem, as implied in their responses in Table 8.21 as well as in Table 8.22 below, which show that over 45 percent of the sample said that there was no problem in obtaining more land to cultivate, but they were restricted by inadequate means of clearing the bush for cultivation. The fact that some 60 percent of the sample still saw land clearing as a threat to agricultural expansion in this basically grassy part of the country makes one wonder about what the government is willing to do for the local farmer, who produces the bulk of the country's agricultural products. This is further compounded by limited financial resources (some 90 percent), limited labor (60 percent), and, for a very significant percentage (70 percent), government restriction. The land restriction by the government in this part of the country has been noted since the colonial era, when the northern land was first vested into the hands of the regional governor. But it was ineffective until the independent government continued to acquire the best land for its distorted agricultural projects, which intensified in the 1970s and 80s, and vested all land to the states under the Land Use Act of 1978, making land unlimitedly available for both foreign and domestic capitalistic investment (chapter 5). Farmers, as a result, are being pushed off of their land, especially in the north, where the land is easier to clear. Since they did not have the resources to back up loans to buy more land, small-holders, who were dispossessed of their land, were either left without any properties to drift to the major cities, or to till the less desirable farmland. These farmers in Sokoto State were, therefore, responding to what they had observed happening to the local farmers and to the impending catastrophe that they themselves face because of the constraints imposed by the government. As a result, local farmers in this part of the country were ambivalent about what might happen to them if this trend continued.

When farmers were asked who was responsible for solving their farm-related problems identified above, a very high percentage (over 80 percent) as shown in Table 8.23 believed in solving their own farm problems. However, the government played a more significant role here in Sokoto State than in Ondo State, as can be seen in the Table. Only 39 percent stated that the government was not responsible for solving their farm problems, compared to the 83 percent rating in Ondo State. Several reasons could be cited to explain this high response in favor of the government: Moslems, in general, do not want to blame their leaders for society's woes, and they trust their leaders to do what can be done. This point can also be extended to explain their response about the weather conditions as well. Some were ready to point out, *"We don't want to blame Allah (God) for the weather. There is nothing the Government can do about the weather or water."* It took a lot of explanation to get them to answer the questions objectively without subverting the intent of the questions. However, with regard to the weather conditions, the statistics in Chapter 4 confirmed their response.

Table 8.21

Importance of Certain Factors in Producing More food in Sokoto State

	Very import.	Import.	Somewhat import.	Not import.
Farm expansion by individual	83.4	13.9	1.7	0.7
More people farming	65.6	30.1	2.0	2.0
Modern methods of farming	68.2	20.9	8.3	2.3
Providing improved seeds	45.7	30.5	20.9	2.6
Providing fertilizer	65.2	23.8	8.9	1.7

Table 8.22

Limiting Factors in Obtaining More Land for Farming in Sokoto State

	Very great extent	Great extent	Some extent	Not at all
Government restriction	46.7	5.3	18.2	29.5
No means to clear bush	25.5	29.5	15.6	29.1
No land to obtain	21.2	8.6	23.8	45.7
Money/credit	66.6	22.2	6.3	4.0
Labor shortage	24.8	12.9	22.2	38.7

Table 8.23

Who is Responsible for Solving Farm Problems in Sokoto State

	Very Great extent	Great extent	Some extent	Not at all
Government	17.5	14.9	28.1	39.1
Extension Service	4.6	7.9	16.2	70.2
Oneself	70.5	10.6	11.6	7.1

Secondly, the ousted President Shagari came from a Moslem ruling class in this part of the country and might have made some impression on the state, it being his home. This point is very important in that it is reflected in the answer to the questions regarding the performances of individual government regimes, as discussed in the following section.

Furthermore, much of the agricultural development that took place in recent years, especially under the Shagari administration regime, had been northern states biased as well, with Sokoto, a partly drought-prone state, presently being the leading food producer in the union. One of the huge irrigation projects the country has successfully participated in is also in this part of the country. This allowed several fortunate nearby farmers, who were not dispossessed, to have access to irrigated plots. And the distribution of fertilizer in the 1982 season, for example, as shown in Tables 8.24 and 8.25, has been northern states' biased. The states of Kaduna and Sokoto, two of the most likely states to be partly drought-stricken, got the greatest share in the distribution of fertilizer. The two states combined accounted for over 35 percent of the total distribution. In addition, the distribution of fertilizer to different government projects shows an equally northern bias, with Sokoto Rima BDA and Hadeija Jamare RBDA, both in the far north, receiving the greater share (Table 8.25).

More important still is the preponderant illiteracy of the community's people, who are little informed about their rights and privileges with regard to government services, and, therefore, may not be aware of the services they deserve. In fact, several of them pointed out that they did not know that the government was involved in their private agricultural venture.

In conclusion, it should be noted that there are several overriding problems in the Sokoto State study area with regard to agricultural expansion. The most often mentioned obstacle is money, which, of course, dictates how the other problems can be properly dealt with. An individual farmer with holdings of two or three acres of land obviously will not have enough finances to solve his problems. Money is needed to pay laborers to help clear the bush, which most of the farmers said was a serious obstacle to an individual farmer who depends only on crude hoes and cutlasses to expand his land area.

Table 8.24

Quantities of Fertilizer Distribution to States, 1982

State	Quantity Projected	Quantity Delivered
Abuja**	5,200	3,310
Anambra	35,000	19,157
Bauchi*	55,000	41,716
Bendel	19,400	10,418
Benue	31,000	42,618
Borno*	25,000	23,314
Cross River	9,000	2,975
Gongola*	28,200	25,962
Imo	15,000	13,077
Kaduna*	160,000	112,289
Kano*	50,000	39,231
Kwara	10,000	9,945
Lagos	2,500	1,035
Niger*	7,000	6,914
Ogun	2,000	5,000
Ondo	2,340	1,670
Oyo	15,000	12,228
Plateau*	60,000	37,237
Rivers	3,400	3,279
Sokoto*	200,000	55,003

Source: Federal Ministry of Agriculture, Annual Report, 1982, pp. 63

Note: * States in the north.
      ** Federal Capital Territory

Secondly, while availability of land is not, per se, a restricting factor, the government control of the land under the Land Use Act is now taking its toll in this part of the country. The fact that some 70 percent of the sample is already ambivalent with regard to the government factor in land acquisition indicates that the Act is already doing a great damage to agricultural expansion and is taking a pervasive course. It was, therefore, no wonder that the Emirs and Chiefs of the ten northern states held a conference and sent a memorandum to the country's Political Bureau with regard to this particular issue along with other areas of concern, where they blatantly stated that the country had learned few lessons from its past or from the expe-

Table 8.25

Quantities of Fertilizer Distribution to Government Projects, 1982

Project	Quantity Projected	Quantity Delivered
Chad Basin RDA	4,200	2,783
Hadeija-Jamare RBDA	11,800	15,041
Lower Benue RBDA	4,000	5,927
Upper Benue RBDA	5,200	6,394
Niger River BDA	15,500	4,361
Sokoto Rima BDA	–	20,040
Anambra/Imo RBDA	–	1,991
Ayangba ADP	2,250	6,789
Bida ADP	12,400	–
Ilorin ADP	4,500	9,211
Lafia ADP	12,100	9,008
Gombe ADP	33,500	2,556
National Grains Production Company, Kaduna	11,450	9,706
Lagos Warehouse	–	30
National Root Crop Co.	1,864	364
Okitipupa Oil Palm Co.	7,650	885
IAR Samaru, Zaria	2,900	3,130
FDA Oyo (Green Revolution)	–	1,075
Cross River BDA	–	108
FDA Ondo (Green Revolution)	–	150
Kano Agricultural Supply Co.	–	8,074
Deputy Speaker, Kaduna	–	730
National Seed Service	–	150
Funtua ADP	8,800	4,106
Ogun/Oshun RBDA	–	710
S.M.U. Oil Palm, P/Harcourt	370	330
Ayipeku Oil Mills	860	160
FDA Enugu (Green Revolution)	–	485
Bauchi State Agric. Co.	–	2,500
Borno ADP (BOADAP)	–	4,310
Texaco-Agro Ind. Ltd.	–	300
Oyo North ADP	–	500

Source: Federal Ministry of Agriculture, Annual Report, 1982, pp. 63-64

riences of other nations (*West Africa November 3, 1986 pp. 2312-2314*). They therefore called for a reformational amendment of the Land Use Decree, in which they strongly recommended to confer on the Council of Chiefs of every state the control of all rural land in trust for all the people. This, according to them, was the only method by which to guarantee that land was allocated to only those who stood in real need of it, and to protect the rural community from being rendered landless.

Farmers seemed to be pressed with these two issues in Sokoto State, which, therefore, seemed to render other problems not as important. This should be well taken, since without money or land and in the face of being threatened with the loss of his only means of survival, nobody would care about those issues on the bottom of the priority list. They therefore in principle had far more immediate pressing issues to be concerned about than in the south, where the Land Use Act has not taken as much of a toll.

Farmers' Opinions about the Role of Government in Agriculture

Included in the field study was the difficult task of getting farmers to voice their opinions about the government's function in agricultural development. Several factors made this aspect of the study quite difficult. First of all, over 95 percent of the rural population was functionally illiterate, being unable to either read or write. In most cases, then, they were unaware of what the government and its functions should be and unable to articulate their rights and privileges as citizens of the country. Relatively speaking, farmers in Sokoto State are far more removed from the government and its services than those in Ondo State. They are more complacent and enduring and knew very little about what had transpired in the government. Many of the farmers did not know who the presidents were, let alone about their activities in government, and even Azikiwe's name had to be differentiated from Tafawa Balewa's, who was then the prime minister from the north, or that of Ahmadu Bello, the then premier of the northern region.

Secondly, it was anticipated that the farmers would be afraid to respond against any government, especially the current regime, because of its oppressive and intimidating practices against the people. Only a few could dare speak against the government, its policies, and services without any threat from the government itself, and, among those who did speak out, there were consequences such as arson, imprisonment, and even murder. Therefore, interviewing the farmers regarding how they felt about the current government was inconceivable and it resulted in grossly biased responses. It was nonetheless undertaken even though, at times, as soon as the government was mentioned, the farmer wanted to halt the interview. This, obviously, was a delicate matter to deal with. A lot of skill in human relations had to be utilized by the researcher so as to try to get the most frank opinion possible from the farmer and yet not worry or offend him.

In addition, unwillingness to speak against the government had its roots in religion, particularly in the north, as it is against Moslem belief to speak against any leader. A lot of farmers in Sokoto State did not want to talk about the government at all. With the exception of some of those farmers who could read and write — most of whom also worked for the government — very few of the farmers tried to give any suggestions as to how things should be made better for them.

A final area of concern was the issue of language. Although the two dominant languages (Yoruba and the *Pidgin English*) encountered in Ondo state were both known to the researcher, so that his intentions could be communicated effectively, the researcher, did not have this advantage in Sokoto, thereby necessitating a dependence on the interpreters in most cases. So, overall, there was always a question as to whether the interviewers, particularly in Sokoto State, were accurately expressing questions and interpreting responses.

These factors mentioned above made this part of the study particularly difficult, and they have to be taken into consideration in analyzing the responses of the farmers. In comparison, the farmers in Ondo State, on the average, tended to be more candid in their opinions of the government than their northern counterparts, and were more willing to communicate these opinions and give suggestions, especially at the end of the interview.

Response to Individual Governments – Biased or Unbiased?

Considering the claims made by each of these administrations regarding the huge amount of money spent on different agricultural projects, an impact study was made with regard to these claims. Several questions were asked, but because the responses were similar, only one regarding whether or not money spent by each of the different administrations benefited the local farmers is presented here. It is interesting to note how the farmers from the two states responded based on political inclination. Not only did many farmers decline to answer the question, but it seemed that the two states were at odds as to which administration had been doing the worse job, even though no single administration survived the test, especially in the more progressive southern state. While the southern state of Ondo perceived the performance of the Shagari Administration (1979-1983) to be the poorest in this respect, as is consistent with popular belief, the administration of Azikiwe (1960-65) was the worst offender in Sokoto State. Farmers in the northern state clearly responded against Azikiwe (an old enemy from the Ibo tribe) probably based upon what had led to the Civil War, fought between 1967 and 1970. On the other hand, the farmers in Ondo State responded to the immediate cause of the problem, which they felt to be Shagari's unresponsive government, Shagari being a rival party leader of the NPN, and the state being a UPN state.

Farmers in Ondo State were indignant about the manner the Second Republic politicians, under Shagari, betrayed the country's population and looted the limited resources of the country. As expressed by one of the more outspoken farmers: "*It would have been better if there had been no government at all.*" Because their feelings for the Shagari administration were so outstandingly negative, this might have influenced the farmers' responses by regarding the other administrations in a somewhat better light than would actually have been the case were they judged in and of themselves.

With respect to the northerners' negative feelings about Azikiwe: in practice, not even many educated people can blame Azikiwe government for what Nigeria experienced in the 1970s and 1980s because hunger was never experienced during his term in office. However, these old wounds reappeared and, therefore, to the northern Sokoto State, the Azikiwe regime was the worst offender, not Shagari, whose administration brought a relatively rich country to its knees. It is quite apparent, then, that any investigation done of these people with regard to individual governments would be grossly biased because of their political and sectoral inclinations.

Tables 8.26 and 8.27 represent an example of how farmers responded in both states. It is clearly shown that farmers did not benefit from the money spent for agricultural purposes by each of the five regimes, especially in Ondo State. In Table 8.26 none of the administrations received less than a 60 percent disapproval rating from the farmers in Ondo State, which, of course, is significantly high; for the last three regimes the disapproval rate was far more indicative, over 70 percent for Obasanjo, 94 percent for Shagari, and 40 percent (or 88 percent for those who responded) for Buhari. Shagari was apparently the worst offender in Ondo State.

Things were perceived differently in Sokoto State (Table 8.27). The Azikiwe government was seen as the enemy. Seventy-seven percent of those who responded disagreed that the Azikiwe administration had spent money to benefit farmers. On the other hand, the Shagari administration, whose activities brought the entire country into complete decay, was given a 50 percent approval, which is significantly higher than the 3.1 percent approval that this administration received from the southern state. The fact that 47 percent of the respondents (a population which, in the main, will not speak against their leaders) disagreed with the statement indicates that a significant number of farmers were disappointed by Shagari.

Table 8.26

Opinion as to Whether or not Money Spent by each Government Regime Benefited Farmers in Ondo State

	Strongly Agree	Agree	Disagree	Strongly Disagree	No Comm.	Don't Know
Azikiwe	0.0	22.1	44.8	16.6	6.1	10.4
Gowon	0.9	27.3	47.8	14.7	4.0	5.2
Obasanjo	4.3	20.2	50.0	21.2	1.2	3.1
Shagari	0.6	2.5	32.8	61.6	0.6	1.8
Buhari	0.9	4.6	27.3	13.2	35.6	18.4

Table 8.27

Opinion as to Whether or not Money Spent by Each Government Regime Benefited Farmers in Sokoto State

	Strongly Agree	Agree	Disagree	Strongly Disagree	No Comm.	Don't Know
Azikiwe	2.3	11.3	24.2	21.5	7.6	33.1
Gowon	9.3	23.5	21.5	23.2	7.6	14.9
Obasanjo	6.6	33.1	23.2	25.2	5.0	7.0
Shagari	15.2	34.8	21.2	25.8	1.7	1.3
Buhari	5.6	19.5	18.9	22.8	25.5	7.6

The Buhari administration also received a very high negative response from Sokoto State. Over 62 percent of those farmers who dared to respond (or 41.7 percent of the total) about the Buhari administration indicated that they did not benefit from the money spent by this administration. That was very high for a government which came to rescue the country from the hands of the Second Republic politicians and had just been in office for only eight months when the farmers were interviewed. The very fact that over 33 percent (54 percent for Ondo State) did not want to comment about this government indicates that there was already mounting disapproval and fear, due to the oppres-

199

sion, about the Buhari administration. Therefore, these possibly biased responses could not be interpreted to prove any hypothesis, though at this time they seem to support the issues raised in this study. Thus a general question was asked relating to the problems of farmers without any mention of a particular administration.

Government and the Problems of Farmers

In the last few sections several points were indirectly raised in regard to the government factor in solving some of the problems of farmers, and it was generally confirmed that government was of little help to the farmers with respect to finances, seed provision, and the clearing of the bush. In addition, farmers, especially in Sokoto State and to a lesser extent in Ondo State, felt that the government was restricting them from expanding their farmland, which was, of course, due to the Land Use Act and the encroachment of farmers through heavy investment on large-scale agricultural programs, as discussed extensively in Chapter 5.

Several matters of concern were identified which farmers thought the government should help them with. The first of these problems was the issue of finances. It was learned from the interviews that farmers generally believed that if they were provided with loans it would help solve some of their most pressing problems. They felt they could use the money to buy what was needed most in their farming business. Over 95 percent of the farmers from both states saw some need for the government to be involved in helping with their finances.

The burden of bush clearing should to a great extent be borne by the government, especially in the thickly forested southern states. Farmers with holdings of a few acres cannot afford to buy the heavy equipment needed to clear such land. The government should purchase such equipment and offer it to those who really need it the most, not to large capitalist farmers who have a greater chance of buying their own and/or having the requirements to obtain such a loan. That is the reason why those farmers who wanted to clear the land and expand their farms resorted to burning the bush. Over 99 percent of the farmers in Ondo and 78 percent in Sokoto State indicated that the government should help them clear some of the land for cultivation.

The majority of the farmers (75 and 90 percent respectively for Ondo and Sokoto States) felt that the government should help them with supplying water, which is needed in virtually all rural areas. Whether for domestic use or farming purposes, a reliable supply of water is necessarily a public sector problem. The government, however, has never seen the need for providing water for the rural population. None of the over 40 village communities in which the research was conducted had safe pipe-borne drinking water, even among the villages which could be called cities in the western world sense (5,000 to 10,000 persons). A large number of the rural population does not know the function of the government in providing safe drinking water for the citizens, and, at times, does not even know that such services are to be provided by the government. This situation is quite disturbing, because in Ondo State adequate rain is received yearly, yet, this abundant natural water supply cannot be provided safely for the citizens in spite of the heavy investment by the Ondo State government in providing safe drinking water. The situation of Sokoto State is even more puzzling in that both the Federal and State governments are engaged in water resource programs especially for farming purposes, through heavy investment in irrigation projects and other water projects.

Farmers, in addition, sought help from the government in the provision of fertilizer, quality seed, pesticides, and insecticides. The provision of fertilizer and seeds has been the only area in which the government in recent years has been involved in making them amply available for farmers. The government, however, admitted that the consumption rate is still less than 2 kilograms of plant nutrients per hectare of cultivated land, which is much lower than the recommended 18.5 kilograms per hectare.

To continue, the farmers were asked how well the government was helping them to solve some of these identified problems. The respondents' answers are presented in Tables 8.28 and 8.29. The supplying of fertilizer seemed to be the only area in which the government was involved. Between 1976 and 1983, the government, out of desperation under the OFN and GR programs discussed earlier, was involved in providing fertilizer for farmers at subsidized prices so that farmers could buy them more cheaply. But the bulk of the fertilizer supplied by the government went to the northern states (Table 5.3 and Tables 8.24 and 8.25), which is reflected in the response of the farmers. While in the southern Ondo State over 55 percent of the sample implicitly said that the government was not doing a good job providing fertilizers for the farmers, only 22.5 percent felt the same in Sokoto State. However, although the supply of fertilizer seemed to be better dealt with in comparison with the other identified problems, in and of itself, it still had a poor performance. The fact that 35 and 36 percent for Ondo and Sokoto States, respectively, could only say that a fair job had been done with regard to fertilizer supply indicates that the government was not doing an encouraging job in providing fertilizer to farmers. Ironically the supply of fertilizer was amply available but most of the time, according to the government, it did not even reach the farmers, or even if it did, it was not

201

delivered in time. This same manner of response is reflected in the case of seed provision, even though, as pointed out earlier in the chapter, over 97 percent of the sample provided their own seeds without any help from the government.

Table 8.28

How Well is Government Helping to Solve these Problems in Ondo State

	Very Good	Good	Fair	Bad	Very Bad	Don't Know
Finances	0.0	2.1	7.7	51.5	38.3	0.3
Water Problem	0.0	8.9	21.5	46.0	19.6	4.0
Providing						
seed	0.6	2.8	38.0	39.6	18.4	0.6
fertilizer	0.9	7.7	35.6	33.7	21.5	0.6
Clearing bush	0.3	0.9	6.7	46.3	44.8	0.6

Table 8.29

How Well is Government Helping to Solve these Problems in Sokoto State

	Very Good	Good	Fair	Bad	Very Bad	Don't Know
Finances	2.0	5.0	12.6	31.5	46.4	1.7
Water Problem	4.0	7.6	24.2	33.4	25.5	4.3
Providing						
seed	3.6	6.6	35.8	24.5	26.8	1.7
fertilizer	13.6	25.5	36.8	8.3	14.2	2.7
Clearing bush	2.6	5.0	18.5	26.2	43.4	3.3

Although the provision of fertilizer and seed is important, it is probably not the most pressing need for most farmers in the country. Again we are brought back to the issue of money. Obviously, farmers have to have money to buy the so-called subsidized fertilizer or seed. But money is most needed to buy other farm materials and to pay the laborers who work for them. Farmers implicitly indicated that money was needed to pay especially those laborers who cleared the bush. This was a difficult problem for them to deal with in that the clearing of the bush is a very hard, tedious, and at times life-threatening job, due to snakes and other environmental hazards, that some people are not willing to do. If one finds such laborers to do the job, they often dictate the wages and they want to be paid immediately. They may even demand their salary before the work is done or, at times, run away without doing the work. Not many of these farmers can afford such problems, and those who accept them must resort to traditional means of borrowing with interest rates so high that, in reality, they end up working for the loaner. Furthermore, most of these loaners demand their money to be paid at the end of the season. It is, therefore, not surprising that the farmers responded the way they did with regard to finances and bush clearance. These two problems seem to be the most pressing ones for them. In Ondo State 91 percent of the sample indicated that the government has been doing a poor performance in this respect. Only four farmers out of 326 said the government was doing a good job. Even in the Sudan Savanna state of Sokoto, where the land is more open, and where the government's agricultural programs have been concentrated, almost 70 percent thought the government was doing a poor job clearing the bush for farmers.

With regard to credit, in Ondo State almost 90 percent of the sample felt that the government was doing a terrible job in providing financial aid in the form of credit to farmers, and some 78 percent said the same in Sokoto State. Likewise, only 2 percent in Ondo and 7 percent in Sokoto thought the government was doing a good job in helping farmers with their finances.

Farmers, especially the relatively more progressive ones in Ondo State, were aware that the government loaned money as credit to farmers. But they were also cognizant of the fact that money allocated to local farmers was being given or diverted to businesspeople in the cities and was then being used for purposes other than farming. None of the farmers mentioned their lack of credit-worthiness as perhaps being a factor in not being able to obtain loans, which is actually due to the unreasonable requirements placed upon them.

We have seen in this section, also, that the government of Nigeria has indeed neglected the farmers who produce to feed the bulk of the population. No single administration from Independence to date has performed well in helping the farmers. However, the farmers identified the worst offenders in their own way. The Shagari administration, which claimed to have done more than the other governments in helping the rural population, was the most notorious in its neglect in Ondo State, while the Azikiwe government was the worst offender in Sokoto State.

Finally, not only was the hypothesis that there was a neglected rural sector confirmed, but the hypothesis of a development priority which discriminated against the agricultural sector was established. Inadequate credit was perceived by farmers as the most serious problem in both states, and, as a matter of fact, the government has not found a way to improve the situation in the face of distorted development strategies and widespread corruption.

Chapter 9

Summary and Conclusion

Summary of Major Findings

The most visible expression of the economy of Nigeria and other countries of Africa is the abiding human creation of social inequality, unemployment, poverty, and hunger, and their related ills. Agriculture, which is the mainstay of the continent's population, is in complete disarray. Nigeria, a country which was self-sufficient in food in the 1950s, 60s, and early 70s has been unable to feed itself since the mid 1970s. Production of all agricultural products has declined. Land area under cultivation in 1981 was less than one-half that of 1965, although the country is still enormously blessed with arable land. The country was once a world leader in exporting several agricultural products, most of which no longer find their way to the export market. The country engaged in substituting domestic production with imported foodstuffs and spent enormous amounts of money importing food that could be produced locally. It even imported some of those same products it used to export. This decline in agricultural activities coincides with the period in which the country became a leading petroleum exporter. With the potential of a more lucrative petroleum export market, the country turned its back on the more lasting agriculture resource base, whose population mass migrates to the cities to share the oil money there.

The petroleum expansion did not, in itself, bring about the decline in the agricultural sector of the Nigerian economy, but its mismanagement contributed to the acceleration of the already existing process. Instead of complementing the agricultural economy through proper management of the oil money, the government neglected the rural based economy and adopted policies that demoralized farmers.

In this work, some of the commonly cited explanations for the problem of agricultural underdevelopment in Nigeria and many other countries on the continent have been disproven. Colonialism and unfavorable climatic conditions, along with the unproductive and inefficient behavior of the rural population, are among those inadequate explanations. They are inad-

205

equate because they do not take into account the mismanagement, corruption, and distorted development strategies prevalent among the leaders of Nigeria and other developing countries. The corrupt practices of men and women in all levels of government and in the private sector, displaced development strategies, and wasteful spending patterns are the invisible monsters devouring the limited resources of the country. Many political leaders in Nigeria and many African countries go into politics to look after their own interests, not those of the country. They close their eyes, minds, and hearts to what is going on around them. In the face of corruption and self-centeredness, individuals cannot be enlightened to see what the problems may be, and if by chance, problems are clearly seen, there is the question of whether or not policies and strategies will be effectively administered. In such an unstable political climate of selfish ambition, not many can do constructive work.

Nigeria has consistently followed development policies that stifle the ability of the local farmer to produce and undermine his innovative capability. Displaced development priorities are made evident by the neglect of the agricultural sector by the government. From the government's investment data, the agricultural sector of the economy received the least attention from the government, but it contributed over 70 percent of the government revenue in the 1960s, and employed about 70 percent of the work force in the country. In addition, the little capital allocated to the agricultural sector and the application of improved practices were export-crop biased.

The smallholder was, and still is, the main producer of all agricultural products in Nigeria, accounting for over 95 percent of the total agricultural output. Plantation-type agriculture by both the government and several private companies and individuals accounts for less than 5 percent of the total output. However, the investment pattern of the government grossly discriminates against the smallholder, who actually sustains the country. Meanwhile all of the agricultural programs, including the credit programs, are designed to benefit the big capitalistic farmers, especially those farmers who produce export crops, rather than the smallholder.

Problems of the Smallholder Farmer

As seen in this investigation, the plight of the smallholder farmer in Nigeria is one brought on by neglect, abuse, and discrimination. The government has never acknowledged the farmer's plight and the circumstances surrounding him as the cause of the declining production of agricultural activities in the country. It has not seen its own creation of social, political, and economic institutions as contributing to the dire state of affairs. And it has never admitted to many of the inequalities and social injustices resulting from its pattern of expenditure and tax policies which favor the urban communities. Instead, the leaders of Nigeria have closed their eyes to the problems of farmers, at the same time exploiting them to the fullest, for the benefit of the urbanites.

Mounting problems exist in the agricultural sector of the economy. Paramount among these are the problems of finances, transportation, storage facilities, water supply, and the clearing of the bush for cultivation. Credit was seen as an endemic problem. The major source of capital was the sale of crops and accrued savings. Money was seen by farmers as a buffer against almost all their farm problems. Farmers with holdings of a very few acres of land cannot be expected to have the adequate resource base to take care of these problems. In addition, the government itself, having abandoned the farmers, has created facilities to remove them from the land, so as to promote its ill-conceived large-scale capital intensive programs that have further depressed the situation — this after having absorbed billions of naira in wasted resources. The Operation Feed the Nation (1976) and the Green Revolution (1980) programs, promoted by the Land Use Act of 1978, were the immediate deliberate actions taken by the government to remove the smallholder from the land. However, in the face of widespread corruption of the ruling class, these programs were never properly administered, nor were their purposes achieved.

Nigeria has the natural and human resources to begin improvements in the country's development. In the national development plans the overriding need stressed by each administration was that for increasing and diversifying agricultural output to achieve self-sufficiency in food supply, and to raise the rural income and living standard. This was followed by the ever increasing amount of money being poured into the sector. However, to follow the word with action has been quite a different matter.

Contrary to what might be expected, the development of agriculture in Nigeria does not require a huge amount of money, such as was spent during the Third and Fourth National Development Plans for wasted resources, making the country worse off than it had been in the periods before and after Independence. Between 1975 and 1984, the period these two plans were in effect, Nigeria spent an average of over one billion naira ($1.7 billion) a year (or ₦11 billion in a 10 year period) importing food that could have been produced locally. In addition, the country's public sector invested probably another ₦10 billion (₦2.1 billion actual expenditure for 1975-80 and unknown amount for 1981-85) in agricultural development over the 10 year period. This does not include what the private sector contributed. Assuming that the total expenditure during the 10 year period was just ₦20 billion — and it is probably far more than that — the country had no need to spend even 50 percent or even 25 percent of this money over the same period to achieve self-sufficiency in all agricultural production for export and domestic needs. What is needed is to make the best use of limited resources and still achieve agricultural self-sufficiency. Well spent money, directed to the vast majority of the farmers who feed the population, would not only bring about the desired result, but help save a huge amount of resources to be utilized for other purposes. The average farmer, who produces the bulk of the agricultural output in Nigeria, needs just ₦50, ₦100 or at most ₦200 each season for his farm activities. But the country is involved in giving credit to those capitalistic farmers who spend the money to finance businesses in the city that have little or nothing to do with agriculture.

Recommendation for Policy Adjustment

Central to the problem of transforming Nigerian agriculture is the status and role of the smallholder farmer, whose problems have not been addressed by the country's leaders. Instead, facilities have been created to alienate him from his only economic base. It has been said by Secretary of State George Schultz (UN Special Session 1986), that "The talents of individual human beings are the greatest resource a society can bring to the tasks of national development" (Chicago Tribune May 29, 1986 p. 16). However, as in Nigeria, the shortcomings of human beings can be the greatest factor in bringing about the decay of a country. The Nigerian government has tried several agricultural policies, all of which in both principle and practice have deliberately excluded the smallholder farmer, who accounts for over 95 percent of the total output of all agricultural products. These types of strategies are distorted, and they demoralize the majority of farmers who feed the country's population. They are neglectful, inhibitive, and exploitative in pushing the real producer to the outskirts of the mainstream of development, and they show a blatant lack of recognition for the people who shoulder the burden of feeding the country.

To help end this rural genocide and transform the agricultural sector, the rural masses need to be liberated from the oppression of the urban elites and the exploitative practices of the government. The core of this liberation would be mass participation by the peasantry in the political processes that would guarantee them political and economic power.

Secondly, the rural sectors bear the burden of providing for the economic development of the urban areas and making a home for the more than 75 percent of the country's population that remains rural. The bulk of the generated revenue should, therefore, be used for the purpose of developing the rural areas. In addition, some of the petroleum revenue, the management of

208

which has been urban biased, should be invested in the rural areas as well, to help solve some of their problems.

Thirdly, since the bulk of the agricultural output is made by the smallholders, any agricultural development strategies should be targeted to them. Included in this are credit programs designed exclusively for the benefit of the smallholder. These programs should be without the rigid requirements set by banks to benefit only a few capitalistic farmers. Smallholder farmers, in general, need just a little financial aid, and do not expect much either. It would be helpful if the government could design some credit programs that would require the small-holder farmer to pay back debts not only in cash, but also in produce. Paying loans back in cash is often too difficult for the smallholder, and the problem is compounded by the exorbitant interest rates private traditional lenders demand for their money.

Fourthly, Nigeria needs to strengthen both its export based agriculture and food production without undue emphasis on one over the other. The present pattern of development strategy in the sector has been that of gross disregard for food crop pro-duction in favor of the export crops. Both of these areas should be emphasized. Export crops are important because a more lasting solid base for the revenue of the country depends on them, as the oil resource will not last forever. Not only are food crops obviously important to feed and sustain the growing population, but the limited resources shouldn't be wasted on importing foodstuffs that can easily be produced domestically. To this effect, also, would be the protection of the farmers' interests as to the prices received for their products. A fair pricing policy for products, which is competitive in relation to other products in the market, should be pursued by the govern-ment. In addition, the government should give a tax break to the farmers who have done more than their share in contribut-ing to the country's development. These policies would help increase rural income.

In the fifth place, mass mobilization of the rural majority should be regarded as a basic imperative, not only for agricul-ture, but for the overall social transformation of the country. In this respect, the present distorted and urban-biased social and economic development priorities should be reoriented to accommodate the rural areas, where over 75 percent of the country's population resides. The establishment of non-farm activities such as small-scale industries (especially those in-dustries relating to agricultural activities) and the provision of appropriate social services needed by any population should be directed to the rural areas, which would help generate employ-ment and arrest rural-urban migration.

And finally, a long-term organizational structure for agriculture should be designed. This should have the small holder as the dominant base, instead of the present large-scale capital-intensive urban based tycoons, who dominate the center in the Nigerian agricultural sector.

Conclusion

Corruption and mismanagement, and a lack of discipline, commitment, and accountability are critical issues for developing countries on the continent of Africa. Progress in the face of any of these multiple evils cannot be possible no matter how naturally and financially blessed the country may be. Considering the enormous importance of the agricultural sector of most of the countries on the African continent, a commensurate growth rate must be achieved through effective rural development policies. The presence of these social and political evils has not only prevented the desired results from occurring, it has forced most of these countries in Africa to settle for being dependent on international food aid programs. Instead of finding and implementing long-term solutions to their food problem, which would gradually dissolve this dependency, they chose to settle for only their immediate needs being met, allowing the evils to continue and heightening their dependency.

The agricultural situation in Nigeria is not a hopeless one, nor was it ever meant to be. In fact, it has a fairly simple solution. The country has all the natural, financial, and human resources available to reverse the present dilemma and to effect a complete turnaround of affairs, probably in a very short time period. Perhaps what is needed is to design a well-planned, integrated, rural development program that involves an active participation of the rural population, especially the smallholder farmers, and a committed leadership to bring about its implementation, based on equity and social justice. The objective of accomplishing self-sufficiency in agricultural production and any meaningful rural development program — stifled under various administrations — cannot be achieved by mere verbal commitment or political rhetoric without action. Neither can the desired objective be reached through exploitation, deceit, and abuse of the masses for the benefit of few urban elites. To emphasize the role of the individual cultivator — the smallholder farmer — is the only practical and feasible way to reverse the situation. To this end, the often inefficient, output-centered approach of the Nigerian government, which benefits only a privileged few capitalistic farmers, should be abolished. The situation will never change for the better unless some concentrated effort is made by the country's leaders to face the issues mentioned above in an honest and open fashion.

210

Appendix

QUESTIONNAIRE (Facts)

General Characteristics

1. Code Number _____

2. Place of Interview   1) Ondo State   2) Sokoto State

3. Language of Interview   1) English   2) Yoruba   3) Hausa   4) Fulani   5) Other

4. Date of Interview

5. Age of Farmer
   1) 15-20   5) 40-50   2) 21-25   6) 50-60
   3) 26-30   7) over 60   4) 31-40

6. Language of Farmer   1) English   2) Yorbua   3) Hausa   4) Fulani   5) Other

7. Where is your permanent hometown? _____

8. When were you last in your permanent home ? _____

9. When do you normally return to your permanent home ? _____

10. Where are your fields? _____

11. How long have you been farming?
    1) Less than 1 year   2) 1-2 years   6) 11-15 years
    3) 3-5 years   5) 9-10 years   4) 6-8 years   8) More than 20 years
    7) 16-20 years

12. Number of Dependents
    a.Total _____   b.Wives _____   c.Children _____
    d.Grandchildren _____   e.Friends _____   f.Other (please specify) _____

13. How many people moved out of your household since you have been farming?
    a.Total _____   b.Wives _____
    c.Children _____   d.Grandchildren _____
    e.Friends _____   f.Other (please specify) _____

211

14. Where did they move to?

	Other Farms 1	Nearby Town 2	Major Cities 3	Other 4
a. Wives				
b. Children				
c. Grandchildren				
d. Friends				
e. Other (please specify)				

15. Why did they move?

	To marry	To go to school	To obtain job	Other
a. Wives				
b. Children				
c. Grandchildren				
d. Friends				
e. Other (please specify				

16. How many of those who moved out are still considered dependents?

a. Total _____   b. Wives _____   c. Children _____

d. Grandchildren _____   e. Friends _____   f. Other (please specify) _____

17. When do they normally come back home:

	Major Weekends 1	Easter/ Traditional Holidays 2	Christmas 3	Other 4
a. Wives				
b. Children				
c. Grandchildren				
d. Friends				
e. Other (please specify)				

18. How many of those who moved out of your household will not come back?

1) Total _____   2) Wives _____   3) Children _____

4) Grandchildren _____   5) Friends _____   6) Other (please specify _____

Farm Characteristics

19. How much land do you farm?

1) less than 1 acre

2) 1-3 acres   3) 4-5 acres   4) 6-10 acres

5) 11-15 acres   6) 16-20 acres   7) more than 20 acres

20. On the average how much of the field that you farm is:

	All 1	Most 2	Half 3	Little 4	None of it 5
a. Owned by you					
b. Owned by family					
c. Rented by you					
d. Not yours but no permission needed to use it					
e. Not yours but permitted by the chief to farm it					
f. Shared					
g. Other (specify)					

21. It is often difficult to assess how much of each crop one grows on the same field. But I would like to know the general idea of what you grow on your farms. How much of the land do you use for growing:

	All 1	Most 2	Half 3	Little 4	None 5
a. Cassava					
b. Rice					
c. Millet					
d. Cocoa					
e. Cotton					
f. Groundnut					
g. Soyabeans					
h. Corn or maize					
i. Guinea corn					
j. Oil palm					
k. Cocoyam					
l. Yam					
m. Rubber					
n. Wheat					
o. Plantain (or banana)					
p. Cowpeas					
q. Vegetables (specify)					
r. Livestock (specify)					
s. Other (specify)					

22. In general how much of your products do you sell?

	All 1	Most 2	Half 3	Little 4	None 5
a.Cassava					
b.Rice					
c.Millet					
d.Cocoa					
e.Cotton					
f.Groundnut					
g.Soyabeans					
h.Corn or maize					
i.Guinea corn					
j.Oil palm					
k.Cocoyam					
l.Yam					
m.Rubber					
n.Wheat					
o.Plantain (or banana)					
p.Cowpeas					
q.Vegetables (specify)					
r.Livestock (specify)					
s.Other (specify)					

23. How much of your products do you sell

	All 1	Most 2	Half 3	Little 4	None 5
a.In the markets					
b.To cooperatives					
c.To individuals					
d.Other (specify)					

24. How many people work for you on your farm?
1) total _____   2) self _____   3) wives _____
4) hired labor _____   5) children _____   6) others (specify) _____

25. What equipment or machines to you use on your farm?
a.hoes   b.matches   c.tractors   d.axes   e.other (specify)

214

26. On the average, how many hours do you or any of those working for you work in a day during the growing period?

	1-2 hrs. 1	3-5 hrs. 2	6-7 hrs. 3	8-9 hrs. 4	over 9 hrs. 5
a.male head	___	___	___	___	___
b.wives	___	___	___	___	___
c.children	___	___	___	___	___
d.hired labor	___	___	___	___	___
e.other	___	___	___	___	___

27. On the average, how many hours do you or any of those working for you work in a day during the harvesting period?

	1-2 hrs. 1	3-5 hrs. 2	6-7 hrs. 3	8-9 hrs. 4	over 9 hrs. 5
a.male head	___	___	___	___	___
b.wives	___	___	___	___	___
c.children	___	___	___	___	___
d.hired labor	___	___	___	___	___
e.other	___	___	___	___	___

28. Money is needed to buy all your farm equipment, seeds and other farm related things. On the average how much of the money that you spend for your farm activities comes from:

	All 1	Most 2	Half 3	Little 4	None 5
a.personal savings	___	___	___	___	___
b.family/friends	___	___	___	___	___
c.cooperative society	___	___	___	___	___
d.government aid	___	___	___	___	___
e.other (specify)	___	___	___	___	___

29. How much of your seeds to you get

	All 1	Most 2	Half 3	Little 4	None 5
a.in the open market	___	___	___	___	___
b.provided locally from previous years	___	___	___	___	___
c.provided by government	___	___	___	___	___
d.provided by cooperatives	___	___	___	___	___
e.other (specify)	___	___	___	___	___

30. What do you use to improve the quality of your crops?

a.buy improved seed   b.apply fertilizer   c.add manure
d.add water   e.pest and weed control   f.other (specify)

QUESTIONNAIRE (Opinion)

General Characteristics

31. In general, how serious are the following problems in your farming business?

	Very Serious 1	Serious 2	Somewhat Serious 3	No problem 4
a Water supply				
b Transportation				
c Marketing				
d Storage				
e Price				
f Labor supply				
g Planting/harvesting				
h Soil fertility				
i Credit/money				
j Pest and weed control				
k Quality seed				
l Other (specify)				

32. Weather is a major factor in agriculture. In general would you say the weather in the past few years was:

	Very good 1	Good 2	Fair 3	Bad 4	Very bad 5	Don't know 6
a.general						
b.1980						
c.1981						
d.1982						
e.1983						
f.1984						

33. Do you think Ondo/Sokoto state is producing:
   1) more than enough food   2) enough food
   3) somewhat enough food   4) not enough food

34. Do you think Nigeria is producing:
   1) more than enough food   2) enough food
   3) somewhat enough food   4) not enough food

35. Do you think Ondo/Sokoto state has:
   1) too many farmers   2) enough farmers   3) not enough farmers

216

36. Do you think Nigeria has:
    1) too many farmers   2) enough farmers   3) not enough farmers

37. If you had the means, do you think you could farm:
    1) a lot more land   2) a little more land   3) no more land

38. In order to produce more food in the country, please tell me how important you think each of the following is. Do you think it's very important, important, somewhat important, important, or not important?

	Very Import. 1	Import. 2	Somewhat Import. 3	Not Import. 4
a. Expansion of farm by individual	___	___	___	___
b. More people farming	___	___	___	___
c. Modern methods of farming	___	___	___	___
d. Improved seeds	___	___	___	___
e. Fertilizer supply	___	___	___	___
f. Other (specify)	___	___	___	___

39. In order to obtain more land for farming, please tell me to what extent you think each of the following is a limiting factor. Do you think it is a limiting factor to a very great extent, to a great extent, to some extent, or not a limiting factor?

	To a very great extent 1	To a great extent 2	To some extent 3	Not at all 4
a. Government restriction	___	___	___	___
b. Have no means to clear the bush	___	___	___	___
c. No land at all to obtain	___	___	___	___
d. Money/credit	___	___	___	___
e. Labor shortage	___	___	___	___
f. Other (specify)	___	___	___	___

40. In your opinion who was responsible for solving the problems you face in your farming business?

	Not at All 1	Some Extent 2	Great Extent 3	Very great Extent 4
a. government	___	___	___	___
b. research/university people	___	___	___	___
c. oneself	___	___	___	___
d. other (specify)	___	___	___	___

41. What are some of your problems you think the government should help you solve?

	Not at All 1	Some 2	Most 3	All 4
a. Money/credit problems				
b. Water problems				
c. Quality seeds				
d. Fertilizer supply				
e. Bush clearing				
f. Other (specify)				

42. What kind of job is the government doing in solving your problems of:

	Very good 1	Good 2	Fair 3	Bad 4	Very Bad 5	Don't know 6
a. money/credit						
b. water problems						
c. quality seed						
d. fertilizer supply						
e. bush clearing						
f. other (specify)						

43. In general the federal government was/is helping the local farmers.

	Strongly Disagree 1	Disagree 2	Don't Know 3	Strongly Agree 4	Agree 5	No Comment 6
a. the old Azikiwe government						
b. Gowon government						
c. Murtala Muhammed/ Obasanjo regime						
d. Shagari government						
e. present regime						

44. On the average the rural areas got/get as fair a share in the distribution of the national wealth as urban areas.

	Strongly Disagree 1	Disagree 2	Don't Know 3	Strongly Agree 4	Agree 5	No Comment 6
a. the old Azikiwe government						
b. Gowon government						
c. Murtala Muhammed/ Obasanjo regime						
d. Shagari government						
e. present regime						

218

	Strongly Disagree 1	Don't Disagree 2	Strongly Know 3	No Agree 4	Agree 5	Comment 6
45. The federal government gave/gives enough financial aid to the farmers.						
a. the old Azikiwe government	||	||	||	||	||	||
b. Gowon government	||	||	||	||	||	||
c. Murtala Muhammed/ Obasanjo regime	|||	|||	|||	|||	|||	|||
d. Shagari government	|||	|||	|||	|||	|||	|||
e. present regime						
46. Ondo/Sokoto state government gave/gives enough aid to the farmers.						
a. the old Azikiwe government	||	||	||	||	||	||
b. Gowon government	||	||	||	||	||	||
c. Murtala Muhammed/ Obasanjo regime	|||	|||	|||	|||	|||	|||
d. Shagari government	|||	|||	|||	|||	|||	|||
e. present regime						
47. The _____ local government gave/gives enough aid to the farmers.						
a. the old Azikiwe government	||	||	||	||	||	||
b. Gowon government	||	||	||	||	||	||
c. Murtala Muhammed/ Obasanjo regime	|||	|||	|||	|||	|||	|||
d. Shagari government	|||	|||	|||	|||	|||	|||
e. present regime						
48. Government bureaucrats in general have too much power in the matters of farming.						
a. the old Azikiwe government	||	||	||	||	||	||
b. Gowon government	||	||	||	||	||	||
c. Murtala Muhammed/ Obasanjo regime	|||	|||	|||	|||	|||	|||
d. Shagari government	|||	|||	|||	|||	|||	|||
e. present regime						

	Strongly Disagree 1	Don't Disagree 2	Strongly Know 3	No Agree 4	Agree 5	Comment 6
49. Much of the money the federal government spent/spends on agriculture benefits the local farmers.						
a. the old Azikiwe government	______	______	______	______	______	______
b. Gowon government	______	______	______	______	______	______
c. Murtala Muhammed/ Obasanjo regime	______	______	______	______	______	______
d. Shagari government	______	______	______	______	______	______
e. present regime	______	______	______	______	______	______
50. The federal government was/is doing what it can do to help the local farmers in solving various problems.						
a. the old Azikiwe government	______	______	______	______	______	______
b. Gowon government	______	______	______	______	______	______
c. Murtala Muhammed/ Obasanjo regime	______	______	______	______	______	______
d. Shagari government	______	______	______	______	______	______
e. present regime	______	______	______	______	______	______
51. The Ondo/Sokoto government was/is doing what it can do to help the local farmers in solving various problems.						
a. the old Azikiwe government	______	______	______	______	______	______
b. Gowon government	______	______	______	______	______	______
c. Murtala Muhammed/ Obasanjo regime	______	______	______	______	______	______
d. Shagari government	______	______	______	______	______	______
e. present regime	______	______	______	______	______	______
52. The Ondo/Sokoto local government was/is doing what it can do to help the local farmers in solving various problems.						
a. the old Azikiwe government	______	______	______	______	______	______
b. Gowon government	______	______	______	______	______	______
c. Murtala Muhammed/ Obasanjo regime	______	______	______	______	______	______
d. Shagari government	______	______	______	______	______	______
e. present regime	______	______	______	______	______	______

	Strongly Disagree 1	Don't Disagree 2	Strongly Know 3	No Agree 4	Agree 5	Comment 6
53. The marketing boards are very effective in handling the prices of farm products in the country.	___	___	___	___	___	___
54. The marketing boards should be eliminated because of ineffectiveness.	___	___	___	___	___	___
55. The problem of water should be solved by the government for the farmers.	___	___	___	___	___	___
56. The government should not be involved in the agricultural sector.	___	___	___	___	___	___

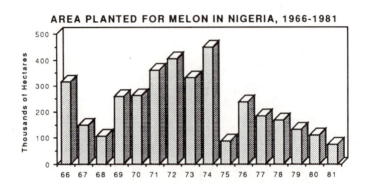

AREA PLANTED FOR MELON IN NIGERIA, 1966-1981

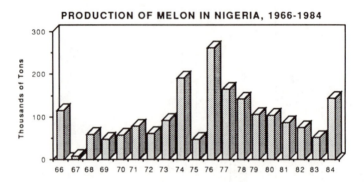

PRODUCTION OF MELON IN NIGERIA, 1966-1984

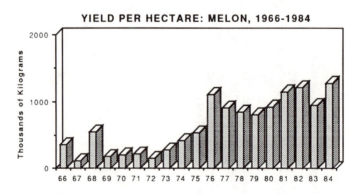

YIELD PER HECTARE: MELON, 1966-1984

APPENDIX FIG. 1

222

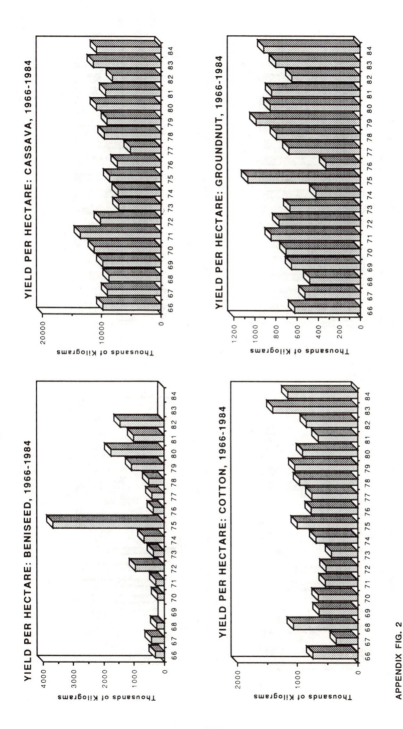

YIELD PER HECTARE: CASSAVA, 1966-1984

YIELD PER HECTARE: GROUNDNUT, 1966-1984

YIELD PER HECTARE: BENISEED, 1966-1984

YIELD PER HECTARE: COTTON, 1966-1984

APPENDIX FIG. 2

223

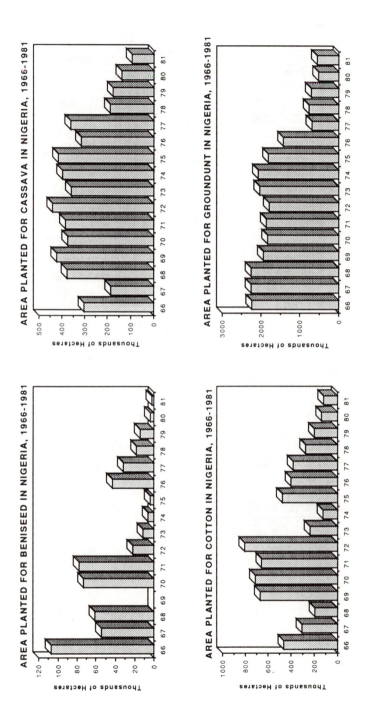

APPENDIX FIG. 3

224

BIBLIOGRAPHY

Adams, R.S. and McNeill, W.H., 1978, Human Migration Patterns and Policies. Bloomington: Indiana University Press.

Adeniran, Tunde, Oct 1982, "Three Years of Nigeria's New Constitution: 2." West Africa, pp. 2768-2769.

Agboola, S.A., December 1968, "Patterns of Food Crop Production in South-Western Nigeria." Nigerian Geographical Journal, pp. 135-151.

Adedeji, Adebayo, May 1986, "Transforming Africa's Economies." Africa Report, pp. 4-8.

Ake, Claude, ed., 1985, Political Economy of Nigeria. London: Longman.

Akinola, Anthony, 1983, "A Test for Nigeria." West Africa, April 11, 1983, pp. 882-883.

Anikpo, Mark, 1985, "Achieving Self-Sufficiency in African Agricultural Food Production: The Case of Nigeria." Africa Today, Food, Famine and Development, 4th Quarter, 32, 4, pp. 29-38.

Arhin, Kwame; Hesp, Paul; and Van der Laan, Laurens, eds., 1985, Marketing Boards in Tropical Africa. London: KPI Limited.

Ayari, Chedly, October 1983, "What Strategy for Africa's Development?" Africa Report, pp. 8-11.

Babalola, A. 1986, "Personal Interview." Federal Ministry of Agriculture, Lagos, Nigeria.

Babangida, I.G., 1985, "Deeper Commitment." West Africa, September 2, 1985, pp. 1791-1792.

Baker, Randall, 1973, "Rwanda." Focus A.G.S., XXIII, 10, pp. 2-8.

Barber, Karin, 1982, "Popular Reactions to the Petro-Naira." The Journal of Modern African Studies, 20, 3, pp. 431-450.

Barbour, K. Michael; Oguntoyinbo, J.S.; Onyemelukwe, J.O.C.; and Nwafor, J.C., 1982, Nigeria in Maps. London: Hodder and Stoughton.

Bayero, Ado and El-Kanemi, M.U. 1986, "Emirs Look to the Future." West Africa, November 3, 1986, pp. 2312-14

Bell, Michael W., 1983, "Government Revenue Stabilisation in Primary-Producing Countries: A Model of Zambia." The Journal of Modern African Studies, 21, 1, pp. 55-76.

Bigelow, Ross E., 1973, "Impact of Selected Agricultural Schemes on the Innovation Patterns Among Traditional Farmers in the Southern Savanna of Ghana." Ph.D. Dissertation, Michigan State University.

Binns, J.A., "The Resources of Rural Africa: A Geographical Perspective." African Affairs, 83, 330, pp. 33-40.

Bolsover, Anne, Feb. 1982, "The Way Ahead for Agriculture." Africa Report, pp. 17-19.

Brain, J. L., "Witchcraft and Development." African Affairs, pp. 371-384.

Brownsberger, William, 1983, "Development and Government Corruption - Materialism and Political Fragmentation in Nigeria." The Journal of Modern African Studies, 21, 2, pp. 215-233.

Bryson, Reid A. and Murray, Thomas J., 1977, Climate and Hunger: Mankind and the World's Changing Climate. Madison: University of Wisconsin Press.

Buhari, Muhammed, 1984, "Buhari's New Year Broadcast." West Africa, January 9, 1984, pp. 56-57.

_____, 1984, "Interview with General Buhari." West Africa, February 27, 1984, pp.424-427.

Buultjens, Ralph, April 1977, "China's Development Efforts and Quest for the Future." Focus. American Geographical Society (AGS), XXVII, 4, pp. 1-8.

Callaway, Barbara J., 1984, "Ambiguous Consequences of the Socialisation and Seclusion of Hausa Women." The Journal of Modern African Studies, 22, 3, pp. 429-450.

Central Bank of Nigeria, Annual Report and Statement of Account, 1980 and 1981.

Central Bank of Nigeria, Import and Export Statistics, Dec. 1980, "Annual Report and Statement of Accounts," p. 89.

Chicago Tribune, "Farm Program Readied for Africa." May 21, 1984.

Chicago Tribune, "West Pushing Reform not Relief, for Africa." Thursday, May 29, 1986, p. 16.

Cobbe, James, 1983, "The Changing Nature of Dependence: Economic Problems In Lesotho." The Journal of Modern African Studies, 21, 2, pp. 293-310.

Cocklin, Chris; Gray, Edward; and Suit, Barry, 1983, "Future Urban Growth and Agricultural Land in Ontario." Applied Geography, 3, pp. 91-104.

Critchfield, Howard J., 1974. General Climatology. Englewood Cliffs, New Jersy: Prentice Hall.

Daily Times of Nigeria, 1979, 13 Years of Military Rule, 1966-79. Lagos, Nigeria: Daily Times Limited.

Daily Times of Nigeria, January 9, 1983.

Derrick, Jonathan, July 1984, "West Africa's Worst Year of Famine." African Affairs, 83, 332, pp. 281-299.

_____, 1986, "The 'Green' Peril." West Africa, April 21, 1986, pp. 829-831.

_____, 1986, "Decline and Fall - 1." West Africa, May 12, 1986, pp. 989-990.

_____, 1986, "Decline and Fall - 2." West Africa, May 19, 1986, pp. 1041-1043.

_____, 1986, "The Green Hope." West Africa, June 23, 1986, pp. 1315-17.

_____, 1986, "Food and Famine." West Africa, November 3, 1986.

Disney, Richard and Elbashir, A.A., 1984, "Mechanisation, Employment and Productivity in Sudanese Agriculture." Journal of Development Economics, 16, pp. 249-262.

Doucet, Lyse, 1986, "Agriculture — What Kind of Future." West Africa, September 22, 1986, pp. 1978-79.

Dumont, R., 1966, False Start in Africa. New York: Praeger.

Easum, Donald B., May-June 1986, "The African Crisis: Whose Challenge?" Africa Report, pp. 40-44.

Eicher, Carl and Witt, Lawrence, 1964, Agricultural in Economic Development. New York, NY: McGraw-Hill Book Company.

Eicher, Carl K., 1970, Research on Agricultural Development in Five English Speaking Countries in West Africa. New York, NY: The Agricultural Development Council.

Eicher, Carl K. and Baker, Doyle C., 1982, MSU International Development Papers, Paper No. 1. East Lansing, MI: Department of Agricultural Economics, Michigan State University.

Ekundare, R. Olufemi, 1973, An Economic History of Nigeria 1860-1960. New York, NY: Africana Publishing Co.

Enabor, Ephraim E., 1976-77, "The Role of Forestry in the Amelioration of Drought in Nigeria." Nigerian Geographical Journal, 20, 2, pp. 153-163.

Encyclopaedia Britannica, 1984, The New Encyclopaedia Britannica. Chicago: Encyclopaedia Britannica, Inc. vol. 13, pp. 85-96.

Encyclopaedia Britannica, 1984, The Encyclopaedia Year book. Chicago: Encyclopaedia Britannica, Inc.

Federal Department of Agriculture, 1982, Moloney Street, Lagos.

Federal Ministry of Agriculture, Department of Agricultural Planning; 1982, Lagos, Nigeria.

Federal Ministry of Agriculture, (ca. 1981-82), An Outline of Nigerian Agricultural Policy. Igbobi, Nigeria: Dependable Press (Nig.) Enterprises.

Federal Ministry of Agriculture, Jan. 1984, Information Bulletin on Nigerian Agriculture. King & George Press, Ltd.

Federal Nigeria, Embassy of Nigeria, Washington, D.C., 4, 1,
July-Sept. 1977, p. 17.

Federal Republic of Nigeria, Annual Abstract of Statistics.
Lagos, Nigeria: Federal Office of Statistics. (Various issues).

Federal Republic of Nigeria, Digest of Statistics. Lagos,
Nigeria: Federal Office of Statistics.

Federal Republic of Nigeria, Nigeria Economic Indicators
1972-76. Lagos, Nigeria: Federal Office of Statistics.

Federal Republic of Nigeria, Nigeria Trade Summary. Lagos,
Nigeria: Federal Office of Statistics. (Various issues).

Federal Republic of Nigeria, Review of External Trade. Lagos, Nigeria: Federal Office of Statistics. (Various issues).

Federal Republic of Nigeria, 1970, Second National Development Plan 1970-74. Lagos, Nigeria: Federal Ministry of
Information.

Federal Republic of Nigeria, 1974, Second National Development Plan 1970-74, Second Progress Report. Lagos,
Nigeria: The Central Planning Office, Federal Ministry
of Economic Development and Reconstruction.

Federal Republic of Nigeria, 1975, Third National Development Plan 1975-80, Lagos, Nigeria: The Central Planning Office, Federal Ministry of Economic Development.

Federal Republic of Nigeria, First Progress Report on Third
National Development Plan 1975-80. Lagos, Nigeria:
The Central Planning Office, Federal Ministry of Eco-
nomic Development.

Federal Republic of Nigeria, 1981, Fourth National Development Plan 1981-85, Lagos, Nigeria: The National
Planning Office, Federal Ministry of National Planning.

Federal Republic of Nigeria, 1982, Annual Report of the Federal Ministry of Agriculture. Ikoyi, Lagos: Federal Ministry of Agriculture.

Food and Agriculture Organisation of the United Nations,
FAO Trade Yearbook, Rome, Italy.

229

Found, W.C., 1972, A Theoretical Approach to Rural Land Use.

Gill and Duffs; 1982, "Cocoa Marketing Reprint", January 1982.

Green, Edward, 1982, "U.S. Population Policies Development, and the Rural Poor of Africa." The Journal of Modern African Studies, 20, 1, pp. 45-67.

Griffiths, J. F., 1975, "Nigeria." World Survey of Climatology, 10, pp. 167-192.

Gusau, Alhaji Ibrahim, August 1981, "Nigeria's Green Revolution." Africa Report, pp. 19-22.

Hance, William A., 1967, African Economic Development.Praeger: New York, NY.

_____, 1970, Population Migration and Urbanization in Africa, New York, NY: Columbia University Press.

_____, 1975, The Geography of Modern Africa, 2nd ed., New York, NY: Columbia University Press.

_____, 1977, Black Africa Develops. Cross Road Press: U.S.A.

Harris, Richard, 1975, The Political Economy of Africa. New York, NY: Halsted Press.

Hart, Keith, 1982, The Political Economy of West African Agriculture. Cambridge University Press, pp. 1-226.

Hawkins, Tony, May-June 1986, "The New Realism in Lagos." Africa Report, pp. 73-76.

Hecht, Robert M., 1983, "The Ivory Coast Economic Miracle: What Benefits for Peasant Farmers?" The Journal of Moderan African Studies, 21, 1, pp. 25-53.

Hinderink, J. and Sterkenburg, JJ, 1983, "Agricultural Policy and Production in Africa: The Aims, the Methods and the Means." The Journal of Modern African Studies, 21, 1, pp. 1-23.

Hodson, H. V. ed., 1981, The Annual Register 1980. Longman, pp. 230-233.

Holdcroft, Lane E., August 1982, "The Role of External Aid." Africa Report, pp. 15-18.

Ikporukpo, C.O., 1983, "Environmental Deterioration and Public Policy in Nigeria." Applied Geography, 3, 303-316.

Innis, Donald Q., 1980, "The Future of Traditional Agriculture." Focus - American Geographical Society AGS, 30, 3, pp. 1-8.

International Marketing Information Series, July 1982, "Foreign Economic Trends in Nigeria and Their Implication to the United States."

Jedrej, M.C., 1983, "The Growth and Decline of a Mechanical Agriculture Scheme in West Africa." African Affairs, 832, 329, pp. 541-558.

Johnson, Glenn L., et al., 1969, "Strategies and Recommendations for Nigerian Rural Development 1969/1985." (East Lansing, MI: Consortium for the Study of Nigerian Rural Development, Michigan State University).

Joint Planning Meeting On Tree Crops, 1982 in Small Holder Rubber Development in Bendel State.

Jones, Ted L.; Gans, A.R.; Hoover, Robert G.; Maxey, Richard P.; Stoneham, A. H.; and Smith, Mervin G., 1966, A Report for the Consortium for the Study of Nigerian Rural Development. "A Proposed Agricultural Credit Program for Nigeria." East Lansing, MI: CSNRD-4, Michigan State University.

Jones, William O., 1960, "Economic Man in Africa." Food Research Institute Studies. (Stanford, CA: Food Research Institute).

Jones, William O., 1969, "Plantations." In, International Encyclopedia of the Social Studies, 12, pp. 154-59.

Joseph, Richard A., 1978, "Affluence and Underdevelopment: The Nigerian Experience." The Journal of Modern African Studies, 16, 2, pp. 222ff.

Kader, Ahmad A., "The Contribution of Oil Exports to Economic Development. A Study of the Major Oil Exporting Countries." n.d., n.p.

Kelly, Kenneth, June 1981, "Agricultural Change in Hooghly, 1850-1910," AAG, 71, 2, pp. 237-254.

Koeppe, Clarence E. and Long, George C. De, 1958, Weather and Climate. New York: McGraw-Hill.

Kopec, Richard J., ed. 1975 ,Atmosphere Quality and Climatic Change. Department of Geography, University of North Carolina at Chapel Hill.

Lacey, Linda, 1981, "Urban Migration in Developing Countries. A Case Study of Three Cities in Nigeria." Ph.D. Dissertation, Cornell University.

Lacey, Linda, 1982, "Interurban Movements and Repeat Migration in Nigeria: Implications for Planners." African Urban Studies, 14, pp. 19-31.

Lockwood, John G., 1974, World Climatology: An Environmental Approach. Great Britain: Edward Arnold.

Lofchie, M.F. and Commins, S.K., 1982, "Food Deficits and Agricultural Policies in Tropical Africa." The Journal of Modern African Studies, 20, 1, pp. 1-25.

Mabogunje, Akin L., 1968, Urbanization in Nigeria. London: London University Press Ltd.

May, Jacques M. (M.D.), 1974, "The Geography of Malnutrition in Africa South of The Sahara." Focus A.G.S., XXV, 1 and 2, pp. 1-10.

Mayer, Jean, November 26, 1984, "An African Nightmare." Newsweek, p. 50-58.

Mengistead, Kidane, 1985, "Food Shortages in Africa: A Critique of Existing Agricultural Strategies." Africa Today, Food, Famine and Development, 4th Quarter, pp. 39-53.

Mills, Frank Leroy, "The Development of Alternative Farming Systems and Prospects for Change in the Structure of Agriculture in St. Kitts, West Indies." Ph.D. Dissertation, Clark University, Worcester, Massachusetts, n.d.

Munishi, Gaspar K. K., 1982, Development Administration in Tanzania: Public Service Planning and Utilization Ph.D. Dissertation, University of Wisconsin-Madison.

Munslow, Barry, 1984, "State Intervention in Agriculture: The Mozambican Experience." The Journal of Modern African Studies, 22, 2, pp. 199-221.

Nigeria Document, February 1982, "The Agricultural Situation." African Report, pp. 39-41.

Nigeria, The Punch, July 1, 1981.

Nigeria, Sunday Sketch, June 17, 1981.

Nigerian Sunday Tribune, "Our Legislators are Greedy," June 14, 1981

Obadan, Michael I., 1982, "Direct Foreign Investment in Nigeria: An Empirical Analysis." African Studies Review, XXV, 1, pp. 68-102.

O'Connor, A.M., 1978, The Geography of Tropical African Development: A Study of Spatial Patterns of Economic Chance Since Independence. Oxford, England: Pergamon Press.

Ogbona, Okoro D., 1979, "The Geographic Consequences of Petroleum in Nigeria with Special Reference to the Rivers State." Ph.D. Dissertation, University of California, Berkley.

Oguntoyimbo, J.S., June 1967, "Rainfall, Evaporation and Cotton Production in Nigeria." Nigerian Geographical Journal, 10, pp. 43-89.

Ojo, G.J.A., December 1963, "Trends Towards Mechanized Agriculture in Yorrubaland." Nigerian Geographical Journal, pp. 116-129.

Okoli, E.J. 1983, "Something Rotten - Corruption in high Places." West Africa, January 24, 1983, pp. 190-192.

Okurume, Godwin, 1969, Consortium for the Study of Nigerian Rural Development. "The Food Crop Economy in Nigerian Agricultural Policy. The Interdependence of Food Crops and Export Crops in Production." East Lansing, MI: CSNRD-31, Michigan State University.

Olatunbosun, Dupe, 1968, The Consortium for the Study of Nigerian Rural Development in Collaboration with The Nigerian Institute for Social and Economic Research. "Nigerian Governments' Policies Affecting Investment in Agriculture." Ibadan, Nigeria: NISER, University of Ibadan.

Olatunbosun, Dupe, 1975, Nigeria's Neglected Rural Majority. Ibadan: Oxford University Press.

Olayide, S.O., ed., 1976, Economic Survey of Nigeria 1960-1975. Ibadan, Nigeria: Aromolaran Publishing Company, Ltd.

Oluwasanmi, H.A., 1966, Agriculture and Nigerian economic Development. London: Oxford University Press.

Ondo State of Nigeria. Ondo State Component of the Third National Development Plan, 1975-80.

Ondo State of Nigeria. Report on The Rural Economic Survey, 1977. Akure, Nigeria: Statistic Division, Ministry of Finance & Economic Development.

Ondo State of Nigeria. Report on Rural Economic Survey, 1978. Akure, Nigeria: Statistics Division, Ministry of Economic Planning and Statistics.

Ondo State of Nigeria. Report on Rural Economic Survey, 1979. Akure, Nigeria: Statistics Division, Ministry of Economic Planning and Statistics.

Ondo State of Nigeria, March 1977. An Interim Report on the Rural Economic Survey, Ondo State, 1976. Akure, Nigeria: The Ministry of Finance and Economic Development.

Ondo State of Nigeria. Digest of Agricultural Statistics 1977. Akure, Nigeria: Statistics Division, Ministry of Economic Planning and Statistics.

Ondo State of Nigeria, Ondo State Component of the Fourth National Development Plan 1981-85.

Ondo State of Nigeria, June 1978. Report on Livestock and Poultry Survey in Ondo State. Akure, Nigeria: Statistics Division, Ministry of Finance & Economic Development.

Onimode, Bade, 1982, Imperialism and Underdevelopment in Nigeria, "The Dialectis of Mass Povery." London: Zed Press.

Onitiri, H.M.A. and Olatunbosun, Dupe, eds., 1974, The Marketing Board System. "Proceedings of an International Conference." Ibadan, Nigeria: Ibadan University Press.

Onoh, J.K., 1983, The Nigerian Oil Economy. New York, NY: St. Martin's Press.

Osundara, Niyi Nov. 1983; "Once Upon a General Election." West Africa, November 14, 1983.

Oyelese, J.O., June 1966, "Some Aspects of Food Crop Cultivation in the Plantations of Barbados-West Indies." Nigerian Geographical Journal, pp. 55-70.

Oyelese, J.O., 1984, "Multiple Deprivation in Cities: The Case of Ilorin, Nigeria." Applied Geography, 4, pp. 71-80.

Palen, J. John, 1981, The Urban World. New York, NY: McGraw-Hill Book Co.

Pierre, P., April 17, 1981, "The Senegal River and its Environment." Marches Tropicaux, pp. 2-35.

Quarterly Economic Review of China. Annual Supplement: China, Hong Kong and North Korea.

Quarterly Economic Review of Nigeria. Annual Supplement: Nigeria (Various Issues)

Richardson, Bonham C., June 1975, "Livelihood in Rural Trinidad in 1900." Annals of the Association of American Geographers, 65, 2, pp. 240-250.

Ruddell, David, Dec 1982, "From Twelve to Nineteen to Forty." West Africa, pp. 3194-3197.

Rumney, George R., 1968. Climatology and the World's Climates. New York, NY: MacMillan.

Saylor, Gerald, 1968, "A study of Obstacles to investment in Oil Palm and Rubber Plantations". East Lansing, Michigan: Consortuim for the Study of Nigerian Rural Development, Michigan State University.

Schatz, Sayre P., 1984, "Pirate Capitalism and the Inert Economy of Nigeria." The Journal of Modern African Studies, 22, 1, pp. 45-57.

Schneider, Stephen H. and Londer, Randi S., 1984, The Co-Evolution of Climate and Life: San Francisco: Sierra Club Books.

Seebohn, Frederic, Jan 1984, "World Hunger." African Affairs, 83, 330, pp. 3-9.

Simko, Robert A., Jan. 1974, "Tanzania: Experiment in Co-operative Effort." Focus A.G.S., XXIV, 5, pp. 1-6.

Smock, David, 1967, "Land Fragmentation and the Possibilities of Consolidation in East Nigeria." Bulletin of Rural Economics and Sociology, XI, 3, pp. 194-210.

Sokoto State of Nigeria, 1981, Programmes of Sokoto State in the 4th National Development Plan, 1981-85. Sokoto, Nigeria: Ministry of Economic Planning.

Sokoto State of Nigeria, Quarterly Report on the Prices of Selected Commodities in Some Towns in Sokoto State. April-Dec. 1981. Sokoto, Nigeria: Statistic Division, Economic Planning Department, Ministry of Finance and Economic Planning.

Sokoto State of Nigeria, Quarterly Report on the Prices of Selected Commodities in Some Towns in Sokoto State. April-Dec. 1982. Sokoto, Nigeria: Statistic Division, Economic Planning Department, Ministry of Finance and Economic Planning.

Stocking, Michael, 1983, "Farming and environmental degradation in Zambia: the human dimension." Applied Geography, 3, pp. 63-77.

Tandon, Yashpa, 1978, "The Food Question in East Africa: A Critical Case in Tanzania," Africa Quarterly, vol. XVII, #4.

Taylor, D.R.F., 1983, "Geography and the Developing Nations." Canadian Geographer, 27, 1, pp. 1-3.

The Guardian, Sunday, September 18, 1983. "Corruption is Sky-High." Lagos, Nigeria. pp. 21-22.

The Milwaukee Journal, "For Parched Africa, Help is too Little and too Late." Sunday, April 15, 1984, p. 1

The Milwaukee Journal, "Socialism's Heyday in Africa Has Ended." Sunday, June 23, 1985, p. 1.

The Milwaukee Journal, "Nigeria sets example worth support." Monday, April 6, 1987, p. 9A.

The Milwaukee Journal, "Pride Kept Nigerians from Taking IMF Loan." Sunday, April 12, 1987, p. 3J.

The 1986 Almanac, 39th Edition. Boston: Houghton Mifflin Company.

Trewartha, Glenn T., 1968, An Introduction to Climatology. New York: McGraw-Hill.

Trewartha, Glenn T., 1970, The Earth's Problem Climates. Madison, Wisconsin: The University of Wisconsin Press.

Trewartha, Glenn T., 1981, The Earth's Problem Climates. Madison, Wisconsin: The University of Wisconsin Press.

Uchendu, Victor, 1967, "Some Issues in African Land Tenure." Tropical Agriculture, 44, 2, pp. 94-96.

United Nations, Demographic Yearbook 1970-76 estimates.

U.S. Department of Agriculture, Nigeria Document, "The Agricultural Situation." Africa Report, January- February 1982, pp. 39-41.

Ugochukwu, Onyema, 1983, "Rich Men, Poor Men." West Africa, October 10, 1983. pp. 848-849.

_____, 1984, "The Return of the Military." West Africa, January 8,1984, pp. 53-56.

_____, 1984, "Rice and the Agriculture Paradox." West Africa, March 19, 1984, pp. 605-606.

Uyanga, Joseph T., 1980, A Geography of Rural Development in Nigeria. Washington, D.C.: University Press of America, Inc.

Vengroff, Richard, "Food and Dependency: P.L. 480 Aid to Black Africa." The Journal of Modern African Studies, pp. 27-43.

Wallace, Tina, 1980, "Agricultural Projects and Land in Northern Nigeria." Review of African Political Economy, 17, pp. 59-70.

West Africa Special Correspondent, 1982, "The Honourable Members." West Africa, April 19, 1982, pp. 1050-1051

_____, "Portents from Nigerian Elections." West Africa, August 15, 1983, pp. 1863-65

_____,1983, "The Governors' Elections." West Africa, August 22 1983, pp. 1924-28.

_____, 1986, "Food Aid as Band- Aid." West Africa, February 21, 1983, p. 456.

_____, 1986, "Nigerian Budget - Spirit of Emergency." West Africa, Jan. 13, 1986, pp. 52-54.

_____, 1986, "Still too Much Government." West Africa, July 28, 1986, p. 1583.

Western State of Nigera, Digest of Agricultural Statistics 1970. Ibadan, Nigeria: Statistics Division, Ministry of Economic Planning and Reconstruction.

Western State of Nigera, Digest of Agricultural Statistics 1971. Ibadan, Nigeria: Statistics Division, Ministry of Economic Planning and Reconstruction.

Western State of Nigera, Digest of Agricultural Statistics 1973. Ibadan, Nigeria: Statistics Division, Ministry of Economic Planning and Reconstruction.

Western State of Nigeria, Report of Agricultural Survey in the Western State of Nigeria 1975. Ministry of Economic Development, Statistics Division, Ibadan.

Wigley, T.M.L., Ingram, M.J., and Farmer, G., eds., 1981, Climate and History. Studies in past climates and their impact on Man. Cambridge, England: Cambridge University Press.

Williams, Maurice J., October 1983, "Toward a Food Strategy for Africa." Africa Report, pp. 22-26.

World Meteorological Organization; Monthly Climatic Data for the World: Asheville, NC: National Climatic Data Center.

Zartman, I. William, ed., 1983, The Political Economy of Nigeria. "A SAIS Study on Africa." New York, NY: Praeger Publishers.

INDEX